27th Modern Artificial Intelligence and Cognitive Science Conference (MAICS 2016)

Dayton, Ohio, USA
22-23 April 2016

ISBN: 978-1-5108-2936-7

Printed from e-media with permission by:

Curran Associates, Inc.
57 Morehouse Lane
Red Hook, NY 12571

Some format issues inherent in the e-media version may also appear in this print version.

Printed by Curran Associates, Inc. (2016)

MAICS
c/o Anca Ralescu
EECS Dept. ML 0030
University of Cincinnati
Cincinnati, OH 45221-0030
USA

Phone: (513) 556-4752
Fax: (513) 556-2569

Anca.ralescu@uc.edu

Additional copies of this publication are available from:

Curran Associates, Inc.
57 Morehouse Lane
Red Hook, NY 12571 USA
Phone: 845-758-0400
Fax: 845-758-2633
Email: curran@proceedings.com
Web: www.proceedings.com

TABLE OF CONTENTS

Knowledge Modeling for Data Sharing, Integration, and Reuse

Pascal Hitzler
Department of Computer Science and Engineering
Wright State University

Abstract

Increasing amounts of data are shared, often publicly on the World Wide Web, for reuse by third parties. Such reuse usually necessitates the integration of this data with other data, or with software, in order to enable data-based applications, fine-grained search, data analytics, etc. This integration is often a significant cost factor due to the wide variance regarding representational choices for data, ranging from syntactic data formats to semantic heterogeneity stemming from different viewpoints of data providers. In this presentation, we will shed light on the role of knowledge modeling for data sharing and reuse. In particular, we will discuss how Semantic Web Technologies make it easier to integrate and thus reuse heterogeneous data.

Biographical Sketch

Pascal Hitzler is (full) Professor and Director of Data Science at the Department of Computer Science and Engineering at Wright State University in Dayton, Ohio, U.S.A. His research record lists over 300 publications in such diverse areas as semantic web, neural-symbolic integration, knowledge representation and reasoning, machine learning, denotational semantics, and set-theoretic topology. He is Editor-in-chief of the Semantic Web journal by IOS Press, and of the IOS Press book series Studies on the Semantic Web. He is co-author of the W3C Recommendation OWL 2 Primer, and of the book Foundations of Semantic Web Technologies by CRC Press, 2010 which was named as one out of seven Outstanding Academic Titles 2010 in Information and Computer Science by the American Library Association's Choice Magazine, and has translations into German and Chinese. He is on the editorial board of several journals and book series and is a founding steering committee member of the Web Reasoning and Rule Systems (RR) conference series, of the Neural-Symbolic Learning and Reasoning (NeSy) workshop series, and of the Association for Ontology Design and Patterns (ODPA). He also frequently acts as conference chair in various functions. For more information, see http://www.pascal-hitzler.de.

Social and Perceptual Fidelity of Avatars and Autonomous Agents in Virtual Reality

Benjamin Kunz
Department of Psychology
University of Dayton

Abstract

Advances in display, computing and sensor technologies have led to a revival of interest and excitement surrounding immersive virtual reality. Here, on the cusp of the arrival of practical and affordable virtual reality technology, are open questions regarding the factors that contribute to compelling and immersive virtual worlds. In order for virtual reality to be useful as a tool for use in training, education, communication, research, content-creation and entertainment, we must understand the degree to which the perception of the virtual environment and virtual characters resembles perception of the real world. Relatedly, virtual realitys utility in these contexts demands evidence that goal-directed behaviors and interpersonal interactions in virtual reality mimic real-world actions and that learning in one domain transfers to the other. In particular, providing the virtual reality user with a compelling sense of self and co-presence with virtual others has implications not just for creating convincing social environments but even for conveying the intended sense of scale and space in virtual environments. This presentation discusses the importance and challenges involved in creating and depicting interactive avatars representing both human and computer-controlled agents. Special attention will be paid to the use of computer-controlled avatars to both investigate interpersonal processes and behaviors and to improve the fidelity and naturalism of these autonomous agents.

Biographical Sketch

Benjamin R. Kunz received his Ph.D. in Cognitive Psychology from the University of Utah in 2010. He is now an assistant professor in the Department of Psychology at the University of Dayton with research interests in visual-spatial perception and action in real and virtual environments, embodied cognition and the body schema, and social influences on spatial cognition.

A Study of Android Malware Detection Techniques and Machine Learning

Balaji Baskaran and Anca Ralescu
EECS Department
University of Cincinnati
Cincinnati, OH 45221 - 0030
baskarbi@mail.uc.edu, anca.ralescu@uc.edu

Abstract

Android OS is one of the widely used mobile Operating Systems. The number of malicious applications and adwares are increasing constantly on par with the number of mobile devices. A great number of commercial signature based tools are available on the market which prevent to an extent the penetration and distribution of malicious applications. Numerous researches have been conducted which claims that traditional signature based detection system work well up to certain level and malware authors use numerous techniques to evade these tools. So given this state of affairs, there is an increasing need for an alternative, really tough malware detection system to complement and rectify the signature based system. Recent substantial research focused on machine learning algorithms that analyze features from malicious application and use those features to classify and detect unknown malicious applications. This study summarizes the evolution of malware detection techniques based on machine learning algorithms focused on the Android OS.

Introduction

According to a 2014 research study (RiskIQ(2014)), malicious applications in Google Play Store have increased 388% between 2011 and 2013.

As the initial part of our research, we conducted an extensive study where we analyze the current trends and approaches on detecting the malwares on Android Systems using Machine Learning techniques. The overall goal of this study is to identify the research so far on Android Malware detections using Machine Leaning Techniques. With this analysis we can formulate a defense mechanism specifically to counteract the Update attack, the most difficult intrusion technique to detect and eliminate.

Update Attack: In Android update attack is defined as the benign application installed in the system downloads malicious payloads while updating itself or downloads third party malicious applications and installs in the system. This type of attack is very hard to detect because the original application is benign. Unless we track the installed previous versions and the application after the update we cannot detect the malicious activity. We aim to give a brief approach on counteracting the update attack with the survey on recent trends on Malware detection.

Based on the current attack trends and analysis of the present literatures, (Raveendranath et al.(2014)Raveendranath, Rajamani, Babu, and Datta) lists the types of malwares as follows:

1. **Information Extraction**
   Compromises the device and steals personal information such as IMEI number, user's personal information, etc.
2. **Automatic Calls and SMS**
   User's phone bill is increased by making calls and sending SMS to some premium numbers
3. **Root Exploits**
   The malware will gain system root privileges and takes control of the system and modifies the information.
4. **Search Engine Optimizations**
   Artificially search for a term and simulates clicks on targeted websites in order to increase the revenue of a search engine or increase the traffic on a website.
5. **Dynamically Downloaded code**
   An installed benign application downloads a malicious code and deploys it in the mobile devices.
6. **Covert channel**
   A vulnerability in the devices that facilitates the information leak between the processes that are not supposed to share the information.
7. **Botnets**
   A network of compromised mobile devices with a Bot-Master which is controlled by Command and Control servers (C&C). Carry out Spam delivery, DDDos attacks on the host devices.

From this point on, the structure of the paper is as follows. Section is a general overview of current security deployed by play-store. Classification of various methods used in detecting malwares in Android systems is presented in Section . The paper concludes in Section

Overview of Android System Security

Google Play Store uses an in-house malicious application detection system called Bouncer. But researchers have proved that Bouncer's ability to detect the malicious application is minimal and they could successfully publish a prototype malicious application in play-store. Android Play-Store uses application's meta data such as user's rating and user's comments to flag a malicious application. But by the time the malicious application is detected, it could have made enough damage to the affected mobile system.

Malware authors use many techniques to evade the detection such as (a) code obfuscation technique, (b) encryption, (c) including permissions which are not needed by the application, (d) requesting for unwanted hardwares, (e) download or update attack in which a benign application updates itself or another application now with malicious payload, which is very tough to detect. This also encourages the need for new researches on the detection techniques, including machine learning based techniques. Many studies have shown that machine learning algorithms to detect the malicious activities are successful in detecting them with very high accuracy.

Android Malware Detection

Based on the features used to classify an application, we can categorize the analysis as Static and Dynamic. Static analysis is done without running an application. Examples of static features include, (a) permissions, (b) API calls which can be extracted from the AndroidManifest.xml file. Dynamic analysis deals with features that were extracted from the application while running, including (a) network traffic, (b) battery usage, (c) IP address, etc. The third type of analysis is hybrid analysis which combines the features from static and dynamic techniques. The rest of this section describes the features extracted from the application and machine learning algorithm used.

Static Analysis

In static analysis, the features are extracted from the application file without executing the application. This methodology is resource and time efficient as the application is not executed. But at the same time, this analysis suffers from code obfuscation techniques the Malware authors employ to evade from static detection techniques. One of very popular evasion technique is the Update Attack: a benign application is installed on the mobile device and when the application gets an update, the malicious content is downloaded and installed as part of the update. This cannot be detected by static analysis techniques which will scan only the benign application.

The most commonly used static features are the Permission and API calls. Since these are extracted from the application *AndroidManifest.xml* and influence the malware detection rate to a high extent, extensive research has been made with these as features as well as combined with other features extracted from meta-data available in Google PlayStore such as version name, version no., author's name, last updated time, etc.,

(Sahs and Khan(2012)) used permissions and Control Flow Graphs(CFG) as features and used One-class Support Vector Machine(SVM). The most of training data are benign applications and the classifier will classify a sample as malicious only if it is sufficiently different from the benign class.

(Shabtai et al.(2010)Shabtai, Fledel, and Elovici) used permission, framework methods and framework classes for their classification system.

(Sanz et al.(2012)Sanz, Santos, Laorden, Ugarte-Pedrero, and Bringas) extracted the strings in the application, permissions, user rating, number of ratings, size of the application and used Bayesian Networks, J48 Decision Tree and Random Forest, SVM with SMO kernel. A total of 820 samples were used to test and the authors concluded that they could achieve a very high accuracy with less false positive rate.

(Ghorbanzadeh et al.(2013)Ghorbanzadeh, Chen, Ma, Clancy, and McGwier) used Neural Networks to detect an application's category from permissions by means of multi layered feed forward networks. A feed forward Neural Network is built with two layers each containing 10 neurons. The hidden layer contains sigmoid transfer function and the output linear transfer functions was deployed. The suthoud assumed that the permissions declared in the manifest file may be manipulated by the malware authors and they may misrepresent the categories declared in the manifest. So to simulate this property, the authors permuted permissions of 50% of the test data and fed into the network.

(Yerima et al.(2013)Yerima, Sezer, McWilliams, and Muttik) used 2000 applications with 1000 malicious and 1000 benign applications. They extracted features like Permissions, API calls, Native Linux System commands and various features from manifest and class files. The malware authors embed native linux commads such as chnown, mount, remount, etc., and run them in the Android system when the application is launched. Mutual information (entropy) is used to rank the features and then a Bayesian Classifier is used for classification.

(Samra et al.(2013)Samra, Yim, and Ghanem) extracted features from AndroidManifest.xml such as count of xml elements, application specific information such as name, category, description, rating, package info, description, rating values, rating counts and price. The information from 18174 android application with 4612 business category and 13535 tools were extracted by using web crawlers. They were clustered using K-Means clustering.

(Peiravian and Zhu(2013)) utilized permission, API calls and the combination of both as features. The two types of permissions in Android, requested permission and required permission are used to express an application as a binary vector where $P_i = 1$ iff the Manifest.xml has the ith permission. Same as permission, API calls are also expressed as a binary vector with $API_i = 1$ iff there is the API call made in the application. These two features are concatenated and the third feature is formed. A total of 2510 samples including 1260 are malicious and 1250 benign are used. The authors concluded that Bagging, an ensemble classification method has the best performance in classifying all created datasets.

(Liu(2013)) investigated three specific types of malware: *SMS-related, control-related and spy-related.* An application's permission and ¡uses-feature¿ xml tag which requests the necessary hardware devices needed to run the application, is extracted and used as features. Information Gain is used to select important features and SVM with the basic classifier is used to detect the malicious application. The authors could detect Spy-related applications with an accuracy of 81%, SMS-related with malicious applications with an accuracy of 97% and Control-related malicious applications with an 100% accuracy and could detect benign applications with an accuracy of 88%.

(Glodek and Harang(2013)) constructed five Random Forests with 5-fold cross validation and compared their performance in detecting malicious applications. They have used 500 malicious and 500 benign from North Carolina State University's malware project. Permission, broadcast receivers and native code embedded in the application are used as features and they concluded that their method outperforms a lot of commercial anti virus detection tools.

(Jerome et al.(2014)Jerome, Allix, State, and Engel) extracted the opcodes from class.dex file and translated into opcode sequences, binary sequences of k-grams that characterize the least functionalities required by a program. They trained their model with Gnome Project dataset and randomly picked 1246 applications from the Google Play Store. The test dataset consists of 25,476 malware samples, 15670 benign applications from VirusTotal. Information Gain was used to select important features among the available ones. The author used a linear implementation of SVM to classify application samples. The results were compared with the detection rate of 25 anti virus tools. The study release an interesting signature patterns of Malware, Goodware, False Positives and False Negatives of their classifier. The false negatives were found out to be adwares and they were also considered a threat by the tool.

(Pehlivan et al.(2014)Pehlivan, Baltaci, Acarturk, and Baykal) used 3748 application packages, developed C# scripts to automatically extract about 182 attributes that include Permissions, version no and version name of the applications. The study compared feature selection methods such as Gain Ratio Attribute Evaluator, Relief Attribute Evaluator, Control Flow Subset Evaluator, and Consistency Subset Evaluator and machine learning algorithms Bayesian classification, Classification and Regression Tree (CART), J48 DT, RF, SMO. Using the feature selection methods, they came up with 97 features that could represent the whole dataset. Finally the authors conclude that, with just 25 features, the Control Flow Subset Evaluator selection gave a good performance and Random forest and J48 performed better than Bayesian classifier.

(Chan and Song(2014)) analyzed 796 benign and 175 malicious applications for their study. Permissions used from the manifest.xml file and API call info from the classes.dex file are extracted and with Information Gain they selected a set of 19 relevant API calls. They compared the results obtained by machine learning algorithms such as Naive Bayes, SVM with SMO algorithm, RBF Network, Multi Layer Perceptron, Liblinear, J48 decision tree and Random Forests.The authors concluded that the were able to get 90% of the accuracy by using the API calls and permission combined than using the individual features alone.

(Liu and Liu(2014)) combined the two types of permissions, required permission and requested permission and designed a two layer approach with these features and employed machine learning algorithms to detect the malicious applications. A total of 28,548 benign applications and 1,536 malicious applications and permission pairs i.e., combination of any two requested permission are analyzed. The two layered approach helped to balance the detection accuracy and detection speed of the classifier. In Phase 1, requested permissions and the J48 Decision Tree algorithm is used in detection and in Phase 2, requested permission pairs and the J48 Decision Tree is used for detection. If there is any contradiction in the results obtained from both the phases, used permission pairs and J48 is used to classify again. The authors achieved a good result with this approach and recommended using the permission in component level than the application level for better detection of malicious activities.

(Ideses and Neuberger(2014)) used permission, broadcast receivers and activities, byte code fragments, system-calls as features and trained SVM with the training dataset. The researchers tested their proposed Malware detection system with a security tester for benchmarking where their system was tested with 7,000 samples. They conclude that their system could achieve about 99.3% positive rate with just 0.14% false alarm rate.

(Yerima et al.(2014a)Yerima, Sezer, and McWilliams) presented and analyzed three Bayesian classification approaches for detecting Android malwares. Permissions and code based properties such as API calls, both Java system based and Android system based, Linux and Android system commands are also extracted from the sample applications. A list of top 20 permissions and top 25 API calls used by benign and malicious applications are presented.

(Fazeen and Dantu(2014)) used combines Intentions of the applications esp., Task Intentions with permission as feature in developing their model. At first the requested permissions are extracted and a histogram is constructed for that task-intention category. Normalizing this results in an I shaped PMF. This shape is used to compare and detect the unknown applications as benign or malicious based on their Task Intentions. The system works as follows:

- **Phase I** trains and uses machine learning algorithms to find the task intentions of the sample applications.
- **Phase II** uses the knowledge from Phase I to find the task intention of an unknown application and classify as benign or malicious. The I shape is compared with the requested permission by using a using a matching ratio, that is generated by a machine learning algorithm. If the ratio is in a threshold, then the application is potentially safe. The authors used Naive Bayes, Multi Layered Perceptron and Random Forests and compared their performances.

(Xiaoyan et al.(2014)Xiaoyan, Juan, and Xiujuan) extracted permissions from the manifest and represented as a binary vector. Then Principle Component Analysis (PCA) is performed to select the best features. A linear SVM is trained to classify the app samples. The author compares the result with other classifiers such as J48 Decision Tree, Naive Bayes, BayesNet, CART, RandomForest and concludes that SVM gives a better performance.

(Yerima et al.(2014b)Yerima, Sezer, and Muttik) came up with a parallel implementation of their system to detect malicious android applications. They used application related feature such as permissions, Standard OS and android framework commands. They developed parallel implementation of Logistic function based classifier, Naive Bayes - probabilistic method and PART, RIDOR which are rule based classifier. with the features extracted, the classification is performed with the individual algorithms and then parallel implementation is carried out. The maximum probability scheme fetched an accuracy of 97.5%.

(Idrees and Rajarajan(2014)) combines permissions and Intents and used 292 applications for training and 340 for testing their model. The study describes some usage statistics of benign and malicious applications with regards to intents and permissions and developed Naive Bayes, Kstar, Prism to detect the maliciuos applications from benign applications.

(Munoz et al.(2015)Munoz, Martin, Guzman, and Hernandez) The authors collected the information from Google Play meta-data such as intrinsic application features, Application category, Developer related feature, certificate related feature, social related feature. They concluded that certificate and developer information, intrinsic application feature are the most promising feature to determine a malware with just meta data.

(Westyarian et al.(2015)Westyarian, Rosmansyah, and Dabarsyah) used 205 benign and 207 malicious application files and extracted API calls that are only related to the permission declared in ¡used-permission¿ label in manifest.xml file. The study concluded that 97% of the malware requests *telephonyManager* and *connectivityManager* are the most important features. Random forest classification obtains 92.4% with cross validation as feature selection algorithm and SVM obtain 91.4% with percentage split as feature selection algorithm.

(Chuang and Wang(2015)) collected API calls from benign application separately and API calls from malicious applications separately and used these as features for classifying an unknown sample. The APIs in the unknown are ranked according to their difference in the number of occurrences in benign and number of occurrences in malicious applications. Then they deploy single a model approach where they will combine the two feature sets into a single vector. In Malicious model approach only the hypothesis from Malicious tended APIs is used for classification. The Hybrid approach combines two separately trained SVM models. These results are then compared to predict whether the unknown sample is malicious. The Hybrid model behaved much better than the Malicious model but the single model obtained from combined features outperformed the Malicious model.

Table 1 shows the top frequent used features in static analysis. Table 2 summarizes the top features that are combined with other features to produce better detection rate. By observing the table 1 and table 2, it can be clearly seen that Permission and API calls, the two features extracted from Manifest file and .dex file produces higher detection rate and inorder to make them more fail safe these can be combined with other features such as mate-data collected from Google Play Store or the features extracted from the XML elements.

Table 1: Topmost used features in static analysis

Sl. No.	Feature
1	Permission
2	API calls
3	Strings extracted
4	Native commands
5	XML elements
6	Meta data
7	Opcodes from .dex file
8	Task Intents

Table 2: Top features combined with other features in static analysis

Feature	Combined With
Permissions	Broadcast receivers Uses-feature tag Android OS commands API calls meta-data opcodes
Features extracted from manifest files and class files	API calls

Dynamic Analysis

(Wei et al.(2012)Wei, Mao, Jeng, Lee, Wang, and Wu) used Droidbox, a tool to monitor the application real time, to dynamically analyze the behavior of android applications. IP address of the source is extracted from the network traffic after then application is run in a sandbox environment. The research concentrated only on the network characteristics of the malwares leveraging the fact that they will find their next target soon. The extracted IP address is used to find the spatial address using external services and to determine the uniformity of geographic distribution of the hosts because infected hosts will be distributed worldwide. After extracting the features, a MxN APP-GEO Matrix is constructed with M representing the android applications(rows) and N network features. ICA (Independent Component Analysis) to extract the latent concept or sparse from the noisy spamming data. The researchers used Weka and FastICA, the two open source libraries to evaluate their model. A total of 310 malware samples were used and they could achieve about 93% accuracy rate.

(Ham and Choi(2013)) used 30 normal apps and 5 malware samples (GoldDream, PJApps, DroidKungFu2, Snake and Angry Birds Rio Unlocker) in this study. The allocated resources when the app starts are monitored and the behavioral pattern is extracted. hese resource data are stored within the device and are converted into feature vectors. Each feature is subdivided to 7 categories, 1. Network, SMS, CPU, and power usage, Process (like ID, Name , running process), memory Native, Dalvik and other and Virtual Memory.32 features are related to malware detection and applied

Information Gain to select features. They used Naive Bayes, Random Forest LR, SVM with 10 fold cross validation.

The authors concluded that Naive Bayes/LRs confusion matrix are irregular in distribution with these features. SVM correctly classified normal type data almost 100% but falsely detected malicious applications as benign. Random Forests outperformed all the algorithms and correctly classifies the majority of normal and malware applications.

(Lu et al.(2013)Lu, Zulie, Jingju, and Yi) compared Bayesian method alone and Bayesian method combined with Chi Square feature selection method results are compared to evaluate the performance of the two ML algorithms. The study concluded that Bayesian method with Chi Squared yielded an accuracy of 89% while Bayesian method alone yielded 80%.

(Tenenboim-Chekina et al.(2013)Tenenboim-Chekina, Barad, Shabtai, Mimran, Rokach, Shapira, and Elovici) used 5 to 10 self-written Trojan malware with two versions of the malware, one benign and other malicious which is repacked version of the benign with malicious code. While the application is running, Many network based features are extracted. The self-written applications are installed in the devices and their behavior was collected and analyzed. This helps the traffic patterns distinguishable from benign and malicious. Feature measurements are performed at fixed time intervals and then aggregation functions are computed over these measurements. Cross feature analysis is used to explore the correlation between features. The deviations caused by abnormal activities from normal activities are observed. With labeled samples a threshold of deviation is obtained during the algorithm formulation. The study could successfully detect the repacked malicious applications using the network features learned.

(Alam and Vuong(2013)) rooted the mobile device to get the details such as, data being sent by applications, IP address being communicated, number of active communications, the system calls and used Random forest with 1330 malicious and 407 benign applications. The authors concluded that with more trees and less feature per tree in the Random Forest, they could achieve an accuracy of 99%.

(Mas'ud et al.(2014)Mas'ud, Sahib, Abdollah, Selamat, and Yusof) monitored the system call of 30 normal applications and 30 malicious applications. The study compares 5 feature selection methods and 5 Machine Learning classifiers KNN, Decision Tree, Multi Layer Perceptron (MLP), Random Forests, Naive Bayes. The applications are run in real devices and are monitored for system calls generated by Strace, an application used to log various system activities in android systems. Then the features are selected by Information Gain and Chi-Square. A set of 5 feature sets are devised and used to compare the efficiency of 5 Machine Learning algorithms. The study concluded that the MLP achieves a highest accuracy and True Positive rate for one feature set while J48 Decision Tree achieves high performance rate for another feature set.

(Ng and Hwang(2014)) also used Strace to monitor the application for 60 secs. The features taken into account were Strace logged ProcessID, system calls, returned values and times between consecutive system calls. The no of times each invoked call is counted. PCA is used in selecting the important feature and then the classifier classifies the application sample malicious or benign based on anomaly score obtained by the input. The author compared their system's performance with classifiers such as Naive Bayes, J48 Decision Tree and SVM and claims that they could achieve 98.4% detection rate.

(Kim and Choi(2014)) Linux based features are extracted from the Android Os and used as feature to detect malicious applications. There were 59 features obtained like, Memory, CPU, Network, etc. 6 malwares were run on the system and the system is monitored to collect the above said features. Every 10 seconds the data is collected and sent over to a server and the server does the classification. Out of 59 features, 36 are selected and the results are compared before and after applying feature selection. It has been said that the feature selection improves the accuracy and reduces the False Positive Rate of the classification.

(Kurniawan et al.(2015)Kurniawan, Rosmansyah, and Dabarsyah) used Logger, a default application which is inbuilt in Android was used to extract the sum of Internet traffic, percentage of battery used and battery temperature for every minute. These information collected as set of features and is fed into weka, a open source learning library for testing and training with Naive Bayes, J48 decision tree and Random Forest algorithms. The author concluded that Random Forest has high accuracy of 85.6% with these features and proposes other features that can be combined with existing system to improve the accuracy.

Table 3 summarizes the most frequently used features in Dynamic analysis. As seen, Network traffic which includes data packets sent, and other behavioral patterns can lead to quick detection of malicious activity. Tracing the IP address can help us to get the geographical landscape of the attack surface. Other than this, SMS, information logged by Logger and Strace is very much helpful in achieving a higher detection rate.

Hybrid Analysis

The hybrid methodology involves combining static and dynamic features collected from analyzing the application and extracting information while the application is running, respectively. Though it could increase the accuracy of the detection rate, it makes the system cumbersome and the analysis process time consuming.

(Shabtai(2010)) extracted opcodes from the executable and proposed a framework that monitors the device state at every instant such as CPU usage, number of packets sent over network, number of running process, battery level. Applications are downloaded from play store. The authors examine the applicability of Knowledge Based Temporal Abstraction (KBTA) which helps continuously monitor and measure events on a mobile system. The study was concluded with 94% detection rate with the feasibility of running such a system with just 3% power consumption. The authors also recommend the implementation of SELinux to enhance the security mechanisms of Android. Efficiency of Machine Learning algorithms such as Decision Trees, Naive

Table 3: Top features used in Dynamic analysis

Sl. No.	Feature	Machine Learning Algorithm
1	Network, SMS, Power Usage, CPU, Process info, Native and Dalvik Memory	Naive Bayes, Random Forest, SVM with SMO algorithm
2	Data packets being sent, IP address, No. of active communications, System calls	Random Forest
3	Process id, System calls collected by Strace, Returned values, Times between consecutive calls	Naive Bayes, Decision Trees, SVM
4	Network Traffic - Destination IP address	Classification
5	System calls collected Strace, Logs of System activities	J48 Decision Trees, KNN, ST, Multi Layer Perceptron
6	Data collected by Logger, Internet traffic, Battery percentage, Temperature collected every minute	Naive Bayes, J48 Decision Trees

Bayes, BayesNet, K-Means, Histogram and Logistic Regression are compared and evaluated.

(Xu et al.(2013)Xu, Yu, Chen, Cao, Dong, Guo, and Cao) proposes a system, MobSafe that combines the dynamic (Android Security Evaluation Framework - ASEF) and static (Static Android Analysis Framework - SAAF) analysis methods. They used 100,000 active android applications from AppChina. Static features include the information from apk files and decoded smali files were analyzed to extract the permissions, heuristic patterns, and program slicing for functions of interest NO ML: analyzing takes within 2mins and For dynamic analysis ADB logging and TCP DUMP were used. The application is launched on a Virtual Machine and subjected to human level interaction simulation. This is then compared with a CVE library and its Internet activity with Google Safe Browser API to check the URLS the app requested is malicious or not.

(Wei et al.(2013)Wei, Zhang, Ge, and Hardy) analyzed 96 benign applications and 92 malware samples to extract static features such as software profiles. Strace is used to record system calls along with the process ID while the application is running for dynamic features. These information are collected and applied over Support Vector Machones and Naive Bayes.

(Feldman et al.(2014)Feldman, Stadther, and Wang) proposes a system, Manilyzer which uses requested permissions, High Prior receivers, Low version numbers and abused services as features and test their model with 617 applications 307 malicious 310 benign applications. Efficiency of Naive Bayes, SVM, K-Nearest Neighbours, J48 Decision Trees are compared and concluded with saying the most number of malware were labelled with 1.x application version number. And also that high priority intent filter were closely associated with SMS malware as 88% of the applications with this characteristics were malicious. Manilyzer is less effective but can be enhanced with other features associated with permissions such as API calls. Manilyzer is effectively used to detect adware spywae and SMS malware.

(Hsieh et al.(2015)Hsieh, Wu, and Kao) studies and summarizes the threat from malware on handheld devices, how malware writers evade the anti virus detection on mobile devices and the techniques that were used to deliver the malicious payload onto the mobile systems. The authors conclude the research by giving out the analysis methodologies in detecting the malwares.

(Lindorfer et al.(2015)Lindorfer, Neugschwandtner, and Platzer) proposes a system MARVIN with large-scale Android malware analysis sandbox ANDRUBIS to provide users with a risk assessment for an application. They developed an end user app into which users will submit their app and receive the score that tells the users how malicious the application is. MARVIN has 98.24% accuracy with less than 0.04% false positives. Static features such as permission, API Calls based on used-permission, reflection API, cryptographic API, dynamic loading of code are combined with dynamic features such as File operations, Network operations, Phone events, Data leaks, Dynamically loaded code, dynamically registered broadcast receivers. SVM with a linear classifier is used as a model of classification. The authors made use of labeled data set obtained from play-store, gnome project and used their system to classify samples from VirusTotal.

Table 4 summarizes the static an dynamic features combined and used as part of hybrid analysis. As seen from Table 1, Permissions is used mostly as a feature along with dynamic features like Logged information, API call traces and Network Traffics.

Future Goals on Counteracting the Update Attack

With this analysis, it can be seen that only very few researches have been conducted which deals with counteracting the update attack. As discussed in the previous section, the update attack is so hard to detect because with the previous version installed on the device is benign and it is not sure when the malicious activity os performed. The key to detect update attack is to keep track of the functions of the previous benign applications that are installed on the android devices. When the application is updated we can find the difference between the old and recent versions of the application and with combining the machine learning techniques and the acquired knowledge from malicious malware files, we can easily detect the update attack and the malicious in-

Table 4: Top features used in Hybrid analysis

Sl. No.	Feature	Machine Learning Algorithm
1	CPU Usage, No. of packets sent, No. of running process, Battery level	Naive Bayes, Decision trees, Random Forest,BayesNet, K-Means, Logistic Regression
2	Static: Information from apk, Decoded smali files Dynamic: ADB Logging, TCP Dump	Random Forest
3	Static: Static: Software profile Dynamic: Strace - system calls and process id,	Naive Bayes, SVM
4	Static: Permission, High priority receivers, version numbers	Naive Bayes, SVM, K-NN, J48 Decision Trees
5	Static: Permission, API Calls based on used-permission, reflection API, cryptographic API, Dynamic: loading, File operations, Network operations, Phone events, Data leaks, Dynamically loaded code, dynamically registered broadcast receivers	SVM with linear function

tent of the malware author.

Figure 1: Counteracting the update attack

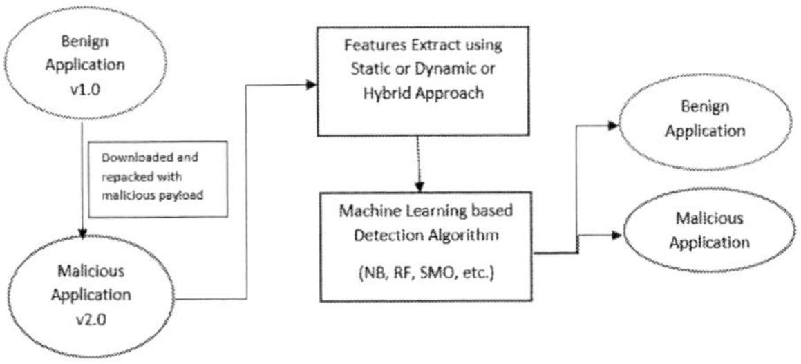

Conclusion

This study summarizes recent developments in android malware detection using machine learning algorithms. Detection techniques and systems that uses static, dynamic and hybrid approaches are discussed and highlighted. A method that could lead to potential counteracting the update attack is discussed. The unavailability of a larger android malware dataset remains a great problem in evaluating various approaches. With a proper dataset shared among researchers, a system that learns a new malware and share that knowledge to all the mobile devices, so that they can protect themselves from future attacks, could be developed.

References

M.S. Alam and S.T. Vuong. Random forest classification for detecting android malware. In *Green Computing and Communications (GreenCom), 2013 IEEE and Internet of Things (iThings/CPSCom), IEEE International Conference on and IEEE Cyber, Physical and Social Computing*, pages 663–669, Aug 2013. doi: 10.1109/GreenCom-iThings-CPSCom.2013.122.

P.P.K. Chan and Wen-Kai Song. Static detection of android malware by using permissions and api calls. In *Machine Learning and Cybernetics (ICMLC), 2014 International Conference on*, volume 1, pages 82–87, July 2014. doi: 10.1109/ICMLC.2014.7009096.

Hsin-Yu Chuang and Sheng-De Wang. Machine learning based hybrid behavior models for android malware analysis. In *Software Quality, Reliability and Security (QRS), 2015 IEEE International Conference on*, pages 201–206, Aug 2015. doi: 10.1109/QRS.2015.37.

M. Fazeen and R. Dantu. Another free app: Does it have the right intentions? In *Privacy, Security and Trust (PST), 2014 Twelfth Annual International Conference on*, pages 282–289, July 2014. doi: 10.1109/PST.2014.6890950.

S. Feldman, D. Stadther, and Bing Wang. Manilyzer: Automated android malware detection through manifest analysis. In *Mobile Ad Hoc and Sensor Systems (MASS), 2014 IEEE 11th International Conference on*, pages 767–772, Oct 2014. doi: 10.1109/MASS.2014.65.

M. Ghorbanzadeh, Yang Chen, Zhongmin Ma, T.C. Clancy, and R. McGwier. A neural network approach to category validation of android applications. In *Computing, Networking and Communications (ICNC), 2013 International Conference on*, pages 740–744, Jan 2013. doi: 10.1109/ICNC.2013.6504180.

W. Glodek and R. Harang. Rapid permissions-based detection and analysis of mobile malware using random decision forests. In *Military Communications Conference, MILCOM 2013 - 2013 IEEE*, pages 980–985, Nov 2013. doi: 10.1109/MILCOM.2013.170.

Hyo-Sik Ham and Mi-Jung Choi. Analysis of android malware detection performance using machine learning classifiers. In *ICT Convergence (ICTC), 2013 International Conference on*, pages 490–495, Oct 2013. doi: 10.1109/ICTC.2013.6675404.

Wan-Chen Hsieh, Chuan-Chi Wu, and Yung-Wei Kao. A study of android malware detection technology evolution.

In *Security Technology (ICCST), 2015 International Carnahan Conference on*, pages 135–140, Sept 2015. doi: 10.1109/CCST.2015.7389671.

I. Ideses and A. Neuberger. Adware detection and privacy control in mobile devices. In *Electrical Electronics Engineers in Israel (IEEEI), 2014 IEEE 28th Convention of*, pages 1–5, Dec 2014. doi: 10.1109/EEEI.2014.7005849.

F. Idrees and M. Rajarajan. Investigating the android intents and permissions for malware detection. In *Wireless and Mobile Computing, Networking and Communications (WiMob), 2014 IEEE 10th International Conference on*, pages 354–358, Oct 2014. doi: 10.1109/WiMOB.2014.6962194.

Q. Jerome, K. Allix, R. State, and T. Engel. Using opcode-sequences to detect malicious android applications. In *Communications (ICC), 2014 IEEE International Conference on*, pages 914–919, June 2014. doi: 10.1109/ICC.2014.6883436.

Hwan-Hee Kim and Mi-Jung Choi. Linux kernel-based feature selection for android malware detection. In *Network Operations and Management Symposium (APNOMS), 2014 16th Asia-Pacific*, pages 1–4, Sept 2014. doi: 10.1109/APNOMS.2014.6996540.

H. Kurniawan, Y. Rosmansyah, and B. Dabarsyah. Android anomaly detection system using machine learning classification. In *Electrical Engineering and Informatics (ICEEI), 2015 International Conference on*, pages 288–293, Aug 2015. doi: 10.1109/ICEEI.2015.7352512.

M. Lindorfer, M. Neugschwandtner, and C. Platzer. Marvin: Efficient and comprehensive mobile app classification through static and dynamic analysis. In *Computer Software and Applications Conference (COMPSAC), 2015 IEEE 39th Annual*, volume 2, pages 422–433, July 2015. doi: 10.1109/COMPSAC.2015.103.

Wen Liu. Mutiple classifier system based android malware detection. In *Machine Learning and Cybernetics (ICMLC), 2013 International Conference on*, volume 01, pages 57–62, July 2013. doi: 10.1109/ICMLC.2013.6890444.

Xing Liu and Jiqiang Liu. A two-layered permission-based android malware detection scheme. In *Mobile Cloud Computing, Services, and Engineering (MobileCloud), 2014 2nd IEEE International Conference on*, pages 142–148, April 2014. doi: 10.1109/MobileCloud.2014.22.

Yu Lu, Pan Zulie, Liu Jingju, and Shen Yi. Android malware detection technology based on improved bayesian classification. In *Instrumentation, Measurement, Computer, Communication and Control (IMCCC), 2013 Third International Conference on*, pages 1338–1341, Sept 2013. doi: 10.1109/IMCCC.2013.297.

M.Z. Mas'ud, S. Sahib, M.F. Abdollah, S.R. Selamat, and R. Yusof. Analysis of features selection and machine learning classifier in android malware detection. In *Information Science and Applications (ICISA), 2014 International Conference on*, pages 1–5, May 2014. doi: 10.1109/ICISA.2014.6847364.

A. Munoz, I. Martin, A. Guzman, and J.A. Hernandez. Android malware detection from google play meta-data: Selection of important features. In *Communications and Network Security (CNS), 2015 IEEE Conference on*, pages 701–702, Sept 2015. doi: 10.1109/CNS.2015.7346893.

D.V. Ng and J.-I.G. Hwang. Android malware detection using the dendritic cell algorithm. In *Machine Learning and Cybernetics (ICMLC), 2014 International Conference on*, volume 1, pages 257–262, July 2014. doi: 10.1109/ICMLC.2014.7009126.

U. Pehlivan, N. Baltaci, C. Acarturk, and N. Baykal. The analysis of feature selection methods and classification algorithms in permission based android malware detection. In *Computational Intelligence in Cyber Security (CICS), 2014 IEEE Symposium on*, pages 1–8, Dec 2014. doi: 10.1109/CICYBS.2014.7013371.

N. Peiravian and Xingquan Zhu. Machine learning for android malware detection using permission and api calls. In *Tools with Artificial Intelligence (ICTAI), 2013 IEEE 25th International Conference on*, pages 300–305, Nov 2013. doi: 10.1109/ICTAI.2013.53.

R. Raveendranath, V. Rajamani, A.J. Babu, and S.K. Datta. Android malware attacks and countermeasures: Current and future directions. In *Control, Instrumentation, Communication and Computational Technologies (ICCICCT), 2014 International Conference on*, pages 137–143, July 2014. doi: 10.1109/ICCICCT.2014.6992944.

RiskIQ. Android malware attacks and countermeasures: Current and future directions. June 2014.

J. Sahs and L. Khan. A machine learning approach to android malware detection. In *Intelligence and Security Informatics Conference (EISIC), 2012 European*, pages 141–147, Aug 2012. doi: 10.1109/EISIC.2012.34.

A.A.A. Samra, Kangbin Yim, and O.A. Ghanem. Analysis of clustering technique in android malware detection. In *Innovative Mobile and Internet Services in Ubiquitous Computing (IMIS), 2013 Seventh International Conference on*, pages 729–733, July 2013. doi: 10.1109/IMIS.2013.111.

B. Sanz, I. Santos, C. Laorden, X. Ugarte-Pedrero, and P.G. Bringas. On the automatic categorisation of android applications. In *Consumer Communications and Networking Conference (CCNC), 2012 IEEE*, pages 149–153, Jan 2012. doi: 10.1109/CCNC.2012.6181075.

A. Shabtai. Malware detection on mobile devices. In *Mobile Data Management (MDM), 2010 Eleventh International Conference on*, pages 289–290, May 2010. doi: 10.1109/MDM.2010.28.

A. Shabtai, Y. Fledel, and Y. Elovici. Automated static code analysis for classifying android applications using machine learning. In *Computational Intelligence and Security (CIS), 2010 International Conference on*, pages 329–333, Dec 2010. doi: 10.1109/CIS.2010.77.

L. Tenenboim-Chekina, O. Barad, A. Shabtai, D. Mimran, L. Rokach, B. Shapira, and Y. Elovici. Detecting application update attack on mobile devices through network featur. In *Computer Communications Workshops (INFOCOM WKSHPS), 2013 IEEE Conference on*, pages 91–92, April 2013. doi: 10.1109/INFCOMW.2013.6970755.

Te-En Wei, Ching-Hao Mao, A.B. Jeng, Hahn-Ming Lee, Horng-Tzer Wang, and Dong-Jie Wu. Android malware detection via a latent network behavior analysis. In *Trust, Security and Privacy in Computing and Communications (TrustCom), 2012 IEEE 11th International Conference on*, pages 1251–1258, June 2012. doi: 10.1109/TrustCom.2012.91.

Yu Wei, Hanlin Zhang, Linqiang Ge, and R. Hardy. On behavior-based detection of malware on android platform. In *Global Communications Conference (GLOBECOM), 2013 IEEE*, pages 814–819, Dec 2013. doi: 10.1109/GLOCOM.2013.6831173.

Westyarian, Y. Rosmansyah, and B. Dabarsyah. Malware detection on android smartphones using api class and machine learning. In *Electrical Engineering and Informatics (ICEEI), 2015 International Conference on*, pages 294–297, Aug 2015. doi: 10.1109/ICEEI.2015.7352513.

Zhao Xiaoyan, Fang Juan, and Wang Xiujuan. Android malware detection based on permissions. In *Information and Communications Technologies (ICT 2014), 2014 International Conference on*, pages 1–5, May 2014. doi: 10.1049/cp.2014.0605.

J. Xu, Y. Yu, Z. Chen, B. Cao, W. Dong, Y. Guo, and J. Cao. Mobsafe: cloud computing based forensic analysis for massive mobile applications using data mining. *Tsinghua Science and Technology*, 18(4):418–427, August 2013. doi: 10.1109/TST.2013.6574680.

S.Y. Yerima, S. Sezer, G. McWilliams, and I. Muttik. A new android malware detection approach using bayesian classification. In *Advanced Information Networking and Applications (AINA), 2013 IEEE 27th International Conference on*, pages 121–128, March 2013. doi: 10.1109/AINA.2013.88.

S.Y. Yerima, S. Sezer, and G. McWilliams. Analysis of bayesian classification-based approaches for android malware detection. *Information Security, IET*, 8(1):25–36, Jan 2014a. ISSN 1751-8709. doi: 10.1049/iet-ifs.2013.0095.

S.Y. Yerima, S. Sezer, and I. Muttik. Android malware detection using parallel machine learning classifiers. In *Next Generation Mobile Apps, Services and Technologies (NGMAST), 2014 Eighth International Conference on*, pages 37–42, Sept 2014b. doi: 10.1109/NGMAST.2014.23.

A Tool for Staging Mixed-initiative Dialogs*

Joshua W. Buck and **Saverio Perugini**
Department of Computer Science
University of Dayton
300 College Park
Dayton, Ohio 45469–2160 USA
Tel: +001 (937) 229–4079, Fax: +001 (937) 229–2193
E-mail: {jbuck1, saverio}@udayton.edu

Abstract

We discuss and demonstrate a tool for prototyping dialog-based systems that, given a high-level specification of a human-computer dialog, stages the dialog for interactive use. The tool enables a dialog designer to evaluate a variety of dialogs without having to program each individual dialog, and serves as a proof-of-concept for our approach to mixed-initiative dialog modeling and implementation from a programming language-based perspective.

Introduction

Mixed-initiative interaction is a flexible interaction strategy where the user and system engage as equal participants in an activity and take turns exchanging initiative, thereby sharing initiative. The strategy has been proposed and studied as a link to bridge artificial intelligence (AI) and human-computer interaction (Hearst, 1999). Mixed-initiative interaction has been studied and applied to keep the human in the learning feedback loop of an intelligent search, particularly, in planning, scheduling, and constraint satisfaction (Ferguson and Allen, 1998; Fleming and Cohen, 1999, 2001; Frank et al., 2001; Pu and Lalanne, 2002; Smith et al., 2005; Wolfman et al., 2001). This paper specifically addresses mixed-initiative dialog (Glass and Seneff, 2003; Lee et al., 2010; Walker and Whittaker, 1990). While "[c]reating an actual dialog system involves a very intensive programming effort" (Guinn, 1999), our tool simplifies that effort so that dialog designers can evaluate a variety of human-computer dialogs, including mixed-initiative dialogs (see figure 1).

A Language-based Approach to Mixed-initiative Dialog Modeling

We approach this problem by casting it in a programming language-based context, using notions from *lambda calculus* (Friedman and Wand, 2008). While not the focus of this paper, we introduce the fundamentals of the approach here to help orient the reader to the overall idea. As the user progresses through a dialog, we think of the steps that she takes as the evaluation of a function. Changing the evaluation method of the function (or transforming the function) then corresponds to different interaction policies (Rudnicky et al., 1999) for the dialog (i.e., ways of mixing initiative). The overall idea is that different function evaluation strategies correspond to different interaction policies for the dialog (i.e., system initiated vs. mixed-initiative) or ways of mixing initiative. For instance, consider a course scheduling dialog where the user must make selections for department, time, and number of credits, among others. We can model this dialog with a function $schedule$ with type signature $(department \times time \times credits) \rightarrow course$, simplified for purposes of succinct presentation. Evaluating this function using the *complete, eager* (Friedman and Wand, 2008) or *applicative-order evaluation* (Abelson and Sussman, 1996) function application evaluation method common in most programming languages (e.g., C, Java, Scheme) requires the user to supply arguments for the complete list of parameters to the function, in one stroke. In interaction terms, this evaluation method corresponds to a user completing, for example, an online, web-based form with multiple input fields (as, e.g., generated by Ajax) and clicking 'submit' once he has provided responses for all of the required fields. Optional fields correspond to (optional) parameters with default values (e.g., as in Python; Sebesta 2015). In general, this evaluation strategy corresponds to providing (possibly) multiple responses in a single utterance. A single utterance with only one response (if the function is a unary function), which is common in confirmation dialog boxes in application software, can also be modeled with this method.

Currying this function corresponds to spreading the interaction required to complete the dialog across a fixed series of multiple, progressive user-system dialog turns (i.e., system solicitation followed by user response, and so on). Currying the function $schedule$ above transforms it into one with type signature

$$department \rightarrow (time \rightarrow (credits \rightarrow course))^1,$$

such that

$$schedule_{uncurried}(\texttt{biology}, \texttt{morning}, 3) =$$

*We thank the four anonymous reviewers of this paper for their helpful comments and suggestions that helped to improve it.

[1] Parentheses included for purposes of clarity.

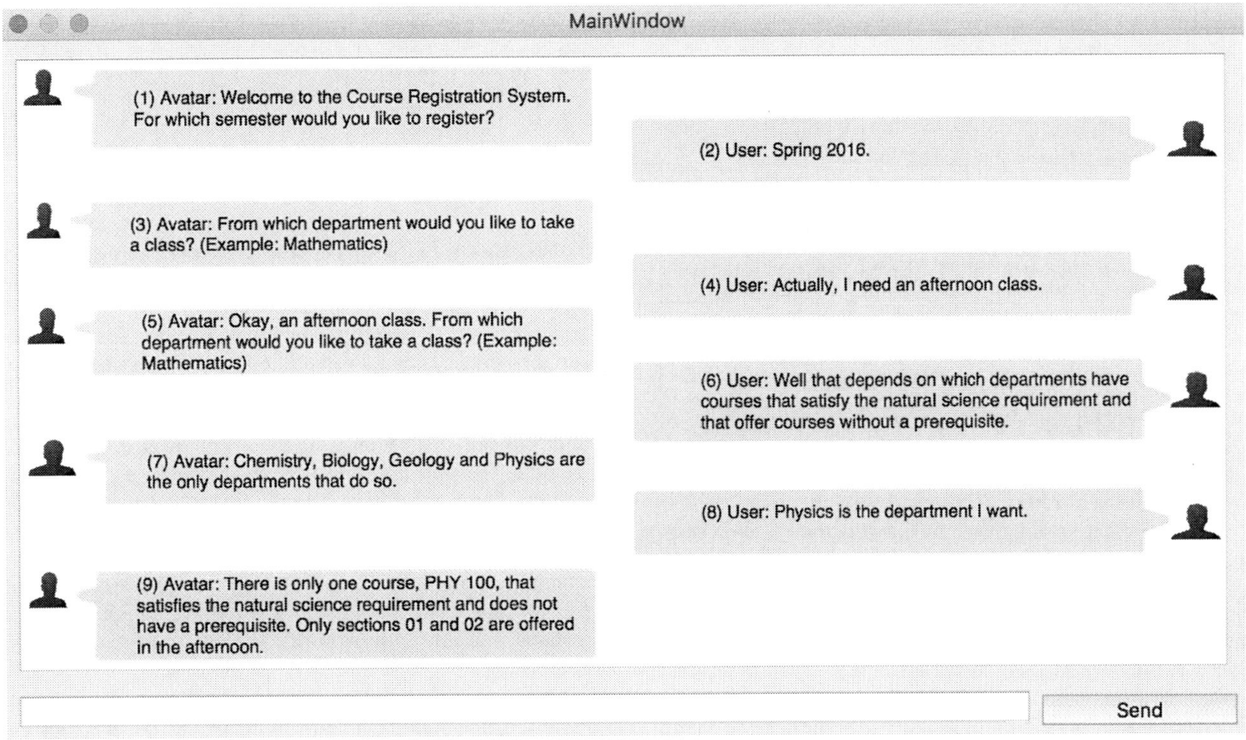

Figure 1: A mixed-initiative dialog.

$$((schedule_{curried}(\texttt{biology}))(\texttt{morning}))(3).$$

In general, *currying* (Scott, 2009) transforms a function $f_{uncurried}$ with type signature

$$f_{uncurried} : (p_1 \times p_2 \times \cdots \times p_n) \rightarrow r$$

into a function $f_{curried}$ with type signature

$$f_{curried} : p_1 \rightarrow (p_2 \rightarrow (\cdots \rightarrow (p_n \rightarrow r) \cdots)),$$

such that

$$f_{uncurried}(a_1, a_2, \cdots, a_n) = (\cdots ((f_{curried}(a_1))(a_2)) \cdots)(a_n).$$

(Uncurrying a curried function inverses the curry operation.) The function resulting from currying a function modeling a dialog corresponds to the interaction common in wizards for installing application software (Hamidi, Andritsos, and Liaskos, 2014) or in ATMs or airport and train kiosks, where the user is required to complete a *fixed*, system-initiated dialog (Allen, 1999) that involves supplying only one response per utterance. (Fixed dialogs have been referred to as *strongly-typed interactions* (Lee et al., 2010), underscoring a connection to the language concept of *strong typing* (Sebesta, 2015).)

Partially applying the function $schedule_{uncurried}$ corresponds to a fixed dialog where the user is afforded the flexibility to provide more than one response per utterance. This mode of interaction is common when providing a telephone, credit card, or PIN number through a voice modality. *Partial function application* states that for any function $f(p_1, p_2, \ldots, p_n)$,

$$f(a_1, a_2, \ldots, a_m) = g(p_{m+1}, p_{m+2}, \ldots, p_n),$$

where $m \leqslant n$, such that

$$g(a_{m+1}, a_{m+2}, \ldots, a_n) = f(a_1, a_2, \ldots, a_m, a_{m+1}, a_{m+2}, \ldots, a_n).$$

(Note that currying $f_{uncurried}$ and progressively applying the resulting $f_{curried}$ function has the same effect as partially applying $f_{uncurried}$.)

Lastly, applying the program transformation partial evaluation (Jones, 1996) to $schedule_{uncurried}$ corresponds to permitting the user to communicate answers to the set of questions in the dialog in utterances corresponding to all possible set partitions of the set of questions, and using all possible permutations of those partitions. *Partial evaluation* generalizes the idea of partial function application from any prefix of the parameter list to any subset of the parameter list and formally states that for any function $f(p_1, p_2, \ldots, p_n)$,

$$f(a, b, \ldots, r) = g(p_1, p_2, \ldots, p_n - a, b, \ldots, r),$$

where $\{a, b, \ldots, r\} \subseteq \{p_1, p_2, \ldots, p_n\}$, such that

$$g(s, t, \ldots, z) = f(a, b, \ldots, z).$$

Table 1 summaries these associations from programming language concepts to human-computer dialogs.

We developed a notation employing these function evaluation strategies for specifying mixed-initiative dialogs. A specification involving multiple functions using different evaluation strategies corresponds to a dialog involving multiple sub-dialogs. We refer the reader interested in additional details to (Perugini, 2015).

System Design and Implementation

While the implementation details are beyond the scope of this paper, we make some remarks. Figure 2 provides a conceptual overview of the design and execution of our dialog system construction tool. The left side of the figure depicts dialog specification and the right side illustrates dialog staging.

At present, the dialog designer must specify the dialog in a textual format using a high-level description language that is a less formal version of our language-based, dialog authoring notation that is then compiled into an XML document (see right side of figure 4). While the visual dialog builder interface through which the designer specifies the dialog to be implemented (see figure 4) is still in development, we use it in scenario 0 below to obviate the need to cover the formal syntax and details of our dialog authoring language. A specification in either format is then compiled into an XML document (see right side of figure 4). The XML document is then parsed into a variety of data structures (see figure 3) for use by the dialog staging engine, which processes user responses and stages the turns of the dialog (i.e., structures the interaction). We use the term *staging* to refer to the process by which the progressive turns of the dialog are structured or layered. For instance, the system starts by soliciting a response from the user to a particular question and then awaits a reply. The user in turn provides a response and the system makes another solicitation. The user then might respond to an unsolicited, yet forthcoming, question that the system accepts, processes, and uses to determine the next prompt to present. Dialog management, conducted through the staging engine here, performs system-action prediction (Lee et al., 2010)—deciding what to prompt for and/or accept next based on the discourse history and the current utterance. In this sense, staging operationalizes the dialog modeled by the specification and can be thought of as an interpreter (in the programming language sense of the word) for the specification.

Though not shown explicitly in figure 2, the dialog designer can also interact directly with the generation engine and the staging engine, in addition to a visual dialog builder, which is why the designer is depicted at the center of the dialog toolkit, especially since the staging engine supports server commands for interacting with user clients. Figure 3 illustrates the data structures used to represent the human-computer dialog demonstrated in the following designer and user scenarios.

Designer and User Scenarios

We use the following six scenarios from student course scheduling at a university to demonstrate our tool.

Scenario 0: Dialog Design

Using a drag-and-drop, split-screen, visual dialog builder (see figure 4), a dialog designer specifies a dialog by opening a new blank dialog project. In a new blank dialog template, a designer may specify aspects of the dialog such as a welcome message and generic (confirmation) responses to user utterances such as 'Okay, you answered ....' The designer can then create the first solicitation. Creating a new solicitation launches a set of boxes in the visual panel (left side of figure 4), by default, prompting the designer for a solicitation (typically a question) and three valid responses to it that the dialog (client) user may provide in response to that solicitation. The first solicitation in a course registration dialog might be 'For which semester would you like to register?' The three valid responses specified by the designer to this solicitation might be 'Fall,' 'Spring,' and 'Summer.' Using the tool, the designer can add and remove solicitations and responses at any time from the dialog specification she is authoring.

Once the dialog designer has specified more than one solicitation, she can establish a total or partial ordering between responses and solicitations by drawing arrows using the visual tool. For instance, the dialog designer might draw a relationship arrow from the 'Mathematics' response of the third solicitation to the fifth solicitation 'For which class would you like to register?' with the mathematics courses as possible responses. This scenario illustrates how a particular response can lead to a different path through a dialog through the inclusion of relationship arrows to associate certain responses to forthcoming solicitations. If no relationships are specified, the default interaction policy is implicit in the visual, top-to-bottom order of the solicitations in the left pane (i.e., a fixed dialog). In other words, if a response is listed without a defined relationship to another solicitation, the next solicitation by default is the solicitation immediately below the given response. Relationships that collectively induce a loop in the dialog specification—such as a relationship between a response and itself—without at least one path out of the loop are not permissible.

As mentioned above, the dialog designer can also create the dialog specification using our dialog authoring notation in a text format. Note that the right pane of the interface shown in figure 4 is a textual XML representation of the dialog specification. The two panes of the split-screen shown in figure 4 are synchronized in real time to be accurate reflections of each other, and the dialog designer always has the option of using either or both, at her discretion. The dialog designer can also dynamically change the interaction policy of a dialog or any sub-dialogs (i.e., evaluation order of the solicitations), as well as perform other operations, by interacting directly with the staging engine though a console, as mentioned above.

Scenario 1: Fixed Dialog with

Table 1: Metaphors from programming language evaluation strategies to a variety of human-computer dialogs.

Evaluation strategy	Responses per utterance	Ordering of utterances	Example(s)	Scenario
complete, eager evaluation	single	only one utterance	confirmation dialog boxes common in application software	–
complete, eager evaluation	multiple	only one utterance	web forms with multiple fields	2
currying	single	totally-ordered	wizards for installing application software or ATMs or airport and train kiosks	1
partial function application	multiple	totally-ordered	communicating a telephone, credit card, or PIN through voice	4
partial evaluation	single	partially-ordered	online test/quiz or survey	5
partial evaluation	multiple	partially-ordered	making a flight, rental car, or hotel reservation with a human agent	3

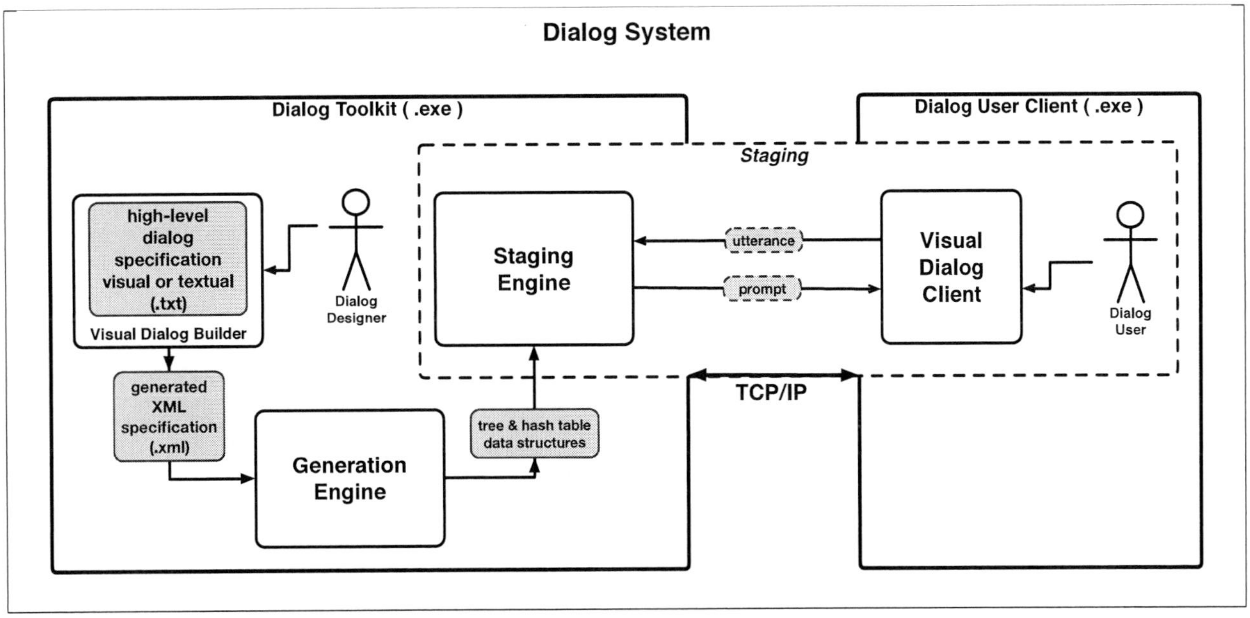

Figure 2: Conceptual design and execution of our dialog system.

Single Response per Utterance

The system solicits for a semester for which to register and the user responds with 'spring 2016.' In a fixed dialog, the user must respond to this question. The next solicitation is for a department in which to register for a course. The user replies with 'mathematics department' and the system solicits for the course level: undergraduate or graduate. The user responds with 'undergraduate' and the system prompts for a course. The user replies '168' and the system responds with 'Okay, mathematics 168. The course is offered from 3:35pm to 4:50pm on Tuesdays and Thursdays. Confirm registration?' If the user responds with 'yes,' the dialog is complete. This scenario illustrates one complete path through the dialog, where the user responds to all of the system solicitations in the order in which they are presented. This scenario corresponds to the third row of table 1 (i.e., currying). Figure 1 illustrates the interface through which the user, in this scenario and all following scenarios, interacts with the system while participating in the dialog.

Scenario 2: Fixed Dialog with All Responses in a Single Utterance

We restart the dialog system. This time, when prompted for a semester, the user responds with 'spring 2016 mathematics 168.' Note that the system accepts utterances containing responses embedded among other non-essential words. For instance, an equivalent response is 'I would like to register for mathematics 168 in spring 2016, please.' The system processes all of the responses in this utterance and responds with 'Okay, mathematics 168 in spring 2016. The course is offered from 3:35pm to 4:50pm on Tuesdays and Thursdays. Confirm registration?' If the user responds with 'yes,' the dialog is complete. This scenario illustrates a complete path through the dialog where the user provides responses to all of the solicitations in a single utterance. This scenario corresponds to the second row of table 1 (i.e., complete, eager evaluation).

Scenario 3: Mixed-initiative Dialog,

Unsolicited Responses

Assume we undo the user utterance in the scenario 2 above. This causes the system to solicit for a semester again. This time, the user does not provide a semester but rather a department in which to register for a course: 'mathematics department.' The system accepts and processes this unsolicited response instead and again solicits for a semester. This demonstrates the ability to provide responses for solicitations that the system has not made yet but will at some point in the dialog—a degree of mixed-initiative interaction known as *unsolicited reporting* (Allen, 1999). The user completes the dialog in one more turn with the utterance: 'mathematics 168 spring 2016.' This scenario corresponds to the fifth and sixth rows of table 1 (i.e., partial evaluation).

Scenario 4: Fixed Dialog with Multiple Responses per Utterance

Assume the dialog designer desires to permit the user to respond to multiple solicitations in a single utterance, but also wants to enforce an ordering on the set of solicitations of the dialog. Here the user could respond first with 'spring 2016 mathematics department' and then with '168.' Responses given in a single utterance are unordered as they are processed at the same time. This scenario illustrates a dialog supporting multiple responses per utterance, but with a fixed order on its solicitations, corresponding to the fourth row of table 1 (i.e., partial function application).

Scenario 5: Unsolicited, Single-response, Utterances

In contrast, the dialog designer might desire to permit the user to respond to solicitations in any order, but with only one response per utterance. In such a dialog, the user could reply with 'mathematics 168,' but could not provide multiple responses in any single utterance; responses such as 'spring 2016 mathematics department' are not permitted. This scenario corresponds to the fifth row of table 1 (i.e., partial evaluation).

Practical Considerations

Our dialog engine automatically infers dependencies between possible dialog responses in an effort to reduce dialog length. For instance, if the user responds with 'mathematics 168,' the system automatically infers that the user wants to register for an undergraduate course in the mathematics department and, thus, it is unnecessary to prompt for course level and department. The user then only needs to select the semester in which to register for the course and confirm the registration.

Our dialog engine uses error recovery strategies (Lee et al., 2010), including (explicit) confirmation, regarding mismatching and/or conflicting user responses. For instance, assume the user desires to register for a physics course. If the user responds first with 'mathematics department' and then with 'physics 168' in the next utterance, the dialog system responds with 'physics 168 is offered in the physics department, not the mathematics department. Would you like to change the department from mathematics to physics? If not, please choose a mathematics course.' This feature obviates the need to undo responses up to the response involving invalid or inconsistent information (e.g., department) and dynamically adjusts the response (e.g., to 'physics department'), if confirmed by the user. Also note that if the user makes an utterance that does not contain any valid responses for the dialog, such as 'I would like to book a flight from New York to Chicago please,' the system responds with 'I am sorry. I did not understand your response. Please reply to the prompt.' We designed our dialog engine to be thread-safe and the data structures that it manipulates to be stateless to allow multiple users to participate in individual instances of the same dialog concurrently.

Related Research

One approach to dialog modeling and implementation is from an artificial intelligence (AI) perspective (Allen et al., 2001), and involves selectively enumerating only those flows of control within the implementation which have been gleaned to be essential through learning algorithms. For instance, researchers have used constraint satisfaction to determine an ordering of dialog prompts (Donaldson and Cohen, 1997) and constraint propagation to implement subdialog invocation (Frank et al., 2001). There are a variety of other learning-based approaches (DeVault, Leuski, and Sagae, 2011; Misu et al., 2012). In contrast, using language-based concepts, including partial evaluation (Jones, 1996), to specify dialogs and to intensionally model multiple paths through a dialog without extensionally hardcoding each into the control flow of the implementation, is a fundamentally different approach to dialog modeling, management, and implementation. It achieves flexible dialog in a cleaner, less conditionally complex, design.

While there is an array of literature on developing (mixed-initiative) dialog systems and dialog management and construction frameworks (Hochberg, Kambhatla, and Roukos, 2002), we mention a few research projects due to their implementation-oriented nature: the DARPA *Communicator*-funded CMU *Sphinx*[2] project (Rudnicky et al., 1999), *RavenClaw* (Bohus and Rudnicky, 2003, 2009; Rudnicky and Xu, 1999) the *TuTalk*[3] project (Jordan, Ringenberg, and Hall, 2006), the *Atlas* dialog management system (Freedman, 2000), and the *Radiobot-CFF* (Leuski and Traum, 2011) and *NPCEditor* (Leuski and Traum, 2011) systems.

Conclusion

Human-computer dialog implementation is a challenging problem. Published literature has highlighted this problem, and discussed how much of a laborious, time-consuming process it can be (Glass and Seneff, 2003; Guinn, 1999; Hochberg, Kambhatla, and Roukos, 2002). Casting this problem on a programming languages landscape has suggested the use of a variety of function evaluation strategies, corresponding to different dialog interaction flow policies (i.e., staging methods) and ways of mixing initiative. It

[2] `http://cmusphinx.sourceforge.net/`

[3] An acronym for *Tutorial Talk*.

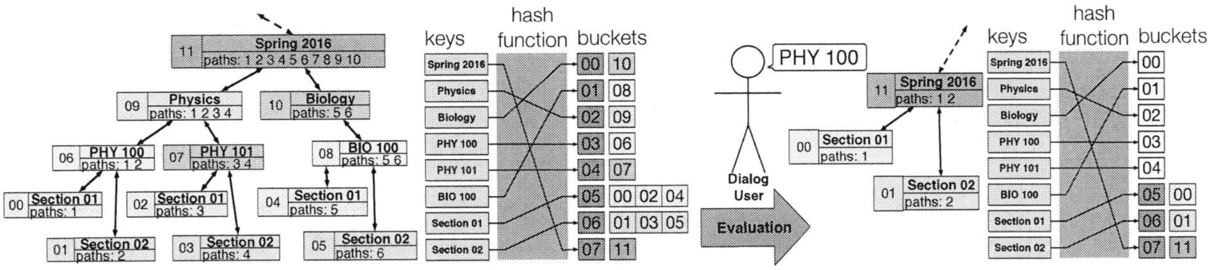

Figure 3: Data structures used to represent a human-computer dialog in our implementation.

has also supported our construction of the tool for automatic dialog implementation addressed here. Our tool can aid human-computer dialog designers in the following ways: i) no programming is required by the designer; only dialog specification is required, and the dialog system is automatically implemented and ii) the resulting dialog system can be reconfigured (e.g., different interaction policies can be applied/realized) (Glass and Seneff, 2003; Jordan, Ringenberg, and Hall, 2006; Polifroni, Chung, and Seneff, 2003) through minor modifications to the dialog specification. These benefits might help a dialog designer prototype and evaluate (Jordan, Ringenberg, and Hall, 2006), through studies with users (Feng et al., 2006), a variety of human-computer dialogs. For instance, evaluating several competing dialog designs with users and monitoring the paths taken by users to dialog completion and mining the results for the most-frequently used can help suggest refinements to the dialog specification (Spiliopoulou, 2000). Evaluating the least-frequently used paths might help the designer identify and isolate aspects of the dialog specification that could benefit from further attention.

This work can be extended in multiple directions. Lifting the problem of mixed-initiative dialog modeling, management, and implementation to a language-based landscape opens up opportunities for enriching not only the supportable dialogs but also the flexibility in interaction afforded in each as we explore additional language concepts and study their analogs in mixed-initiative interaction. Specifically, we plan to explore the use of *computational reflection* (Maes, 1987), and particularly *introspection* (i.e., read-only reflection), to support the user in *meta*-dialog inquiries, a higher-order degree of mixed-initiative interaction where the user may ask the system questions about the status of the dialog versus the typical reverse—only the system asking questions (Kronenberg and Regel-Brietzman, 2001). For instance, a user might inquire: 'How many more questions are you going to require me to answer?' We also intend to explore *meta*-dialog operations, such as 'Let us save the current status of this dialog and start over.' The capture, storage, invocation of *first-class continuations* (e.g., as provided by the `call/cc` facility in Scheme) (Friedman and Wand, 2008) can support *meta*-dialog operations such as the capture and reuse of frequently accessed dialog branches as macros as discussed by Quan et al. (2003), though in a slightly different context.

Coroutines and threads, and the actor model of concurrency with its message-passing motif, especially as used in the functional languages Elixir (Thomas, 2014) and Erlang (Armstrong, 2013), may help us specify and stage complex, problem-solving dialogs, where the system or user must engage each other in multiple (sub-)dialogs in parallel to solve the task at hand.

Our long-term goal is to develop a catalog of concepts of programming languages that are helpful metaphors for specifying and staging mixed-initiative dialogs, and formalizing their synergistic effects on dialog management and system design, and empirically studying the desirability of the interactions they support and enable.

References

Abelson, H., and Sussman, G. 1996. *Structure and Interpretation of Computer Programs*. Cambridge, MA: The MIT Press, second edition.

Allen, J.; Byron, D.; Dzikovska, M.; Ferguson, G.; Galescu, L.; and Stent, A. 2001. Towards conversational human-computer interaction. *AI Magazine* 22(4):27–37.

Allen, J. 1999. Mixed-initiative interaction. *IEEE Intelligent Systems* 14(5):14–16.

Armstrong, J. 2013. *Programming Erlang: Software for a Concurrent World*. Dallas, TX: Pragmatic Bookshelf, second edition.

Bohus, D., and Rudnicky, A. 2003. RavenClaw: Dialog management using hierarchical task decomposition and an expectation agenda. In *Proceedings of the Sixth Annual INTERSPEECH Conference*. International Speech Communication Association.

Bohus, D., and Rudnicky, A. 2009. The ravenclaw dialog management framework: Architecture and systems. *Computer Speech and Language* 23(3):332–361.

DeVault, D.; Leuski, A.; and Sagae, K. 2011. Toward learning and evaluation of dialogue policies with text examples. In *Proceedings of the Twelfth Association for Computational Linguistics (ACL) SIGDIAL Workshop on Discourse and Dialogue*, 39–48. Portland, OR: Association for Computational Linguistics.

Donaldson, T., and Cohen, R. 1997. A constraint satisfaction framework for managing mixed-initiative discourse.

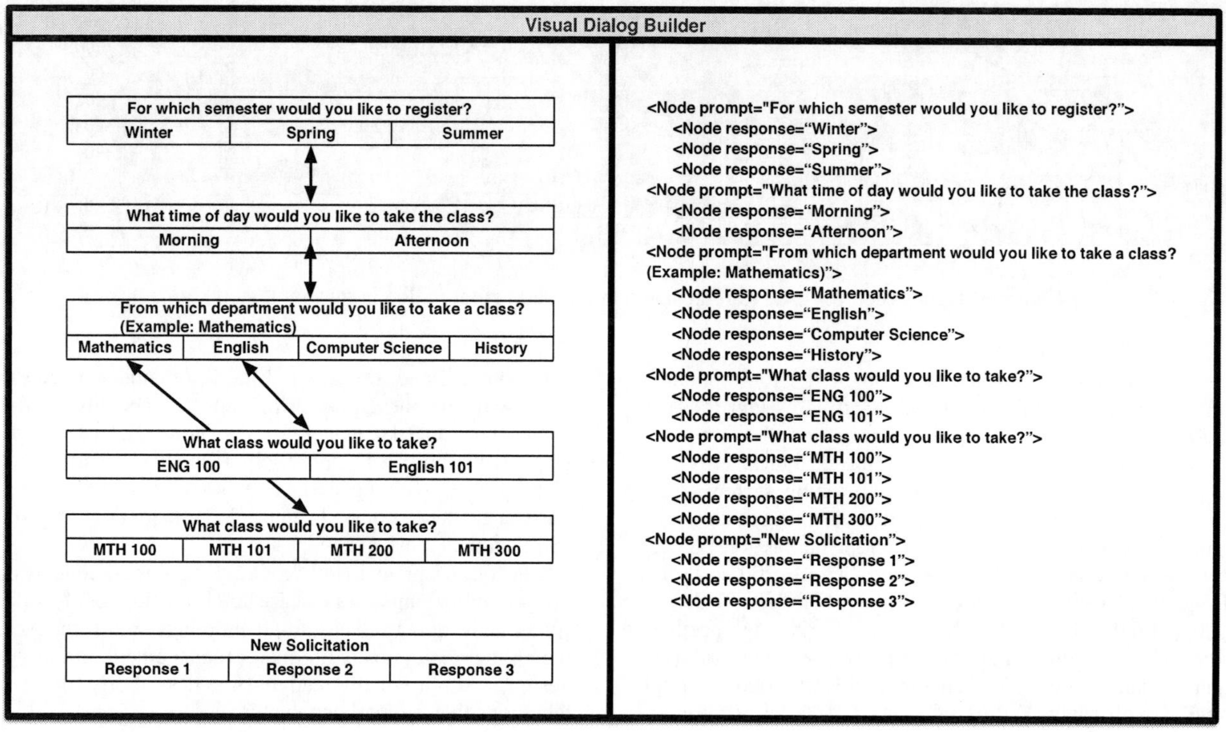

Figure 4: Sketch of a split-screen, visual/textual user interface for dialog specification. An incomplete/partial dialog is shown here (i.e., what is shown here is not the final representation of the dialog).

In *Proceedings of the AAAI Spring Symposium on Computational Models for Mixed Initiative Interactions*, number SS-97-04, 37–43. Menlo Park, CA: AAAI Press.

Feng, J.; Hakkani-Tür, D.; Fabbrizio, G. D.; Gilbert, M.; and Beutnagel, M. 2006. Webtalk: Towards automatically building spoken dialog systems through mining websites. In *Proceedings of the IEEE International Conference on Acoustics, Speech and Signal Processing (ICASSP)*, 573–576. Los Alamitos, CA: IEEE Computer Society Press.

Ferguson, G., and Allen, J. 1998. Trips: An integrated intelligent problem-solving assistant. In *Proceedings of the Fifteenth National Conference on Artificial Intelligence (AAAI)*. Menlo Park, CA: AAAI Press.

Fleming, M., and Cohen, R. 1999. Towards a methodology for designing and evaluating mixed-initiative AI systems. In *Proceedings of the AAAI Workshop on Mixed-initiative Intelligence*, 130–134. Menlo Park, CA: AAAI Press.

Fleming, M., and Cohen, R. 2001. A user modeling approach to determining system initiative in mixed-initiative ai systems. In Bauer, M.; Gmytrasiewicz, P.; and Vassileva, J., eds., *Proceedings of the Eighth International Conference on User Modeling (UM)*, 54–63. Sonthofen, Germany: Springer.

Frank, M.; Muslea, M.; Oh, J.; Minton, S.; and Knoblock, C. 2001. An intelligent user interface for mixed-initiative multi-source travel planning. In *Proceedings of the Sixth ACM International Conference on Intelligent User Interfaces (IUI)*, 85–86. New York, NY: ACM Press.

Freedman, R. 2000. Using a reactive planner as the basis for a dialogue agent. In *Proceedings of the Thirteenth International Florida Artificial Intelligence Research Society Conference*, 203–208.

Friedman, D., and Wand, M. 2008. *Essentials of Programming Languages*. Cambridge, MA: MIT Press, third edition.

Glass, J., and Seneff, S. 2003. Flexible and personalizable mixed-initiative dialogue systems. In *Proceedings of the North American Chapter of the Association for Computational Linguistics (ACL): Human Language Technologies (NAACL-HLT) Workshop on Research Directions in Dialogue Processing*, 19–21. Stroudsburg, PA: Association for Computational Linguistics.

Guinn, C. 1999. Evaluating mixed-initiative dialog. *IEEE Intelligent Systems* 14(5):21–23.

Hamidi, S.; Andritsos, P.; and Liaskos, S. 2014. Constructing adaptive configuration dialogs using crowd data. In *Proceedings of the Twenty-ninth ACM/IEEE International Conference on Automated Software Engineering (ASE)*, 485–490. New York, NY: ACM Press.

Hearst, M. 1999. Mixed-initiative interaction. *IEEE Intelligent Systems* 14(5):14–16.

Hochberg, J.; Kambhatla, N.; and Roukos, S. 2002. A flexible framework for developing mixed-initiative dialog systems. In *Proceedings of the Third Association for Computational Linguistics (ACL) SIGDIAL Workshop on Discourse and Dialogue*, 60–63. Stroudsburg, PA: Association for Computational Linguistics.

Jones, N. 1996. An Introduction to Partial Evaluation. *ACM Computing Surveys* 28(3):480–503.

Jordan, P.; Ringenberg, M.; and Hall, B. 2006. Rapidly developing dialogue systems that support learning studies. In *Proceedings of Intelligent Tutoring Systems (ITS) Workshop on Teaching with Robots, Agents, and NLP*, 1–8.

Kronenberg, S., and Regel-Brietzman, P. 2001. Bridging the gap between mixed-initiative dialogs and reusable subdialogs. In *Proceedings of the IEEE Workshop on Automatic Speech Recognition and Understanding (ASRU)*, 276–279. Los Alamitos, CA: IEEE Computer Society Press.

Lee, C.; Jung, S.; Kim, K.; Lee, D.; and Lee, G. 2010. Recent approaches to dialog management for spoken dialog systems. *Journal of Computing Science and Engineering* 4(1):1–22.

Leuski, A., and Traum, D. 2011. NPCEditor: Creating virtual human dialogue using information retrieval techniques. *AI Magazine* 32(2):42–56.

Maes, P. 1987. Concepts and experiments in computational reflection. In *Proceedings of the International ACM Conference on Object-Oriented Programming Systems, Languages and Applications*, 147–155. New York, NY: ACM Press.

Misu, T.; Georgila, K.; Leuski, A.; and Traum, D. 2012. Reinforcement learning of question-answering dialogue policies for virtual museum guides. In *Proceedings of the Thirteenth Annual Meeting of the Special Interest Group on Discourse and Dialogue*, 84–93. Stroudsburg, PA: Association for Computational Linguistics.

Perugini, S. 2015. Staging mixed-initiative dialogs by program generation and transformation. Technical Report arXiv:1108.0476v5 [cs.PL], Computing Research Repository (CoRR). Available from `http://lanl.arXiv.org/abs/1108.0476v5`.

Polifroni, J.; Chung, G.; and Seneff, S. 2003. Towards the automatic generation of mixed-initiative dialogue systems from web content. In *Proceedings of the Eighth European Conference on Speech Communication and Technology (EUROSPEECH)*, 193–196. International Speech Communication Association.

Pu, P., and Lalanne, D. 2002. Design visual thinking tools for mixed-initiative systems. In *Proceedings of the Seventh International Conference on Intelligent User Interfaces (IUI)*, 119–126. New York, NY: ACM Press.

Quan, D.; Huynh, D.; Karger, D.; and Miller, R. 2003. User interface continuations. In *Proceedings of the Sixteenth Annual ACM Symposium on User Interface Software and Technology (UIST)*, 145–148. New York, NY: ACM Press.

Rudnicky, A., and Xu, W. 1999. An agenda-based dialog management architecture for spoken language systems. *IEEE Automatic Speech Recognition and Understanding Workshop* 13(4).

Rudnicky, A.; Thayer, E.; Constantinides, P.; Tchou, C.; Stern, R.; Lenzo, K.; Xu, W.; and Oh, A. 1999. Creating natural dialogs in the carnegie mellon communicator system. In *Proceedings of the Sixth European Conference on Speech Communication and Technology (EUROSPEECH)*. International Speech Communication Association.

Scott, M. 2009. *Programming Language Pragmatics*. Amsterdam: Morgan Kaufmann, third edition.

Sebesta, R. 2015. *Concepts of Programming Languages*. Boston, MA: Addison Wesley, eleventh edition.

Smith, S.; Cortellessa, G.; Hildum, D.; and Ohler, C. 2005. Using a scheduling domain ontology to compute user-oriented explanations. In Castillo, L.; Barrajo, D.; Salido, M.; and Oddi, A., eds., *Planning, Scheduling, and Constraint Satisfaction: From Theory to Practice*. IOS Press.

Spiliopoulou, M. 2000. Web usage mining for web site evaluation. *Communications of the ACM* 43(8):127–134.

Thomas, D. 2014. *Programming Elixir: Functional, Concurrent, Pragmatic, Fun*. Dallas, TX: Pragmatic Bookshelf.

Walker, M., and Whittaker, S. 1990. Mixed-initiative in dialogue: An investigation into discourse segmentation. In *Proceedings of the Twenty-eighth Annual Meeting on Association for Computational Linguistics (ACL)*, 70–78. Stroudsburg, PA: Association for Computational Linguistics.

Wolfman, S.; Lau, T.; Domingos, P.; and Weld, D. 2001. Mixed initiative interfaces for learning tasks: Smartedit talks back. In *Proceedings of the Sixth ACM International Conference on Intelligent User Interfaces (IUI)*, 167–174. New York, NY: ACM Press.

Fuzzy Algorithms: Applying Fuzzy Logic to the Golden Ratio Search to Find Solutions Faster

Stephany Coffman-Wolph
West Virginia University Institute of Technology
405 Fayette Pike, Montgomery, West Virginia 25136
sscoffmanwolph@mail.wvu.edu

Abstract

Applying the concept of fuzzy logic (an abstract version of Boolean logic) to well-known algorithms generates an abstract version (i.e., fuzzy algorithm) that often results in computational improvements. Precision may be reduced but counteracted by gaining computational efficiency. The trade-offs (e.g., small increase in space, loss of precision) for a variety of applications are deemed acceptable. The fuzzification of an algorithm can be accomplished using a simple three-step framework. Creating a new fuzzy algorithm goes beyond simply converting the data from raw data into fuzzy data by additionally converting the operators and concepts into their abstract equivalents. This paper demonstrates: (1) how to apply the general framework by developing a fuzzy algorithm for a simple linear search algorithm and (2) the success of this process through the development of the Fuzzy Golden Ratio Section Search.

Background

Fuzzy logic is a set of rules and techniques for dealing with logic beyond a two-value (yes/no, on/off, true/false) system. In other words, fuzzy logic is an abstraction of two-value logic and allows for not only multiple values but also an overlap of values between fuzzy sets. Therefore, fuzzy logic can mimic a more human-like approach to decision making. L. Zadeh introduced fuzzy logic in the 1960s as an expansion of Boolean logic in his paper entitled "Fuzzy Sets" (Zadeh 1965).

Applying the concepts of fuzzy logic to an algorithm essentially creates an abstract version of the original algorithm. The abstract version allows for faster processing by taking advantage of integer calculations, reduced search trees, etc. A fuzzy algorithm can (potentially) find multiple similar solutions while the non-fuzzy version of the algorithm generates only one solution. Fuzzification of an algorithm is extremely advantageous when components or solutions naturally contain a high level of similarity/symmetry or form natural groups/clusters.

This process has already been successfully applied to the following algorithms: (1) a concept-oriented fuzzification for finding fuzzy patterns (Coffman-Wolph & Kountanis 2013c), (2) a fuzzification of both data and the operators for a fuzzy process particle swarm optimization (FP2SO) (Coffman-Wolph & Kountanis 2013a), (3) a fuzzification of multiple algorithm components to find strategies for adversarial situations from game theory (Coffman-Wolph 2013), and (4) a fuzzification of the simple simplex method for the transportation problem (Coffman-Wolph & Coffman, Jr 2014). All of the above fuzzy algorithms were generated using a simple three-step framework (Coffman-Wolph & Kountanis 2013b). Similarly, other researchers have used fuzzy logic controls with various evolutionary algorithms (Sabzi, et al 2016). The author previously asserted that the general framework technique could be successfully applied to many other algorithms to take advantage of the power of fuzzy logic. This paper demonstrates the successful application of the framework to one-dimensional search algorithms with the Golden Ratio Section Search used to illustrate the process.

Fuzzification of Algorithms

There are three main categories of components within an algorithm that can be fuzzified: (1) data, (2) operators, and (3) concepts. As stated earlier, fuzzification is a method of adding abstraction. The fuzzification of data is the process of taking "raw"/non-fuzzy data and converting it into fuzzy data. The fuzzification of operators is the process of converting a mathematical, logical, or comparative operator to its fuzzy counterpart, which operates on fuzzy sets instead of pure numbers. The fuzzification of concepts, the most difficult of the three, is the conversion of an idea into a similar fuzzy idea. These three techniques, together, will be used within the framework to create a fuzzy algorithm.

Fuzzification of Data

The process of fuzzifying data (also known as fuzzification of data) is a simple two-step process. The first is scaling or normalizing the data. The second is assigning each data point to a fuzzy set. When the process is complete the data is ready to be used within a fuzzy algorithm.

Begin by scaling each of the data points. For easier conversion from raw data to fuzzy data, scale or normalize the data first. There are many ways to scale data. For example, scale each data point x_i, using the following standard normalization equation:

The Normalized value:
$x_{inorm} = ((x_i - min) / (max - min))$,
Where:
max is the maximum value of all data points
min is the minimum value of all the data points

After the data is normalized, the fuzzification process can begin. There are two important decisions that need to be made during this phase: (1) the total number of fuzzy sets and (2) the amount of overlap between the sets. The higher the number of fuzzy sets and the smaller the overlap between the sets, the more precise the system is (i.e., less fuzziness). If each fuzzy set only represents one value and there is no overlap, then the system is essentially the same as the original non-fuzzy version. Often these two values are left as user defined parameters in the final algorithm.

There are numerous ways to define fuzzy sets. It is common to define the fuzzy sets using an equation. It is possible to have "uneven" fuzzy sets (i.e., the fuzzy set size is not a constant or the overlap is not consistent). However, the most common approach to create fuzzy sets is to divide the range of values evenly with consistent overlap.

Fuzzification of Operators

Any calculation using fuzzy data requires that all operators are also fuzzified. Changing all the operators from the traditional version to the equivalent fuzzy version causes the end calculation to be more abstract. The term operator does not simply refer to mathematical operators, but also logical and comparative operators.

Writing fuzzy operators can be challenging on a number of levels and requires many decisions to be made. For example, when defining the comparative operators, decisions will need to be made regarding what makes two sets equal, not equal, less than, greater than, etc. Additionally, a fuzzy operator needs to deal with the overlap that can exist between fuzzy sets.

Within fuzzy logic there exists several predefined operators – the majority of them are logical operators. Each of these well-defined fuzzy operators' behavior is based on the equivalent operators from traditional set theory. Operators are most commonly associated with numbers, but in the fuzzy world, operators can deal with a greater range of data representations. Often the user needs to expand these predefined operators into special operators specifically defined for the context of the data.

Fuzzy operators can either be written as an equation or as a set of if/then rules. Both methods are common. Equations are computationally faster than if/then rules, providing greater speed advantages within an algorithm. On the other hand, if/then rules are often easier to write, providing an advantage design-wise.

Fuzzification of Concepts

The fuzzification of a given concept is the most challenging of the three presented in this paper mainly because a concept can be difficult to define. A concept is an essential element from the algorithm. Like the fuzzification of data or an operator, the purpose is to create an abstract version of the non-fuzzy "concept". To identify concepts that are candidates for the fuzzification process, look for places where items could be represented by a set or look for items that only differ by a small amount. Another way to identify concepts that would benefit from being fuzzified is to notice repeated information or items that could be categorized. Fuzzification (i.e., the creation of fuzzy sets) lends itself well to these types of situations.

Fuzzy Algorithm

Many researchers refer to a "fuzzy algorithm" as one in which the data has been fuzzified (for example: Koteshwariah et al 2015). This paper excludes algorithms where only the data has been fuzzified resulting in a more strict definition of a fuzzy algorithm. Specifically, to be considered fuzzy, an algorithm must go beyond simply using fuzzy data. To truly make the algorithm fuzzy, either the operators and/or the concepts within the algorithm need to be fuzzified. When the algorithm is modified to includes a fuzzy concept, the algorithm is undeniable a fuzzy algorithm. It is trickier to determine if the algorithm is fuzzy when only the operators have been fuzzified because of the fine line between a traditional operator and a fuzzy operator – even when operating on fuzzy data. A fuzzy operator is differentiated from the basic operator by being re-written to accommodate the meaning of the fuzzy data.

Fuzzy Algorithm Framework

The following describes the general framework for the fuzzfication of any algorithm and provides the steps to convert any algorithm from a traditional non-fuzzy version to a fuzzy version. The framework is written as a general procedure so it can be applied to a broad spectrum of algorithm types.

The three steps of the framework:

1. Decide what can/should be fuzzified and determine the category of each piece to be fuzzified
2. Fuzzify each piece (identified in step 1) based on the category
   a. Scale/normalize the data, then fuzzify the data
   b. Fuzzify the operators
   c. Fuzzify the concepts
3. Defuzzification (if needed/applicable)

The first step is to make an in-depth examination of the algorithm (which is to be fuzzified) and decide which elements to fuzzify. It is helpful to determine what the solution will look like in the fuzzy form. This will lay the foundation for the entire fuzzified algorithm. Therefore, it can be helpful to work backwards through the algorithm to determine what elements (data, operators, or concepts) need to be changed in order for the solution to be produced.

As mentioned in previous sections, data, operators, and concepts can be fuzzified. Simply fuzzifying the data is not necessarily a complete fuzzification of an algorithm. Conversely, not everything needs to be fuzzified. The challenge is selecting which elements should be fuzzified and which elements should not. Almost everything numeric could be fuzzified (by the process provided in the section on fuzzification of data). Elements that are essential to the fundamentals of the algorithm are generally not fuzzified. For example, in an algorithm for finding the shortest path from a starting location to a destination location, the starting and ending locations should not be fuzzified. However, the distances between locations could be fuzzified and, additionally, the concept of ordering might be fuzzified. Of course, these decisions may depend greatly on the application of the algorithm.

The final optional step is defuzzification. Defuzzification, the opposite of fuzzification, is used to convert the result back to a non-fuzzy result. In some cases, this step might be unnecessary. The determination of needing defuzzification is both problem dependent and usage dependent. If the algorithm is being used to narrow the solution space and the information will be fed into a non-fuzzy algorithm, then it is important to develop a method of defuzzification. Defuzzification can be applied to data or concepts.

The Golden Ratio Section Search

In this paper, the Golden Ratio Section Search will be fuzzified. The Golden Ratio Section Search belongs to a class of problems known as the one-dimensional search algorithms. One-dimensional search methods are used to find the minimum or maximum of a function within a particular interval. Other similar searches include: Dichotomous Search (bisection method), Uniform Search Method, Equal Interval Method, Fibonacci Search Method, Quadratic (or polynomial) Interpolation, and Newton's Method. The Golden Ratio Section Search has the advantage of faster convergence than most simple algorithms without requiring function derivatives making the method more versatile.

For this paper, two problems will be run on both a fuzzy and traditional version of the Golden Ratio Section Search. The two versions will be compared in terms of computation complexity, number of iterations, and an evaluation of advantages and disadvantages. A walkthrough will be provided so the reader and compare the fuzzy and non-fuzzy versions of the algorithm.

Application of One-dimensional Search Algorithms

There are many types of problems that can be formulated so that searching for a minimum or maximum of a function yields the desired result. Thus, this type of search has far reaching applications. One example is finding the roots of a polynomial, which can be challenging if $n>3$. One-dimensional searches are used to find the "fixed point" of a function (i.e., given a function f(x), then a fixed point c is a point that satisfies $f(c) = c$). Similarly, it can be used to find the "zeros" of a function (i.e., given a function f(x), then a zero of the function is any point where $f(x) = 0$). In non-linear constrained or unconstrained optimization, one-dimensional search algorithms are used to find the step size to move in the "improving" direction (e.g., in steepest descent, the improving direction is the gradient).

The (Non-Fuzzy) Algorithm

Golden Ratio Section Search works similar to most bisection searches but there is more than one internal point. (And, thus, more than two segments). One common application of this algorithm is to find the absolute minimum (or maximum) of a mathematical function. The algorithm begins by finding (or calculating) the upper and lower bounds of the area that contains the minimum (or maximum) value. Calculate the two interior points using the bounds forming three sub-segments. The algorithm then decides which sub-segment contains the minimum (or maximum) value. The upper and lower bounds are narrowed and the process is repeated until the minimum (or maximum) value is located within a specific tolerance. The Golden Ratio is defined as follows:

Golden Ratio = $\varphi = (1 + \sqrt{5})/2 \approx 1.6180339$

The Golden Ratio Section Search uses τ:
$\tau = (\sqrt{5} - 1)/2 \approx .6180339$
(Which is the Golden Ratio minus one)

This value, τ, will be used to subdivide the line such that the ratio of the lengths of the segments is the Golden Ratio. With a lower bound of LB and an upper bound of UB, calculate the two points x_1 and x_2 that subdivide the line into three segments. The general formulas for this are:

$x_1 = LB + (1 - \tau)(UB-LB)$
$x_2 = LB + \tau(UB-LB)$

The Fuzzy Algorithm

As mentioned in an earlier section, the preliminary research for fuzzy algorithms began with a fuzzy PSO for solving the Traveling Salesperson problem (Coffman-Wolph & Kountanis 2013a) and continued in the author's dissertation (Coffman-Wolph 2013). This research continues exploring what algorithms can benefit from being fuzzifed using the framework.

To fuzzify the Golden Ratio Search, we must consider what should and should not be fuzzified. A fuzzy algorithm produces a fuzzy solution (unless a defuzzification process is applied to the solution). The fuzzy solution for this type of problem is a fuzzy minimum (or maximum). Thus, we must ask ourselves if a precise minimum (or maximum) is required. Often, a precise minimum (or maximum) is not required. Generally, the Golden Ratio Search (and other bi-sectioning algorithms) are used as a feeder into other algorithms (e.g., curve fitting, finding minimum of a polynomial) and do not require the absolute best solution – a "good enough" solution is all that is required. In some cases, the fuzzy version of an algorithm can be used to eliminate a significant portion of the search space and then be used as a starting range in a precise non-fuzzy algorithm to find the absolute minimum (or maximum). We can conclude that the concept of fuzzy minimum (or maximum) is an appropriate concept to be fuzzified for the algorithm.

The next concept to consider for fuzzification is the calculated points. For the traditional Golden Ratio Section Search, we calculate 2 precise points (and thus create 3 exact segments). In the fuzzified version, these 2 precise points would be represented by 2 fuzzy sets (and 3 fuzzy segments). These sets are not necessarily distinct and may contain overlap. Earlier, the crisp calculations were provided to find the 2 precise points. These formulas, operators, and values will be converted to an abstract fuzzified version. (A subscript f will be used to denote a fuzzified value or operator. Note that 1_f is a "fuzzy" 1 and is actually a set). The value of φ and τ will remain crisp and non-fuzzified as these values are essential to the algorithm.

Golden Ratio = $\varphi = (1 + \sqrt{5})/2 \approx 1.6180339$
$\tau = (\sqrt{5} - 1)/2 \approx .6180339$
$x_{1f} =_f LB_f +_f (1-\tau) *_f (UB_f -_f LB_f)$
$x_{2f} =_f LB_f +_f (\tau) *_f (UB_f -_f LB_f)$

Example #1: Simple Polynomial

The Fuzzy Golden Ratio Section Search will first be tested using the problem: find the minimum of the polynomial: x2 - y +2 = 0 (see figure 1). The lower bound (LB) and upper bound (UB) will be set to -3 and 3 respectively. This polynomial will be used to provide the reader with a full example for comparison purposes of the non-fuzzy traditional algorithm and the fuzzified version.

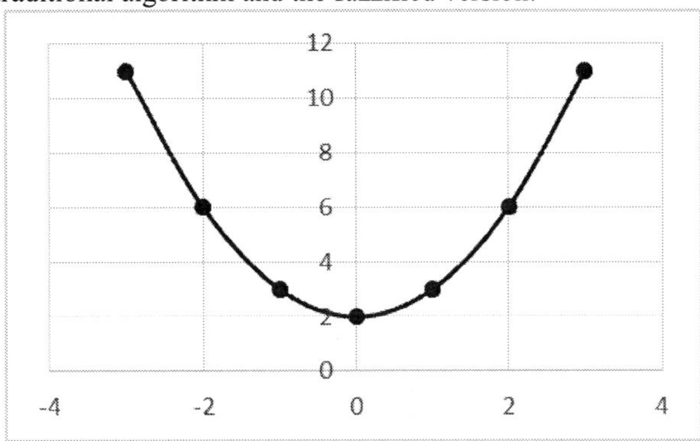

Figure 1: $x^2 - y + 2 = 0$.

Non-Fuzzy Walkthrough

Using the bounds -3 and 3, begin by calculating the two points x_1 and x_2 to subdivide the line:

$x_1 = LB + (1 - \tau)(UB-LB) = -3 + (1-.618)(3-(-3)) = -.708$
$x_2 = LB + \tau(UB-LB) = -3 + .618(3-(-3)) = .708$

There are now three line segments (-3 to -.708), (-.708 to .708), and (.708 to 3). Evaluate the f(UB), $f(x_1)$, $f(x_2)$, and f(LB):

f(UB) = 11
$f(x_1) = 2.501$
$f(x_2) = 2.501$
f(LB) = 11

Since both $f(x_1)$ and $f(x_2)$ are less than both f(LB) and f(UB), the minimum must be between x_1 and x_2 and, thus, they will become the new LB and UB respectively. The algorithm continues by repeating the previous process to find the next x_1 and x_2 but using the new more restricted lower and upper bounds. Using the same formulas, calculate the next x_1 and x_2:

$x_1 = -.708 + (1 - .618)(.708-(-.708)) = -0.167$

$x_2 = -.708 + .618(.708-(-.708)) = .167$

Next we evaluate the f(UB), $f(x_1)$, $f(x_2)$, and f(LB):

f(UB) = 2.501

$f(x_1) = 2.02$

$f(x_2) = 2.02$

f(LB) = 2.501

Using these values, the new lower and upper bounds are determined to be:

LB = -.167

UP = .167

The algorithm proceeds by calculating the next new values of x_1 and x_2 and the corresponding evaluations:

$x_1 = -.167 + (1-.618)(.167-(-.167)) = -.039$

$x_2 =-.167 +.618(.167-(-.167)) = .039$

$f(x_1) = 2.001$

$f(x_2) = 2.001$

Given the above x_1 and x_2, the new lower and upper bounds become:

LB = -.039

UP = .039

The algorithm will make another pass to further tighten the lower and upper bounds to find the minimum of the polynomial. The algorithm will calculate the next values of x_1 and x_2 and the corresponding evaluations:

$x_1 = -.039 + (1-.618)(.039-(-.039)) = -.009$

$x_2 =-.039 +.618(.039-(-.039)) = .009$

$f(x_1) = 2.000$

$f(x_2) = 2.000$

Given the above x_1 and x_2, the new lower and upper bounds become:

LB = -.009

UP = .009

One can continue the algorithm further to find a more precise results. Otherwise, the algorithm can be stopped at this point. As can been seen from figure 1, the minimum value of the polynomial is 2 at the point x = 0. The value we calculated is approximately 2.000. For many purposes (as mentioned earlier), this value is accurate enough and we can consider the algorithm complete.

Fuzzy Walkthrough

The author will now proceed with the Fuzzy Golden Ratio Section Search to find the minimum of the polynomial: $x^2 - y + 2 = 0$ with the initial LB (lower bound) and UB (upper bound) of -3 and 3, respectively. All fuzzy data and operators will be denoted with a subscript f. It is important to remember that the fuzzy values represent a set, but for simplification purposes will be represented in the write-up as a single integer value with a subscript f.

During the setup of the algorithm, a few decisions need to be made: (1) size of the fuzzy sets and (2) allowing overlap between fuzzy sets. Both of these values control the level of precision for the algorithm. (For example: crisp, traditional numbers could be represented with a fuzzy set size of only one value with no overlaps). Additionally, the size of the fuzzy sets does not need to remain constant throughout the algorithm execution. Keeping in the spirit of the Golden Ratio Section Search algorithm, this example will hold the size of the fuzzy sets constant at +/- τ and, thus, create an overlap of approximately .236 between fuzzy sets. For example, -1_f is defined as -1.618 to -.382, 0_f is defined as -.618 to .618, and 1_f is defined as .382 to 1.618.

The algorithm begins the same as the traditional algorithm, with the calculation of the internal two points based on the fuzzified lower and upper bounds of -3_f and 3_f. (As previously mentioned: the value of τ will remain crisp as well as the calculation of 1- τ. The value of τ is essential to the original algorithm and not fuzzified. Additionally, this value is essential to the definition of the fuzzy set size). The values are calculated as follows:

$x_{1f} =_f LB_f +_f (1 - \tau) *_f (UB_f -_f LB_f)$

$=_f -3_f +_f (1- .618) *_f (3_f -_f -3_f)$

$=_f -1_f$

$x_{2f} =_f LB_f +_f (\tau) *_f (UB_f -_f LB_f)$

$=_f -3_f +_f (.618) *_f (3_f -_f -3_f)$

$=_f 1_f$

There are now three line segments (-3_f to -1_f), (-1_f to 1_f), and (1_f to 3_f). We now evaluate the f(UB), $f(x_1)$, $f(x_2)$, and f(LB):

$f_f(UB_f) =_f 11_f$

$f_f(x_{1f}) =_f 3_f$

$f_f(x_{2f}) =_f 3_f$

$f_f(LB_f) =_f 11_f$

Both $f_f(x_{1f})$ and $f_f(x_{2f})$ are less than both $f_f(LB_f)$ and $f_f(UB_f)$. The minimum must be between x_{1f} and x_{2f} and they will become the new LB_f and UB_f. The process repeats and the next x_{1f} and x_{2f} are calculated:

$x_{1f} =_f LB_f +_f (1-\tau) *_f (UB_f -_f LB_f)$

$=_f -1_f +_f (1-\tau) *_f (1_f -_f -1_f)$

$=_f 0_f$

$x_{2f} =_f LB_f +_f (\tau) *_f (UB_f -_f LB_f)$

$=_f -1_f +_f (\tau) *_f (1_f -_f -1_f)$

$=_f 0_f$

There are now three line segments (-1_f to 0_f), (0_f to 0_f), and (0_f to 1_f). Next, evaluate the f(UB), $f(x_1)$, $f(x_2)$, and f(LB):

$f_f(UB_f) =_f 11_f$
$f_f(x_{1f}) =_f 2_f$
$f_f(x_{2f}) =_f 2_f$
$f_f(LB_f) =_f 11_f$

The algorithm will be stopped at this point. As can been seen from figure 1, the minimum value of the polynomial is 2. The value we found is approximately 2 (i.e., the fuzzy set 2). (In general, the algorithm would continue, like the non-fuzzy version, until reaching the desired level of accuracy).

Example #2: More Complex Polynomial

In this example, the Fuzzy Golden Ratio Section Search will be tested with a more complex polynomial. The example was run using two simple Java programs: (1) the traditional Golden Ratio Section Search and (2) the Fuzzy Golden Ratio Section Search. The results of the fuzzy version will be compared to the traditional version.

This second example is to find the maximum of the polynomial: $f(x) = 12x - 3x^4 - 2x^6$ (Hillier and Lieberman 1990). The lower and upper bounds are defined as 0 and 2 (which are the two points where the function begins to be negative). The traditional algorithm ran the function as defined. The fuzzy version of the algorithm used a scaled version of the problem which allows the algorithm to take advantage of integer calculations. The algorithm can be scaled to any number of "decimal points" (denoted as d) of precision by dividing each x by 10^d and then multiplying the entire equation by 10^d.

The maximum value of the $f(x) = 12x - 3x^4 - 2x^6$ occurs in the range of 0.828 and 0.843 and is approximately 0.836 (Hillier and Lieberman 1990). The traditional version of the Golden Ratio Section Search required 5 iterations and computes the maximum to fall in the range of 0.833 and 0.839. The fuzzy version of the Golden Ratio Section Search uses only 3 iterations and computes that the maximum falls in the range of 8 and 9 (on the scaled problem) which is .8 and .9 on the non-scaled version.

The computation complexity of the algorithm is not increased by adding fuzzification to the algorithm. The Java code for the fuzzy algorithm contains only one additional method - a customized Java code to determine the fuzzy equivalence between fuzzy sets. This extra method is called only twice during each iteration and contains 8 lines of code most of which are a series of branching statements. This adds minimal execution time to the overall algorithm.

Testing Environment

The programming code for both the Fuzzy and Traditional version of the Golden Ratio Section Search was written in Java. The testing environment is as follows: Eclipse Mars, SDK 4.5.1 using Java version 1.8 on a HP Spectre running Windows 10 with 2.5 GHz Intel Core i7.

Discussion and Concluding Remarks

The Golden Ratio Section Search algorithm was successfully converted into a fuzzified version of the algorithm using the Framework for Fuzzification of Algorithms (Coffman-Wolph and Kountanis 2013b). For both example polynomials, the fuzzy version of the Golden Ratio Section Search performed better since it required fewer iterations to find a suitable range for the minimum or maximum solution. As stated before, these ranges are sufficient for many of the applications that use Golden Ratio Section Search and other similar one-dimensional search methods. For example, in each iteration of a non-linear optimization algorithm, one is required to use these types of techniques to estimate the best step size in the improving direction. The fuzzy version of the Golden Ratio Section Search takes advantage of the computer's natural high speed of integer calculations. (The traditional version uses the Java double data type for the calculations).

There are two disadvantages to using the fuzzy algorithm over the traditional. The fuzzy algorithm often requires scaling (but this scaling can be controlled by the user to their desired level of precision). The second disadvantages is that in cases where precise answers are needed, the fuzzy algorithm would only be able to provide a starting lower and upper bound and is unable to provide extremely high levels of accuracy.

Future Work

The work done in this paper focuses on only two specific polynomials and provides only the beginning of exploration into the use of the fuzzy framework for this kind of search algorithm. Since these preliminary results show great potential, the next step would be to expand to larger and more varied polynomials as well as non-polynomial functions. Further work could be conducted on other similar algorithms including: Dichotomous Search (bisection method), Uniform Search Method, Equal Interval Method, Fibonacci Search Method, and Quadratic (or polynomial) Interpolation. Additionally, the author would like to expand to other even more general search algorithms (e.g., Tabu search) and sorting algorithms.

References

Coffman-Wolph, S. 2015. The Hunch Factor: Exploration into Using Fuzzy Logic to Model Intuition in Particle Swarm Optimization. In the Proceedings of the 26th Modern AI and Cognitive Science Conference (MAICS 2015).

Coffman-Wolph, S and Coffman, Jr, P. 2014. Fuzzification of the Special Simplex Method for the Transportation Problem. Conference Presentation. In the Proceedings of the INFORMS Annual Meeting, San Francisco, California.

Coffman-Wolph, S. 2013. Fuzzy Search Strategy Generation for Adversarial Systems using Fuzzy Process Particle Swarm Optimization, Fuzzy Patterns, and a Hunch Factor. Ph.D. diss., Department of Computer Science, Western Michigan University, Kalamazoo, MI.

Coffman-Wolph, S. and Kountanis, D. 2013a. Fuzzy Process Particle Swarm Optimization. In the Proceedings of the 43rd Southeastern Conference on Combinatorics, Graph Theory, & Computing. Winnipeg: Utilitas Mathematica Pub. Inc.

Coffman-Wolph, S. and Kountanis, D. 2013b. A General Framework for the Fuzzification of Algorithms. In the Proceedings of the 4th biennial Michigan Celebration of Women in Computing (MICWIC 2013).

Coffman-Wolph, S. and Kountanis, D. 2013c. Finding Strategies in Adversarial Situations. In the Proceedings of the 24th Modern AI and Cognitive Science Conference (MAICS 2013).

Hillier, F. S., and Lieberman, G. J. 1990. *Introduction to Operations Research*. McGraw-Hill.

Kennedy, J., and Eberhart, R. C. 2001. *Swarm Intelligence*. San Francisco, CA: Morgan Kaufmann Publishers, Inc.

Koteshwariah, C. B., Kisore, N. R., Ravi, V., 2015. A Fuzzy Version of Generalized DBSCAN Clustering Algorithm. In the Proceedings of the Second ACM IKDD Conference on Data Sciences (CoDS 15). New York: ACM.

Lasden, L. (1970) *Optimization Theory for Large Systems*. New York, NY: Macmillan Publishing Co, Inc.

Luenberger, D. 1973. *Introduction to Linear and Nonlinear Programming*. Reading, MA: Addison-Wesley Publishing Company.

Sabzi, H. Z., Humberson, D., Abudu, S., King, J. P., 2016. Optimization of Adaptive Fuzzy Logic Controller Using Novel Combined Evolutionary Algorithms, and Its Application in Diez Lagos Food Controlling System, Southern New Mexico. *Expert Systems With Applications*. 43: 154-164.

Wismer, D. and Chattergy, R. 1978. *Introduction to Nonlinear Optimization*. New York, NY: Elsevier North-Holland, Inc.

Zadeh, L.A. 1965. Fuzzy Sets. *Information and Control*. 8: 338-353.

Towards the Development of a Cyber Analysis & Advisement Tool (CAAT) for Mitigating De-Anonymization Attacks

Siobahn C. Day, Henry Williams, Joseph Shelton, Gerry Dozier
Department of Computer Science, North Carolina A&T State University, Greensboro, U.S.A
Center for Advanced Studies in Identity Science
{scday, hcwillia, jashelt1} @aggies.ncat.edu , {gvdozier} @ncat.edu

Abstract

We are seeing a rise in the number of Anonymous Social Networks (ASN) that claim to provide a sense of user anonymity. However, what many users of ASNs do not know that a person can be identified by their writing style.
In this paper, we provide an overview of a number of author concealment techniques, their impact on the semantic meaning of an author's original text, and introduce AuthorCAAT, an application for mitigating de-anonymization attacks. Our results show that iterative paraphrasing performs the best in terms of author concealment and performs well with respect to Latent Semantic Analysis.

Introduction

Anonymous Social Networks (ASN) can provide users with a false sense of anonymity; however, research in the area of Author Identification (Attribution) has shown that users can be identified simply by their writing style (Stamatatos 2009). Narayanan et al. (2012), introduces the concept of a de-anonymization attack where hackers apply sophisticated Author Identification techniques (AITs) in an effort to uncover the identity of an author of a text. Once this occurs the hackers can track a victim across the web and even through other ASNs.

Recently researchers, M. Brennan, Afroz, and Greenstadt (2012); Kacmarcik and Gamon (2006); Rao and Rohatgi (2000), have developed a number of techniques for author concealment. These techniques as well as their ability to conceal one's writing style are as follows: adversarial stylometry, iterative language translation and iterative paraphrasing.

Presently there exist two forms of adversarial stylometry (Afroz, Brennan, and Greenstadt 2012; M. Brennan et al. 2012; M. R. Brennan and Greenstadt 2009). The first form, obfuscation, is when an author tries not to write like themselves while the second form, imitation, is when an author tries to 'mimic' the writing style of another author. Research shows that both of these techniques are effective in concealing one's writing style. In the case of disguising one's writing style, M. Brennan et al. (2012) demonstrate that obfuscation and imitation are easy on the short term but more difficult to maintain on the long term. In Section IV, it will be shown how AuthorCAAT can be used to provide authors with the ability to perform long-term adversarial stylometry.

Another form of author concealment is Iterative Language Translation (ILT) (Mack, Bowers, Williams, Dozier, and Shelton 2015). ILT is where an original text is translated to another language and then back to its original language. This technique was first presented in Rao and Rohatgi (2000), where the authors describe this approach as being "somewhat facetious" and "drastic." They believed that this approach would change the meaning of a message thus making it an impractical approach. It was also mentioned by Kacmarcik and Gamon (2006), that this approach could be a good starting point for someone looking to "scramble" their words. ILT is effective in concealing the writing style of an author; however, it is vulnerable to fingerprinting, (Caliskan and Greenstadt 2012). If one knows the language used in translating the text, one can then recover the original writing style of the author.

The last form of author concealment is Iterative Paraphrasing (IP). The use of IP was originally mentioned in Kacmarcik and Gamon (2006). In IP, one will take the original text and use a paraphrasing tool to convert it into a paraphrased text. Concerning IP, to the authors' knowledge, no one has as of yet analyzed its effectiveness in author concealment, semantics, and its vulnerability to fingerprinting (this will be discussed in Section III).

The remainder of the paper will be as follows. In Section II, we discuss our experiments. In Section III, we discuss our results. In Section IV, we provide a brief discussion of AuthorCAAT. In Section V, we provide our conclusion and future work.

Author Concealment & Fingerprinting Experiments

Our Dataset

The datasets we used for our experiments were gathered from blogs written by 100 different authors. For every author in our dataset, there are 4 instances. Those instances in the dataset are as follows: the first instance served as the probe and the remaining 3 instances served as the gallery. This results in 100 instances in the probe set and 300 instances in the gallery set.

Our Translators & Paraphrasers

Our ILT dataset, used Google translation tools for English to Spanish, Spanish to English, English to Chinese, and Chinese to English. The ILT text was prepared in iterations. We consider an iteration to be a full round trip cycle of translation (e.g. English-Spanish-English and English-Chinese-English). Therefore, Iteration 1 would be E-X-E, Iteration 2 would be E-X-E-X-E, and Iteration 3 would be E-X-E-X-E-X-E, where E stands for English and $X \in \{Spanish, Chinese\}$. Therefore, a total of six ILT datasets were developed consisting of 300 gallery instances of the 100 authors.

Our IP dataset was created using an online tool known as Plagarisma. The Iterations for IP are similar to ILT. Combining ILT with IP we have $X \in \{Spanish, Chinese, Paraphraser\}$. Therefore, three IP datasets were developed consisting of 300 gallery instances of the 100 authors. For ILT/IP, there were a total of nine datasets.

Experiment I: Author Concealment via ILT/IP

For Experiment I, the feature extractor used in Mack, Bowers, Williams, Dozier, and Shelton (2015), referred to as the Hybrid-II Author Identification System (AIS), was applied to the instances of the nine datasets (and the probe set) to create feature vectors where each feature vector consisted of 1282 features. The Hybrid-II AIS, is composed of 95 features from the Unigram feature extractor (Forsyth 1997), 170 stylometric features from De Vel, Anderson, Corney, and Mohay (2001) feature extractor, as well as 256 features in the form of function words and 761 features that come from the Stanford Parser in the form of Parts-of-Speech parent child pairs for a total of 1282 features.

In Experiment I, the baseline performance was the author recognition rate of the 100 authors (English only) using no ILT/IP iterations. While, the ILT/IP experiments were used to determine how well ILT/IP reduces the author recognition rate with respect to the baseline.

Experiment II: Fingerprinting the Translators and the Paraphrasers

For Experiment II, a tool known as JGAAP, Java Graphical Author Attribution Program, (Juola, Sofko, and Brennan 2006) was used to fingerprint the translators and the paraphraser. This tool allows for text analysis using various stylometry and textometry techniques. We used the first 100 authors from each ILT/IP Iteration using the first gallery instance as the 'unknown' author and the remaining two instances from the gallery as the 'known' authors. The 'known' authors were labeled by languages and/or paraphraser. This was used for all three Iterations of ILT/IP. The analysis was processed by using WEKA SMO, with the results ordered with event culling from most to least. Character N Grams, where n=2, was used as the event driver.

Experiment III: Fingerprinting the Number of Iterations Used to Conceal an Author's Writing Style

In Experiment III, the 'unknown' authors were chosen from the first gallery instances of all Iterations of ILT/IP. The 'known' authors were chosen from the remaining two instances of the gallery and were labeled by the number of ILT/IP Iterations that were applied. The same settings as Experiment II were used with respect to the event driver, analysis, and event culling.

Results

Results of Experiment I

The results of Experiment I, Author Concealment via ILT/IP, are shown in Figure 1. Figure 1 shows the affect that ILT/IP has on the accuracy of the AIS. In Figure 1, the x-axis represents the iteration number (Iteration 1, Iteration 2, Iteration 3) and the y-axis represents the accuracy of the AIS.

In Figure 1, the accuracy of the AIS is 54% percent. In the first iteration of ILT/IP, the author identification rates drop. At Iteration 1, ILT-Spanish has the best performance in terms of reducing the AIS rate to 6%, followed by IP at 7% and ILT-Chinese at 10%. In the second iteration, IP has the best performance in reducing the AIS rate to 1%, followed by ILT-Chinese at 11% and ILT-Spanish at 6%. At Iteration 3, IP continues to outperform ILT. At Iteration 3, IP reduces the AIS rate to 6 %, followed by ILT-Spanish at 7% and ILT-Chinese at 11%. These results show the effectiveness of ILT/IP in concealing an authors identity.

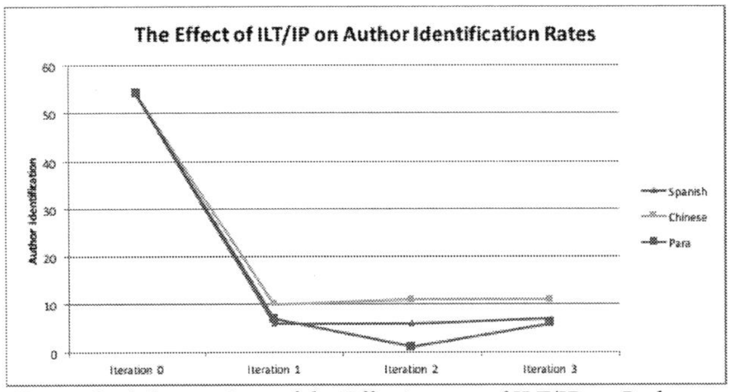

Figure 1: A Comparison of the Effectiveness of ILT/IP on Reducing Author Recognition Rates

Prior research suggests, (Caliskan and Greenstadt 2012; Kacmarcik and Gamon 2006; Rao and Rohatgi 2000), that ILT/IP is naïve as well as problematic due to the resulting text being unable to retain its original meaning. In in order to address this issue, we applied Latent Semantic Analysis (LSA) on all iterations of the dataset.

Latent Semantic Analysis (LSA) "...is a theory and method for extracting and representing the contextual-usage meaning of words by statistical computations applied to a large corpus of text" (Landauer, Foltz, and Laham 1998). Using a LSA tool developed by the University of Colorado Boulder, we compared our original text with the resulting text of ILT/IP.

In the Table 1, the results of using the LSA tool on our dataset are shown. Given two samples of text, the LSA tool will provide an output of 1 if the semantics of the two text samples are exact and -1 if the semantics of the two text samples do not match at all. Given the output of the LSA tool on our dataset, we ran an ANOVA test as well a t-test to break the performances of ILT/IP into equivalence classes as shown in Table 1.

In Table 1, the first column represents the ILT/IP method used, the second column represents the average output of the LSA tool with the standard deviation in parenthesis, and the third column, labeled EC, represents the equivalence class. The equivalence classes are ordered from best to worst in terms of performance. The equivalent classes were determined by applying ANOVA and a t-test to check for statistical significance. The p-value used for the ANOVA test was 0.05.

The results displayed in Table 1, show that the resulting text from ILT-Spanish is closest to the semantics of the original text with an output of 0.862 followed by IP at 0.802 and ILT-Chinese at 0.773. This indicates that ILT/IP is not only non-problematic but effective at preserving the semantics of the original text.

Table 1: LSA Results from Comparing the Original Text with Resulting Text from ILT/IP

ILT/IP Method	LSA Results	EC
Spanish	0.862 (0.11)	1
Paraphraser	0.802 (0.09)	2
Chinese	0.773.16)	3

Results of Experiment II

The results of Experiment II, Fingerprinting the Translators and the Paraphrasers, are shown in Figure 2. In Figure 2, the x-axis shows the iterations (Iteration 1, Iteration 2, Iteration 3) and on the y-axis it shows the accuracy in determining the ILT/IP method used. In Figure 2, one can see as the number of iterations increases so does the accuracy for each ILT/IP method that is being used.

In Figure 2, at Iteration 1, ILT-Spanish has the best fingerprinting accuracy at 93%, followed by ILT-Chinese at 90%, and IP at 86%. In Iteration 2, ILT-Spanish leads at 98% followed by ILT-Chinese 97%, and IP at 91%. In Iteration 3, ILT-Chinese comes in at 99%, followed by ILT-Spanish at 98%, and IP at 95%. The results not only show that the translators can be accurately fingerprinted, but they also show that of the three IP is hardest to fingerprint but only at the first iteration. On the other hand, these results show that the translator and paraphrasers are able to be identified which can potentially allow for reversibility or the uncovering of the original text, thus revealing an authors writing style.

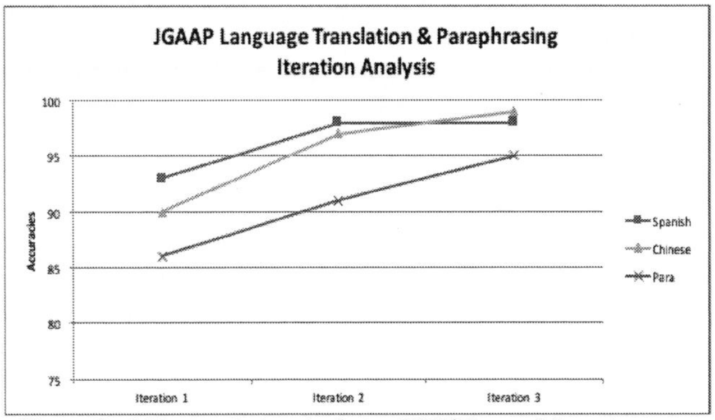

Figure 2: A Fingerprinting Analysis of ILT/IP over 3 Iterations

Results of Experiment III

The results of Experiment III, Fingerprinting the Number of Iterations Used to Conceal an Author's Writing Style, are shown in Figure 3. In Figure 3, the x-axis shows the iterations (Iteration 1, Iteration 2, Iteration 3) and the y-axis shows the accuracy of an iteration of ILT/IP in being fingerprinted. Figure 3 shows determining which Iteration of ILT/IP of a given text proves to be more difficult; however, the accuracy rises over iterations.

In Figure 3, at Iteration 1, ILT-Spanish leads at 70%, followed by ILT-Chinese at 61%, and IP at 47%. At Iteration 2, IP performs best at 31%, followed by ILT-Spanish at 18%, and ILT-Chinese at 15%. At Iteration 3, ILT-Chinese is the best performer at 60%, followed by ILT-Spanish at 53 % and IP at 49% making it the worst performer. The results show that fingerprinting ILT/IP by iteration is harder to fingerprint but not impossible. Thus allowing an original text and author to be revealed.

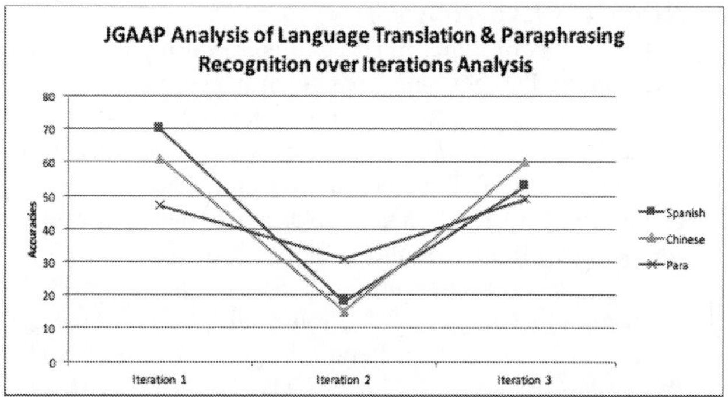

Figure 3: A Fingerprinting Analysis of the Number of Iterations of ILT/IP over 3 Iterations

DISCUSSION: THE DEVELOPMENT OF AUTHORCAAT

The results presented earlier show that translators and paraphrasers can be fingerprinted. Even the iterations can be fingerprinted. In order to conceal one's identity in an efficient and effective way, the authors' believe that a system must be developed that will allow a user to use all of the author concealment methods mentioned in this paper simultaneously while authoring a text. The Center for Advanced Studies in Identity Sciences (CASIS) has developed such a system for author concealment known as AuthorCAAT (Author Cyber Analysis & Advisement Tool).

Figure 5 provides a screenshot of AuthorCAAT. AuthorCAAT has a window that allows an author to type in text. As the author types, their writing style is analyzed. The feature vector associated with their writing style is shown just below the window. To the right of the window, is a pane that displays the author samples that match the sample written within the window based on a user specified by the slide bar. For example, if the slide bar is at '10' this means that the pane will display the authors whose writing samples are within the closest 10% to the author sample that was typed in the window.

Below the Matches to, pane is a drop-down box that will allow an author to translate what is currently in the window in either Spanish, Chinese, or Paraphrase and back to English. Once a language or paraphraser has been selected, the user (author) presses the 'Translate' button to execute one cycle of ILT on the text currently within the author window.

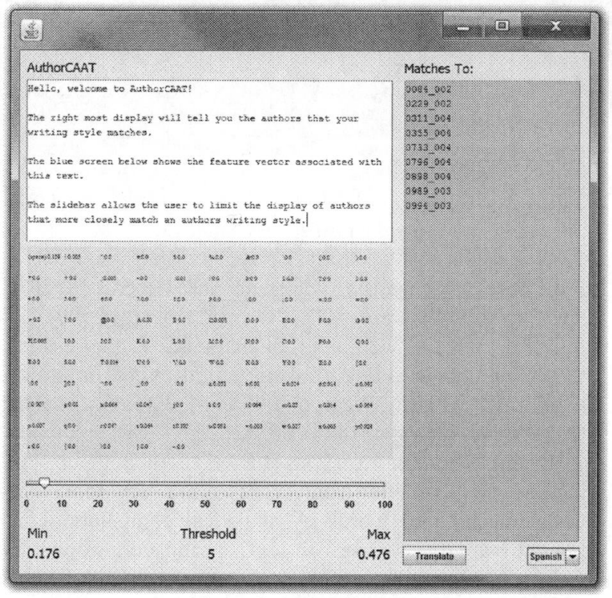

Figure 5: AuthorCAAT

In Figure 5, one can see that AuthorCAAT allows a user to perform both forms of Adversarial Stylometry. If the user sees that their writing style is detected and shown in the pane, then they can choose to re-write their text is such a way that it is not shown in the pane. A user can also monitor the pane in an effort to perform imitation authorship. As long as a particular author ID is shown in the pane (while their author ID is not in the pane) then they are writing like that particular author.

Finally, AuthorCAAT allows for ILT/IP at the sentence level. For example, an author can type in the first sentence and apply ILT/IP to that sentence. After this, the author can add a second sentence and then apply ILT/IP to both sentences in the window and/or edit the resulting sentences further (Adversarial Stylometry).

Conclusions and Future Work

In this paper, ILT/IP dramatically reduces the author recognition rate. Secondly, translators and paraphraser are good enough to preserve the semantics. This is based on our results from our LSA table. Thirdly that not only can language translators be fingerprinted but we can fingerprint paraphrasers too. Lastly we show that the iteration of a particular ILT/IP can be fingerprinted as well. This all leads to a development tool, AuthorCAAT that can do all of things at the sentence level. This will allow fingerprinting to be more difficult. Our Future work will include increasing our dataset from 100 to 1000 to see if the fingerprinting becomes more accurate with more authors in terms of ILT/IP. We suspect the accuracy of fingerprinting iterations at Iteration 1 and 2 will increase with the number of authors analyzed. This is a contrast to what was stated in Caliskan and Greenstadt (2012).

Acknowledgments

This research is based upon work supported by the United States Government including the National Science Foundation. The views and conclusions contained herein are those of the authors and should not be interpreted as necessarily representing the official policies or endorsements, either expressed or implied, of the U.S. Government. The U.S. Government is authorized to reproduce and distribute reprints for Governmental purposes notwithstanding any copyright annotation thereon.

References

Afroz, S., Brennan, M., & Greenstadt, R. (2012, May). Detecting hoaxes, frauds, and deception in writing style online. In Security and Privacy (SP), 2012 IEEE Symposium on (pp. 461-475). IEEE.

Brennan, M. R., & Greenstadt, R. (2009, July). Practical Attacks Against Authorship Recognition Techniques. In *IAAI.*

Brennan, M., Afroz, S., & Greenstadt, R. (2012). Adversarial stylometry: Circumventing authorship recognition to preserve privacy and anonymity.*ACM Transactions on Information and System Security (TISSEC)*, *15*(3), 12.

Caliskan, A., & Greenstadt, R. (2012, September). Translate once, translate twice, translate thrice and attribute: Identifying authors and machine translation tools in translated text. In *Semantic Computing (ICSC), 2012 IEEE Sixth International Conference on* (pp. 121-125). IEEE.

De Vel, O., Anderson, A., Corney, M., & Mohay, G. (2001). Mining e-mail content for author identification forensics. *ACM Sigmod Record*, *30*(4), 55-64.

Forsyth, R. S. (1997). Short substrings as document discriminators: An empirical study. In *ACH-ALLC* (Vol. 97).

Free Online Plagiarism Checker for Students, Teachers, Scholars, Educators, Scientists, Essayists, Writers. Free TurnItIn and Copyscape Alternative. (n.d.). Retrieved February 02, 2016, from http://plagiarisma.net/

Google Translate. (n.d.). Retrieved February 04, 2016, from https://translate.google.com/

Juola, P., Sofko, J., & Brennan, P. (2006). A prototype for authorship attribution studies. *Literary and Linguistic Computing*, *21*(2), 169-178.

Kacmarcik, G., & Gamon, M. (2006). Obfuscating document stylometry to preserve author anonymity. Paper presented at the Proceedings of the COLING/ACL on Main conference poster sessions.

Landauer, T. K., Foltz, P. W., & Laham, D. (1998). Introduction to Latent Semantic Analysis. *Discourse* Processes, **25**, 259-284.

LSA @ CU Boulder. (n.d.). Retrieved February 02, 2016, from http://lsa.colorado.edu/

Narayanan, A., Paskov, H., Gong, N. Z., Bethencourt, J., Stefanov, E., Shin, E. C. R., & Song, D. (2012, May). On the feasibility of internet-scale author identification. In *Security and Privacy (SP), 2012 IEEE Symposium on* (pp. 300-314). IEEE.

Nathan Mack, Jasmine Bowers, Henry Williams, Gerry Dozier, and Joseph Shelton, "The Best Way to a Strong Defense is a Strong Offense: Mitigating Deanonymization Attacks via Iterative Language Translation," *International Journal of Machine Learning and Computing* vol.5, no. 5, pp. 409-413, 2015.

Rao, J. R., & Rohatgi, P. (2000). Can pseudonymity really guarantee privacy? Paper presented at the USENIX Security Symposium.

Stamatatos, E. (2009). A survey of modern authorship attribution methods.*Journal of the American Society for information Science and Technology*,*60*(3), 538-556.

Real-time Unsupervised Clustering

Gabriel J. Ferrer
Department of Mathematics and Computer Science
Hendrix College
1600 Washington Ave.
Conway, Arkansas 72032

Abstract

In our research program, we are developing machine learning algorithms to enable a mobile robot to build a compact representation of its environment. This requires the processing of each new input to terminate in constant time. Existing machine learning algorithms are either incapable of meeting this constraint or deliver problematic results. In this paper, we describe a new algorithm for real-time unsupervised clustering, Bounded Self-Organizing Clustering. It executes in constant time for each input, and it produces clusterings that are significantly better than those created by the Self-Organizing Map, its closest competitor, on sensor data acquired from a physically embodied mobile robot.

Clustering algorithms are unsupervised learning algorithms that employ a distance metric to organize their training inputs into clusters. The classification of a previously unseen input is determined by the cluster to which it is closest, again based on the distance metric. This enables a large input space to be compressed into a more compact representation. A useful application of this technique is to create models of mobile robot environments based on the robot's sensor inputs.

In both training and classification, the distances between the input and the representative example of each cluster must be calculated. By placing a fixed upper bound on the number of clusters, we limit the total number of calculations required by each training and classification operation. This, in turn, enables us to predict the cycle time of the algorithm, a necessity for the practical deployment of such an algorithm aboard a mobile robot.

In this paper, we introduce a novel clustering algorithm, Bounded Self-Organizing Clusters (BSOC), that is designed to meet these constraints. In the robotics literature, the Kohonen Self-Organizing Map (SOM) has been used for this purpose as well. We argue that the design of the SOM leads to a relatively poor clustering, and that BSOC represents a significant improvement. We demonstrate this experimentally using both sonar and image data captured from a mobile robot.

We begin with some background and describe related work. Next, we describe our physical system hardware, with an eye towards making clear the technical limitations to which any solution must conform. We then describe our learning algorithm, followed by our experiments and results. We then give our conclusions and speculations on future work.

Background

Clustering algorithms have long been an appealing machine learning technique for robotics applications, due to their potential for incremental machine learning in combination as well as their ability to reduce complex continuous sensor input values to a smaller number of discrete values. Several examples of this approach employ the Kohonen Self-Organizing Map (SOM) (Kohonen 2001) to reduce the sensor inputs into a finite number of discrete states to facilitate the Q-learning algorithm.

Each SOM is a neural network consisting of a single two-dimensional layer of nodes arranged in a rectangular grid. The number of nodes and their arrangement is fixed. Each node is an object of the same specifications as a network input, which represents the reference input for that node. A distance metric is defined for the space of possible inputs. Typically, this distance metric will be the sum-of-squared-differences. The output node whose reference input that is closest in distance to an input presented to the network is considered the winning node; its coordinates are the output of the SOM.

To train a SOM, a training input is presented to the network. The winning output node's reference input, along with some of its neighbors, is then combined with the input value. The difference vector between the values is calculated and multiplied by a learning rate. The resulting value is then added to the reference input of the learning node. For each affected SOM node i and input vector element j, the update equation for the weight vector w of the reference input (given a learning rate $\alpha, 0 < \alpha < 1$) is:

$$w_{ij} = w_{ij} + \alpha * (input_{ij} - w_{ij})$$

The α parameter is determined by the neighborhood scheme of the specific SOM implementation. Many implementations (e.g. (Smith 2002)) make multiple passes over the input, slowly reducing α on each pass. (Touzet 1997) trains the winning node with $\alpha = 0.9$, and the four cardinal neighbors are trained with $\alpha = 0.5$. As α remains constant throughout, this formulation of the SOM lends itself well to real-time implementation aboard a robot. Since the number of nodes and topology are fixed, one can define a SOM output map that guarantees that the robot's cycle time will reliably meet its timing requirements. This will be the variation of the SOM that will serve as a baseline in our experiments for assessing our own algorithm.

The earliest application of the SOM to robotics was that of (Touzet 1997), in which a tiny (6 cm diameter) Khepera mobile robot equipped with eight infrared sensors for object detection learned to move forward while avoiding obstacles. The continuous values from the IR sensors were routed into a 4x4 SOM. The SOM output node was then employed as a state index for Q-learning. Touzet later scaled up this work to a much larger robot (Touzet 2006) employing a ring of 16 sonars. In this later work, Q-learning was abandoned; instead of using reinforcement rewards, the desired behavior was specified in terms of an acceptable range of sensor values. (Smith 2002) did similar work, with two major differences: a different definition of the SOM learning neighborhood than that of Touzet, and implementation in simulation rather than on a physical robot. Instead of using immediate neighbors, all nodes in the network were affected, with the learning rate combined with a Gaussian smoothing function. (Ferrer 2010) implemented both approaches on a mobile robot and compared the results. He found that both approaches worked respectably well, but that both were surpassed by Q-Learning without the use of clustering.

(Provost, Kuipers, and Miikkulainen 2006) undertook similar work in simulation, but replaced the SOM with the closely related Growing Neural Gas (GNG) algorithm (Fritzke 1995). The GNG is appealing in this context because of its flexible topology. It starts with two nodes. Additional nodes are incorporated into the network as needed to represent inputs that correspond to significant previously-unseen aspects of the input space.

(Ferrer 2014a) also applied the GNG algorithm to robot learning. A robot built a GNG as it drove through its environment. A human then examined each GNG node, specifying an appropriate action based on a visual inspection of the node's reference input. This work was reasonably successful for behavior specification on a physical robot. However, the manual specification of an action for each node was found to be laborious. (Ferrer 2014b) further advanced the concept of employing a GNG for learning an environment. A human pilots a robot through an environment, learning a GNG representation of the environment and associating actions from the human with the GNG nodes. When running autonomously, the robot selects its action based on which GNG node is the winner for the current input image.

Because the GNG adapts the number of clusters based on the inputs it receives, it is not possible to guarantee that the robot will complete each round of processing within a specified target time. While one appealing aspect of the GNG algorithm is the elimination of underutilized nodes, the specifics of this elimination process are too unpredictable to enable us to make guarantees about timing.

The problem of learning from a real-time input stream is also of interest outside the robotics community. (Hapfelmeier et al. 2012) mention application domains such as real-time scientific data processing, finance, web applications, and telecommunications.

Figure 1: Robot

The most prominent clustering algorithm in the literature is arguably k-means (Forgey 1965) (MacQueen 1967). For our application domain, we did not consider this approach at all, as it requires multiple passes through the input data. As each of these multiple passes requires visiting every input sample, our target constraint of constant-time execution cannot be satisfied. Also related to our approach is bottom-up agglomeration as described, for example, by (Koivistoinen, Ruuska, and Elomaa 2006). We do not seek to perform a full bottom-up agglomeration; instead, we use agglomeration as a strategy to help us execute in constant time while retaining good relationships with the inputs.

Hardware

Our robot is a Lego Mindstorms EV3 equipped with a Logitech C270 webcam and three sonar sensors. The EV3 has a 300 MHz ARM9 CPU and 64 MB of RAM. Its OS is a version of Linux. We implemented our software in Java using LeJOS 0.9.0. The webcam is connected to the EV3 via its USB 1.1 port. As the webcam is designed to be used with a USB 2.0 port or better, it is limited to grabbing 160x120 YUYV images at about 14 frames per second. We configured the robot as shown in Figure 1.

Bounded Self-Organizing Clusters

Basic Version

We introduce a novel clustering algorithm called *Bounded Self-Organizing Clusters* (BSOC) (see Figure 2). Each BSOC is a complete undirected weighted graph. Each node in the graph contains the reference input for a cluster (comparable to the nodes in a Self-Organizing Map (Kohonen 2001)). Each edge weight denotes the distance between the reference inputs of the clusters.

Each BSOC is given a maximum number of clusters it can represent. When training, each training input is added to the set of clusters as a reference input. If adding the training input causes the number of nodes to exceed the maximum, the two nodes in the graph with the shortest edge are merged by computing a weighted average of their numerical representations.

The edges are stored in a red-black tree. They are primarily ordered by their distances, and secondarily ordered by the indices of their node endpoints. This enables us to quickly find the smallest edge when needed in the `train` method. When two nodes are merged (and removed from the main graph), their edges are also removed from the red-black tree.

```
setup(max-nodes)
  edges = new red-black-tree
  nodes = map of node-indexes to inputs

lookup(input)
  for each node
    find distance from input to node
  return (node-index, distance) of
     closest node

train(input)
  insert(input)
  if number of nodes exceeds max-nodes
     edge = edges.remove(smallest edge)
     (n1, n2) = endpoints of edge
     Remove n1 and n2 and their edges
     insert(merged(n1,n2))

insert(image, count)
  add (image, count) to nodes
  for each existing node n
     Create and insert a new edge:
     - First vertex is image
     - Second vertex is n
     - Weight = distance from image to n

merged(n1, n2)
  img = (n1.image + n2.image) / 2
  return img
```

Figure 2: Pseudocode for Basic BSOC Training

Let M be the maximum number of nodes for a BSOC. Each call to `lookup` or `insert` makes no more than M calls to the distance function. Each call to `insert` performs up to $M \log M^2 = 2M \log M$ numerical comparisons when inserting an edge connecting the input to each of up to M existing nodes. Each call to `train` makes up to two calls to `insert`, along with a comparison, $2M$ edge removals (each requiring $2 \log M$ comparisons in a red-black tree), and two hash table removals. Consequently, given that M can be fixed as a constant, we can say that each call to `train` or `lookup` takes constant time.

Weighted-Input Variation

A potential drawback of the above algorithm is that clusters that are the result of repeated averages are given the same importance in the merging stage as clusters that are the result of single inputs. We find it intuitive that clusters that are the result of repeated merges would be closer in distance to a larger number of inputs from the input space. The following variation is an attempt to codify this intuition.

In addition to a reference input, each node in the graph contains a counter, initially set to one. Each counter denotes the number of input samples that contributed to the current node. These counters serve two major roles. First, they will be used as weights when merging nodes. Second, each edge weight (i.e., the distance between the reference inputs of the connected nodes) will be multiplied by the larger of the two counters for the connected nodes.

We expect these roles to achieve two things. First, by employing the larger counter as an edge weight multiplier, nodes that are derived from larger numbers of input samples will be less likely to be selected for merging. Second, by weighting the merge based on the counters, when they are selected they will preserve more of the broad influence of the inputs from which they were generated.

The revised BSOC algorithm is given in Figure 3. Note that `setup` and `lookup` are unchanged (and hence omitted). The additional arithmetic calculations have no asymptotic impact on performance.

```
train(input)
  insert(input, 1)
  if number of nodes exceeds max-nodes
     edge = edges.remove(smallest edge)
     (n1, n2) = endpoints of edge
     insert(merged(n1,n2),
            n1.count + n2.count)

insert(image, count)
  add (image, count) to nodes
  for each existing node n
     d = distance from image to n
     Create and insert a new edge:
     - First vertex is image
     - Second vertex is n
     - Weight is d * max(count(image),
                         count(n))

merged(n1, n2)
  w1 = n1.count / (n1.count + n2.count)
  w2 = n2.count / (n1.count + n2.count)
  img = w1 * n1.image + w2 * n2.image
  return img
```

Figure 3: Pseudocode for Weighted BSOC Training

Experiments and Evaluation

Robot Environment

We gathered two different types of sensor data from our robot: triples of distance values from the sonars, and images from the webcam. To gather the sonar data set and the first

Figure 4: Office, Carpeted Floor

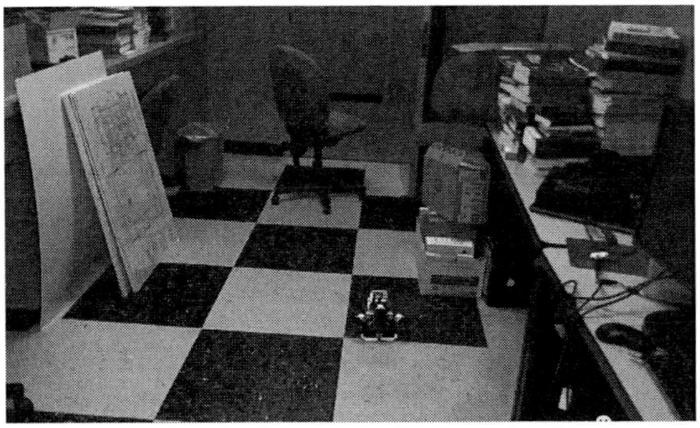

Figure 5: Office, Tile Floor

video data set, we navigated the robot through the cluttered office environment depicted in Figure 4.

For the second video data set, we navigated the robot through a different office environment. While the first environment has a carpeted floor, the second environment has a tile floor of alternating colors, as we can see in Figure 5.

Each video sequence is 700 frames. Each frame is a 160x120 image in YUYV format. As YUYV uses 2 bytes per pixel, the total size of each frame is 38400 bytes. The sonar data set was created from a sequence of 1304 sonar triples. The sonars are configured as follows: One points about 45 degrees to the left of the robot, one points forward, and one points about 45 degrees to the right. The effective range of each sonar is from 0 to 2.5 meters. In all cases, the robot visited many different areas of the office, so as to ensure that each sequence was reasonably representative of the environment.

For both types of data, distance values between samples are calculated as sum-of-squared differences. For computing the distance between two triples of sonar distance values, the differences between the distance values of each corresponding sonar position are computed. For the YUYV images, the differences between each corresponding byte are computed.

Sonar (m^2)			
Nodes	SOM	BSOC1	BSOC2
16	1.812×10^3	2.310×10^1	2.451×10^1
32	1.523×10^3	4.978	2.998
64	7.361×10^1	9.120×10^{-1}	5.473×10^{-1}

Figure 6: Sonar: SSD

When creating clusters, the merging process requires averaging the inputs. In both cases, the averaging is analogous to the computation of the distance. For the sonar triples, the weighted mean values are computed for each sonar position. For the images, the weighted mean values are computed for each byte. Since the byte values are 8-bit unsigned integers, the result of each division is truncated.

Experiments

In this section, the basic version of BSOC is denoted `BSOC1`, and the BSOC variation weighted by input sample counts is `BSOC2`.

We constructed our experiments to test the following hypotheses:

1. Given the same number of clusters, BSOC1 will provide closer matches to its source inputs than the SOM as formulated by (Touzet 1997), and BSOC2 will provide closer matches than BSOC1. We define "closer matches" to be the sum-of-squared-differences (SSD) between each input and the reference input for the closest matching cluster.
2. Given the same number of clusters, BSOC2 will exhibit more consistent performance than the SOM or BSOC1 regardless of the ordering of the input data. We measure "consistent performance" as the ratio of the standard deviation to the mean. Smaller values indicate more consistent performance.

We tested each of our input sequences with clustering algorithms configured with 16, 32, and 64 nodes. For testing the SOMs, we used 4x4, 4x8, and 8x8 grids. The SSD values for the sonar experiments are in units of meters squared. For the video experiments, the units are pixel intensity values squared. For presentation purposes, all entries have been rounded to four significant figures.

Results

Hypothesis 1 As we can see from Figures 6 through 11, Hypothesis 1 was confirmed, with some qualifications. BSOC1 consistently outperformed the SOM in the sonar experiments by multiple orders of magnitude, a compelling improvement. In the first video experiments, it outperformed the SOM by factors ranging from slightly over one to slightly over two, a much less compelling improvement, but still consistently superior. The second video was more favorable, performing 3-4 times better.

Sonar Ratio		
Nodes	BSOC1	BSOC2
16	7.844×10^1	7.393×10^1
32	3.059×10^2	5.080×10^2
64	8.071×10^1	1.345×10^2

Figure 7: Sonar: SOM SSD / BSOC SSD

Video 1			
Nodes	SOM	BSOC1	BSOC2
16	5.465×10^{18}	4.749×10^{18}	1.754×10^{18}
32	4.257×10^{18}	2.524×10^{18}	1.113×10^{18}
64	2.703×10^{18}	1.125×10^{18}	6.765×10^{17}

Figure 8: Video 1: SSD

Video 2			
Nodes	SOM	BSOC1	BSOC2
16	1.404×10^{19}	3.739×10^{18}	1.199×10^{18}
32	5.390×10^{19}	1.806×10^{18}	6.745×10^{17}
64	4.554×10^{18}	1.058×10^{18}	2.838×10^{17}

Figure 10: Video 2: SSD

Video 2 Ratio		
Nodes	SOM/BSOC1	SOM/BSOC2
16	3.75	1.17×10^1
32	2.98	7.99
64	4.30	1.60×10^1

Figure 11: Video 2: SOM SSD / BSOC SSD

BSOC2 outperformed both of the other algorithms very consistently, with the exception of the 16-node sonar experiment, in which its performance was very close to BSOC1. In the other two sonar experiments, it outperformed BSOC1 by about 65%.

In the video experiments, BSOC2 consistently outperformed both the SOM and BSOC1. In the first video, it was about 3-4 times better than the SOM, while with the second video it was 8-16 times better.

All of these clustering algorithms show significant improvement in performance as additional nodes are added. This demonstrates that those engineering a robotic system incorporating a clustering algorithm do have a clearly defined trade-off between cycle time and clustering accuracy. This improvement was less consistent with the second video stream, as the 32-node solution was more favorable to BSOC than the 64-node solution.

Hypothesis 2 We ran a separate set of experiments to test Hypothesis 2, as all of the previous experiments trained the learner by showing the inputs in the order that they were acquired by the robot. While we consider that to be the expected deployment situation of these algorithms, the sensitivity to ordering is also worthwhile to measure. To this end, we trained the 64-node version of each algorithm on six different randomly generated permutations of the input samples. We employ here the same performance metric as our earlier experiments, namely, the sum-of-squared-differences between each input and its closest matching cluster. Figure 12 shows the mean, standard deviation, and ratio for the sonar experiments, and Figures 13 and 14 show the same values for the video experiments.

In all three cases, BSOC2 had a much tighter standard deviation than the other algorithms, showing a more consistent performance regardless of move ordering. In spite of this clear result, in all cases the performance on the non-permuted input is much worse. Figures 15, 16, and 17 highlight this phenomenon. For all of these algorithms, processing the inputs in the order they were acquired creates a highly idiosyncratic statistical outlier.

Potential Applications

We are in the process of developing several different robot learning systems that would employ BSOC as a component. Our first goal is to replicate the learning scheme described by (Touzet 2006). He employed two different SOMs to represent the robot's environment as sensed by a ring of sonars. One SOM was used to represent the environment itself, while the second SOM was used for modeling the result of action selection. The robot's goals are specified in terms of sensor values. The robot then attempts to move itself to a SOM state that is compatible with those values. We have found that while the underlying concept is compelling, there is not sufficient detail to represent the role of the second SOM. We believe that replacing the first SOM with a BSOC will result in improved modeling accuracy, while replacing the second SOM with a Markov chain should prove

Video 1 Ratio		
Nodes	SOM/BSOC1	SOM/BSOC2
16	1.151	3.116
32	1.687	3.825
64	2.403	3.996

Figure 9: Video 1: SOM SSD / BSOC SSD

Permuted sonar			
Algorithm	$\bar{x}$	σ	$\frac{\sigma}{\bar{x}}$
SOM	4.585×10^1	1.008×10^1	2.200×10^{-1}
BSOC1	6.695×10^{-1}	2.043×10^{-1}	3.051×10^{-1}
BSOC2	2.477×10^{-1}	2.717×10^{-2}	1.097×10^{-1}

Figure 12: Sonar, with permuted inputs

Permuted video 1			
Algorithm	$\bar{x}$	σ	$\frac{\sigma}{\bar{x}}$
SOM	1.27×10^{18}	1.455×10^{17}	1.15×10^{-1}
BSOC1	9.82×10^{17}	1.990×10^{17}	2.03×10^{-1}
BSOC2	2.84×10^{17}	6.421×10^{15}	2.26×10^{-2}

Figure 13: Video 1, with permuted inputs

Permuted video 2			
Algorithm	$\bar{x}$	σ	$\frac{\sigma}{\bar{x}}$
SOM	1.13×10^{18}	1.455×10^{17}	1.29×10^{-1}
BSOC1	3.74×10^{17}	4.835×10^{16}	1.29×10^{-1}
BSOC2	1.41×10^{17}	8.661×10^{15}	6.12×10^{-2}

Figure 14: Video 2, with permuted inputs

Sonar: Comparisons of SSD			
Algorithm	Original	Permuted $\bar{x}$	$\frac{Original}{Permuted}$
SOM	7.361×10^{1}	4.585×10^{1}	1.606
BSOC1	9.120×10^{-1}	6.695×10^{-1}	1.362
BSOC2	5.473×10^{-1}	2.477×10^{-1}	2.209

Figure 15: Sonar: Comparisons of SSD

Video 1: Comparisons of SSD			
Algorithm	Original	Permuted $\bar{x}$	$\frac{Original}{Permuted}$
SOM	2.702×10^{18}	1.27×10^{18}	2.12
BSOC1	1.125×10^{18}	9.82×10^{17}	1.14
BSOC2	6.765×10^{17}	2.84×10^{17}	2.38

Figure 16: Video 1: Comparisons of SSD

Video 2: Comparisons of SSD			
Algorithm	Original	Permuted $\bar{x}$	$\frac{Original}{Permuted}$
SOM	4.553×10^{18}	1.13×10^{18}	4.02
BSOC1	1.058×10^{18}	3.74×10^{17}	2.83
BSOC2	2.838×10^{17}	1.41×10^{17}	2.01

Figure 17: Video 2: Comparisons of SSD

effective. We plan to employ Dijkstra's Algorithm to find paths in the Markov chain through the BSOC states that it discovers.

Once the above system proves workable with sonars, we plan to employ video as the primary input. We believe this will enable us to do two things. First, we hope to be able to define robot behaviors in terms of video input, potentially opening up a wider array of possibilities than those given by sonar. Second, we would like to investigate the possibility of using the nodes for small-scale navigation of an environment.

We are also interested in using BSOC as a component to a supervised-learning system. In this way, BSOC would enable a scheme along the lines of k-nearest-neighbor (Saunders, Nehaniv, and Dautenhahn 2006) to be implemented in constant time.

We speculate that this algorithm could be useful for informing human decision-makers in situations requiring rapid responses where sensors are widely distributed and submitting information. Examples of such scenarios could include environmental assessment in the wake of a disaster or any number of military or law-enforcement scenarios[1].

Conclusion

For the purpose of modeling a robot environment in constant time using a sequence of sensor inputs, we have shown that Bounded Self-Organizing Clusters (BSOC) is a compelling alternative to the Kohonen Self-Organizing Map, the existing approach, for both sonar and video inputs. The variation of BSOC that weights the results based on the input sources is a particularly clear winner in our experiments; we consider this to be the definitive variation of the algorithm.

We believe that improved clustering has great potential to improve robot learning as a component of several possible larger systems. We would also be interested in finding applications for this algorithm in other domains beyond robotics that would benefit from real-time clustering.

Significant additional work remains in the development of this algorithm. First, many robot vision systems employ preprocessed features rather than raw pixel data, with the goal of improving recognition robustness across many different robot poses. We plan to investigate using ORB (Rublee et al. 2011) for this purpose. Second, many practical learning situations involve supervised learning. We believe that BSOC could be used as a component of a real-time supervised learning system designed along the lines of k-nearest-neighbor. Third, a system that utilizes BSOC clusters and maintains references to those clusters will need to preserve information as clusters merge. We currently have a prototype system in place to address this employing the Observer design pattern, but have not yet conducted an assessment of its utility.

Anyone who would like to experiment with our code and data sets is welcome to do so. It is archived at `https://github.com/gjf2a/maics2016`. The code is in the public domain.

[1]We would like to thank one of our anonymous reviewers for suggesting these possibilities.

Acknowledgements

We would like to thank the three anonymous reviewers for many helpful comments on our initial submission. We would also like to thank Mark Goadrich for proofreading this paper and giving many helpful suggestions, most specifically the idea to assess performance based on random permutations of the inputs.

References

Ferrer, G. J. 2010. Encoding robotic sensor states for Q-Learning using the self-organizing map. *Journal of Computing Sciences in Colleges* 25(5).

Ferrer, G. J. 2014a. Creating visual reactive robot behaviors using growing neural gas. In *Proceedings of the 25th Modern Artificial Intelligence and Cognitive Science Conference*, 39–44.

Ferrer, G. J. 2014b. Towards human-induced vision-guided robot behavior. In *Proceedings of the 2014 AAAI Fall Symposium: Knowledge, Skill, and Behavior Transfer in Autonomous Robots*.

Forgey, E. 1965. Cluster analysis of multivariate data: Efficiency vs. interpretability of classification. *Biometrics* 21(768).

Fritzke, B. 1995. A growing neural gas network learns topologies. In *Advances in Neural Information Processing Systems 7*, 625–632. MIT Press.

Hapfelmeier, A.; Mertes, C.; Schmidtl, J.; and Kramer, S. 2012. Towards real-time machine learning. In *Proceedings of the ECML PKDD 2012 Workshop on Instant Interactive Data Mining*.

Kohonen, T. 2001. *Self-Organizing Maps*. Springer, 3rd edition.

Koivistoinen, H.; Ruuska, M.; and Elomaa, T. 2006. A Voronoi diagram approach to autonomous clustering. In *Proceedings of the 9th International Conference on Discovery Science*, 149–160.

MacQueen, J. 1967. Some methods for classification and analysis of multivariate observations. In *Proc. of the Fifth Berkeley Symposium on Math. Stat. and Prob.*, 281–296.

Provost, J.; Kuipers, B. J.; and Miikkulainen, R. 2006. Developing navigation behavior through self-organizing distinctive state abstraction. *Connection Science* 18(2):159–172.

Rublee, E.; Rabaud, V.; Konolige, K.; and Bradski, G. 2011. ORB: An efficient alternative to SIFT or SURF. In *Proceedings of the IEEE International Conference on Computer Vision*.

Saunders, J.; Nehaniv, C. L.; and Dautenhahn, K. 2006. Teaching robots by moulding behavior and scaffolding the environment. In *Proceedings of the 1st ACM SIGCHI/SIGART Conference on Human-robot Interaction*, HRI '06, 118–125. New York, NY, USA: ACM.

Smith, A. 2002. Applications of the self-organizing map to reinforcement learning. *Neural Networks* 15:1107–1124.

Touzet, C. 1997. Neural reinforcement learning for behavior synthesis. *Robotics and Autonomous Systems* 22(3-4).

Touzet, C. 2006. Modeling and simulation of elementary robot behaviors using associative memories. *International Journal of Advanced Robotic Systems* 3(2):165–170.

Exploring Web-based Visual Interfaces for Searching Research Articles on Digital Library Systems

Maxwell Fowler, Chris Bellis, Christopher Perry, Beomjin Kim
Department of Computer Science
Indiana University-Purdue University
Fort Wayne, IN, U.S.A.
maxfwlr@gmail.com, kimb@ipfw.edu

Abstract

Previous studies that present information archived in digital libraries have used either document meta-data or document content. The current search mechanisms commonly return text-based results that were compiled from the meta-data without reflecting the underlying content. Visual analytics is a possible solution for improving searches by presenting a large amount of information, including document content alongside meta-data, in a limited screen space. This paper introduces a multi-tiered visual interface for searching research articles stored in Digital Library systems. The goals of this system are to allow users to find research papers about their interests in a large work space, to see how document content relates to a search terms, and to refine their search queries using document content. The current, under development pilot system successfully presents graphical illustrations of search results produced from both meta-data and underlying content in an intuitive visual interface that will assist user's search activities. With minor modification, the proposed system can be applied to a variety of other text-based data repositories.

Keywords - Digital libraries; Visualization; Unstructured text content; Visual analytics

Introduction

Academic paper writing leverages online corpora as one of the sources for references to prior work and to build upon previous results. Most corpora are hosted on services aimed at easing the search process; digital libraries such as the ACM Digital Library and the Library of Congress provide books, articles, and other forms of media, while services such as Google Scholar focus on journal papers. While valuable as knowledge repositories, these services lack in their ability to present information in a way that helps lead to easier, more informed decisions when determining which academic papers to read and reference.

Current digital library systems suffer from limiting standards and provide only superficial information in their search results. Most archiving systems display the title of a work, authors, the publication the work appeared in if applicable, and other basic meta-data at first. No profile of underlying document content is provided, which can make finding the best sources a tedious task which requires reading through the plaintext directly. Further, some search systems do not adequately search document content, instead relying upon users to already know the document they wish to retrieve.

The lack of search depth caused by not searching document content is exacerbated by the use of non-intuitive, text based results. This is not an effective form of data representation. Displaying a large amount of text in a column does not provide an efficient way to traverse search results and pinpoint desired content. At best, text based searches can prioritize results on the title that best matches the desired search terms or upon a hidden document relevance score, which does not help a user see why a given paper is the best choice. Further, many text based search systems on digital libraries lack an intuitive way to determine the relationships between titles, the content in documents, and the relationships between different documents.

Visualizations allow data to be presented in manners that are more interconnected and readily processable. This is accomplished by leveraging users' perceptual cognition. Studies have already shown such leveraging leads to faster data consumption and a higher quality of understanding (Card 1999, Veerasamy 1997). Such visualization work has already been applied to some forms of digital libraries in the past. University of Maryland's GRIDL, for example, presents digital libraries using two hierarchical axes with topics on one axis and publication years on another (Shneiderman 2000). The density of documents for that topic and publication year are then displayed as bar graphs, split between the different kinds of digital media in the library. Visualizations, such as GRIDL, allow large quantities of data to be displayed in a coherent format that is tailored for user ease and document content exploration.

Visualization has been used in the past in order to simplify searching document repositories. Most of these visual approaches have used some form of graphical representation to better show links between papers within a document and the overall document spread in a repository.

Some visualization work used a graphing approach with axes. ActiveGraph, developed by Marks et al, used scatter plots with customizable axes (Marks 2005). These axes, the X, Y, and Z axes, could be set to any of the kinds of meta-data discussed earlier. ActiveGraph took a repository wide approach; it did not get into underlying document content, but did allow an at-a-glance look at the entire repository based on specific meta-data.

Others used different graphical representations. Rushall et al. and Lin focused on self-organizing maps that could be directed at a document repository or single book to display the types of documents in a workspace or the topics contained in a repository (Rushall 1996, Lin 1996). These maps were useful for quickly searching for documents in a visual fashion. The search showed the contents of a workspace in a visual form, allowing the user to quickly parse out the kinds of documents provided. This system still lacked a link between the superficial meta-data and document content, though. While preferable to a text search, the work was still plagued by the limiting factor of judging a book by its cover - using the title, but not the actual content within the document.

To address the limitations of only leveraging meta-data and not document content, Short et al. developed a multi-tiered visual interface for digital libraries (Short 2014). This work used the indices of textbooks to index books based upon their overall content and content by chapter. The multiple tiers focused on different representations. The first tier compared books to each other based on desired search terms. This tier was similar to work such as ActiveGraph, leveraging a similar overall interface with a more regimented coordinate system rather than a scatterplot. This allowed for document screening based on meta-data like before. Clearly unrelated titles, works that were too old to be useful, or works with bad reviews could be safely ignored.

Other tiers took a content based approach to visualization. By leveraging the index of textbooks, Short et al. were able to directly allow exploration of document content. The visualizations showed the layout of the book's index and the presence of search terms on a by-chapter basis using the book's index. Searching for topics showed not only books on the subject, but also exposed the relevant content within. This allowed the search to be used to more easily select the best sources, based on how much they covered the desired search topic.

While the work already done is valuable, we see a place for future development. The current visualization work can be applied to other data domains, such as social networking data and unstructured text content. Unstructured content presents a number of issues. Such documents can have different layouts from one another. Even within a specific domain, such as research articles, the structure can be different. While most articles contain similar sections, such as an introduction and a method section, there is no guarantee articles use the same layout. Sacks-Davis and Ron et al. discussed the subject of structuring text content to be indexable and queryable, but did not consider visual approaches or building indexes for journal papers dynamically (Sacks-Davis 1997). Development in this field, utilizing visual analytic techniques, will assist researchers in finding references for their work.

To assist researchers, a visual search focused on research articles in Digital Library systems would be useful. This system requires indices to exist for the content in the papers. These indices need to be searched in a way that will help users make educated decisions on their paper selections. Papers do not tend to have indices, which mandates that an index is built for papers in some fashion in order to be reasonably searched. This is work previously undone, as prior systems that used indices used pre-built ones, such as Greg et al.'s work, and is a topic we need to address.

In addition, a good search term must support the ability for users' queries to undergo search refinement. A search should not only find documents related to given topics, but should allow the user to refine their search using different terms they discovered during the search. Short et al. approached this subject by showing chapter content from books. This is a limitation as current search refinement focuses specifically on content that is searched for. Related content and words that may be synonymous to desired content are currently unexplored angles for search refinement.

We propose a system which will bring the visual aspect and automatic indexing aspect together into one, targeted at assisting researchers in searching text corpora and refining their searches through intermediate results. This paper will introduce an ongoing development of a system; a two-tiered visualization web application that displays research articles with titles and associated content in a graphical format. The first tier will provide a high level profile of the kinds of documents in a repository and how related these documents are to desired search terms. These relationships will also show a relationship between papers, by proxy. The second tier has been designed with the idea of search refinement in mind. It displays the frequency of search terms in the paper, as well as synonyms, terms related to the search terms, and compound terms created by coexisting words. This paper presents the current prototype of the system developed to assist users' searches on research articles in Digital Library systems.

Methodology

The prototype system consists of three major components: index generation, query processing, and visualization. The index generation module analyzes the underlying content of a Digital Library's research papers and constructs an index for each of them. Query processing is an underlying process that connects the indices with the visualizations. The visualization itself is implemented in two tiers. Tier 1 presents an overview of the document base and the high level relationships among the documents and the query's search terms to guide user' selection of documents. Tier 2 provides a content analysis of a specific document from the Tier 1, showing terms related to the search query for the sake of search refinement. The methodology section is designed around looking for information about thread-based programming and architectures. We used the terms "thread," "process," and "cpu" as our search terms.

Index Generation

Our indexing system was developed using well known Lucene libraries and is not a major focus of our research (Apache 2015b). The documents are first extracted into plain text in order to ensure a consistent format. Using Lucene, common words and other characters deemed to be garbage are removed from the text. This is to prevent such words impeding the index searching process. The text is then stored into a data structure which maintains a word count, as well as information on which sentences in each document contain which words. Together, these structures serve as a searchable index for the document base.

Tier 1 Visualization

The Tier 1 visualization provides a profile of the entire document base. The intent of Tier 1 is to show the best papers for a user's search query in the digital library being used. Tier 1's search is based upon title info and the indices of each document. The aspects considered for each document are the length of the document, the relevancy the documents have to specific terms in a search query, and the relevancy the documents have to the entire search as a whole.

The user's search query is directly represented in the visualization. Each search query is three terms, with each term going into a different colored box. The colored boxes are red, green, and blue, which are the primary additive colors used in computer science. In our examples below, "thread," is the green term, "process," is the red term, and "cpu," is the blue term. Each search term is shown in the visualization in a circle of the term's color. From this point forward, all shapes in the visualization are referred to as nodes.

The documents appear in the visualization as nodes as well. Only documents that include at least one of the aforementioned search terms are placed on the visualization. Node size is determined absolutely, with the largest document in a repository having the largest node and the smallest document the smallest node. Node size is capped at 30 pixels, with any documents that would have a larger size being set to 30. The number of documents displayed by the search is a user defined number, using a slider to change for more tightly focused or broader reaching searches.

The nodes are positioned to show correlation between each document and the search terms in the query. A force directed graph is used for the layout, specifically d3's implementation of Dwyer's algorithm (Bostock 2011, Dwyer 2009). Each document has tension directed towards the search query nodes. The tension force is directly linked to the relation between a document and a term. A search term that a document has no relation to will provide 0 tension. Documents that feature all three terms will tend to be pushed into the middle of the visualization, while documents that only feature two terms will appear between only those two terms and not appear in the middle. We also use a simple collision algorithm to prevent node overlap. The document is placed in the triangle defined by the search term nodes. Documents with all three search terms equally weighted within it will be placed in the middle, equidistantly. Papers more related to a specific term will be placed closer to them, as they have a higher tension toward that search term than the others.

Document relevancy is determined using Lucene's Term Frequency-Inverse Document Frequency (TF-IDF) algorithm. TF-IDF is frequently used in data and text mining applications. The score for a term increases if a term appears often in a document or if that particular word is uncommon (Apache 2015a). Overall, documents are favored for having a large number of desired words. The score for words is used for both document relevancy to a single search term, for the node positioning, and overall document relevancy.

Overall document relevancy combines the relevancy scores for all three search terms to give each document node a color. The most relevant paper, determined by having the highest overall score for all search terms, will be black. Less relevant papers appear white, with papers in the middle falling somewhere on the grayscale in between. Black contrasts well with lighter colored nodes around it, making it a good color to indicate the best papers. Our basis for this decision came from color theory and digital graphics design (Foley 1996).

When a node is selected on the visualization, the node is highlighted and the paper's supplementary data is shown in a tooltip. Figure 2.1 shows a sample of the Tier 1 visualization with the best paper selected. Note that the best paper is not necessarily the largest, as in our sample query one of the smaller papers has the best overall search results. When a paper is selected, the title of the paper is shown, which acts as a link to the PDF. The author and conference are provided as well. Finally, a link to the second tier visualization is provided to link between the two tiers.

The formula scores the probability of a potential term being related to a base term by comparing how many hits the potential and the base have together over the number of hits only the base does in the document set. For each of the two terms that use the score, we will go into specific detail.

Related terms are defined as non-synonyms that appear in the same sentence as a search query's term. These terms can help refine a user's search query by showing them words that commonly appear together.

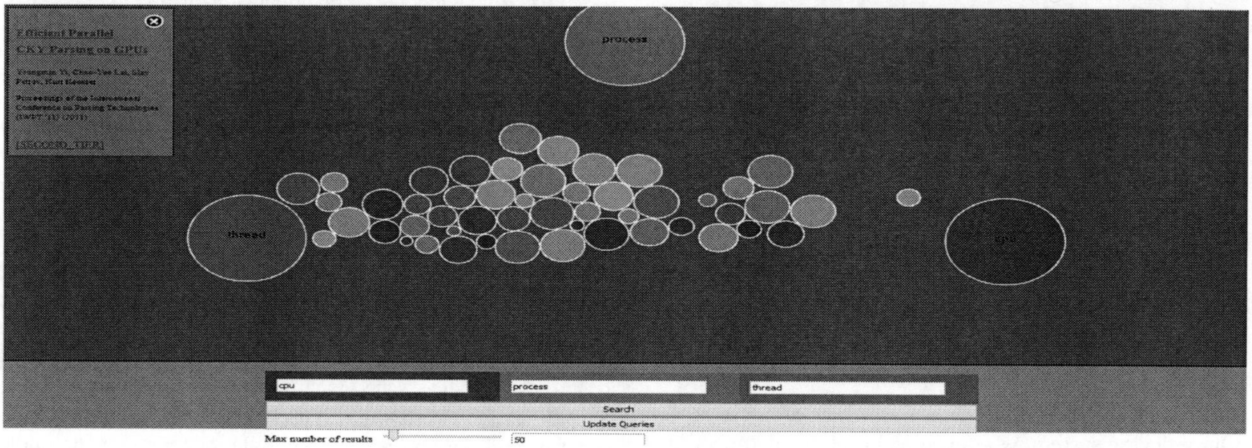

Figure 2.1 Sample view of Tier 1

Tier 2 Visualization

The Tier 2 visualization provides a closer look into specific documents. It relates the search terms to the content in the document itself. This way, the user can see precisely how prevalent a given term is in a document. This serves to increase user confidence in the document they have selected as being a useful document. In addition to directly showing term prevalence, the system provides coexisting words, related terms, and the synonyms for the search terms. The intent is to help users' with the task of search refinement by selecting better words for their queries. Synonyms and compound words are a new consideration in this research. While prior studies did not consider them useful, both serve to allow the user to phrase the same query in multiple ways to find the best results possible for their search.

Both related terms and compound terms using a scoring algorithm called Pointwise Mutual Information-Information Retrieval (PMI-IR). PMI-IR was developed by Peter D. Turney for developing automatic indices of non-structured content (Turney 2001). Our algorithm specifically implements PMI-IR 3, with some modifications:

$$P(potential|base) = \frac{Hits(potential\ AND\ base)}{Hits(base)}$$

This can then be used in a new search to refine the documents returned in a specific direction. In order to determine related terms, all the documents in the database are first stripped down to just contain the sentences containing a specific term.

Each of the remaining words is scored as the potential, with the search term as the base, using PMI-IR 3. The higher the score, the more relevant a specific related term is deemed to be. The current system allows all related terms with a score higher than 0 to appear in the visualization.

Compound terms are similar to related terms, but are specifically terms made up of two words; a query term and either the term directly before or directly after the query term in a sentence. These terms are intended to expand a specific search term. For example, a search can be refined to use "cloud computing," rather than "cloud," after finding the former as a compound term of the latter. Given the query "machine," one might get both, "machine learning," and, "autonomous machine." The same PMI-IR 3 scoring is used on compound terms as is used on related terms.

Synonyms are generated by searching through a synonym database. Our algorithm uses WordNet for collecting synonyms (Fellbaum, C). WordNet returns synsets of potential matches. As synonyms tend to be small in number, there is no threshold number in place for limiting the number of synonyms displayed.

The visualization is consistent between Tier 1 and Tier 2. The same force graph rules still apply. However, data in this tier is only related to one term node. This means that document content nodes that tend toward the middle are weakly related to their term. Content with a high relatedness to a search term, though, appears close to the term's node. Likewise, node size remains consistent in that it shows size, but the size is the count of specific terms, rather than document size.

The size of each object, including the search terms themselves, are how relevant they are to the overall paper. This is the word count from Lucene's index. It is possible to have a paper where a search term has relevance 0, which would make the shape have 0 size. Likewise, it is possible to have related, compound, or synonym terms be larger than the search query nodes if they appear in the current document more than the query terms do. The largest nodes in Tier 2 are the terms that are most likely to help refine a search by replacing a search term.

Each of the term types is represented with its own node shape. Synonyms are given circular nodes, to show they are directly related in meaning to the search query terms. Related terms and compound terms, meanwhile, are squares and triangles respectively. This decision was made to draw distinction between term types.

Figure 2.2 shows an example of a Tier 2 visualization, specifically from the last figure's best document. The size of the three search term nodes shows that they are, in fact, all three prevalent in the paper. Thread is the most relevant, though, as shown by the size. We can see what the terms are by hovering over their nodes. The term will appear in a tooltip above the node.

Discussion

The proposed system has made ground towards reaching the goals set for it. The visualization successfully functions on unstructured text content, such as the journal papers used in this study, which has yet to be done in this way. The Tier 1 visualization does provide a visually accessible look at the entire document repository. It manages to capture the legibility of previous systems while improving upon the visualization's ability to aid in selecting documents. Further, the Tier 2 visualization does make strides towards helping users refine their search in meaningful ways.

The Tier 1 visualization is quite strong at this point. It is useful for finding papers that span across multiple related domains, as shown in the methodology section. The overview is scalable, allowing users to search for a large number of papers or select only a small subset refined to be the best for a given search. Further, the white to black color scale for least to most relevant allows the most relevant paper to stand out easily, making finding the best options in any sized search an easy task.

Tier 1's strength is obvious when we compare the visual search to a text based alternative. Figure 3.1 shows a search for the terms "simulate", "transform", and "automata". The search provides the same information the visualization does, but the best paper's relation to terms is shown as numeric scores. This is less intuitive than the visualization's black to white color scale and position algorithm.

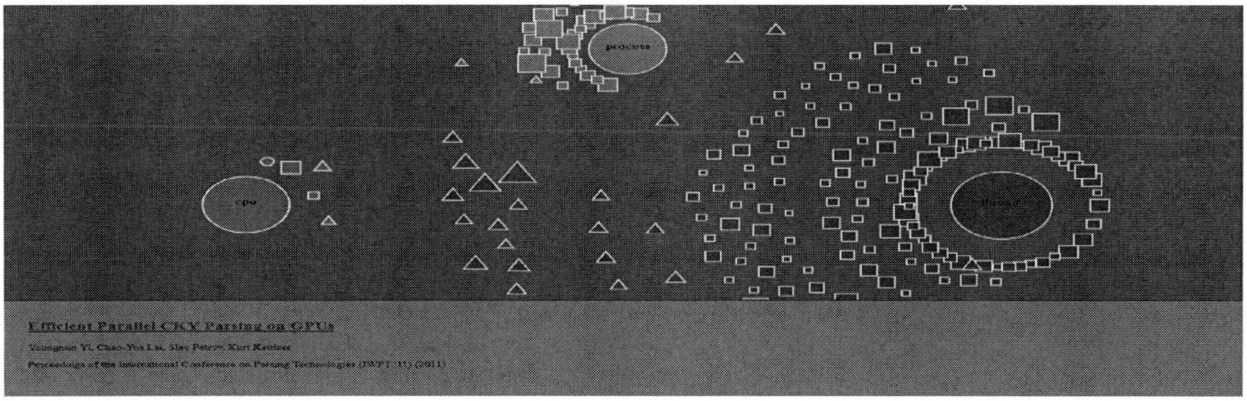

Figure 2.2 Sample view of Tier 2

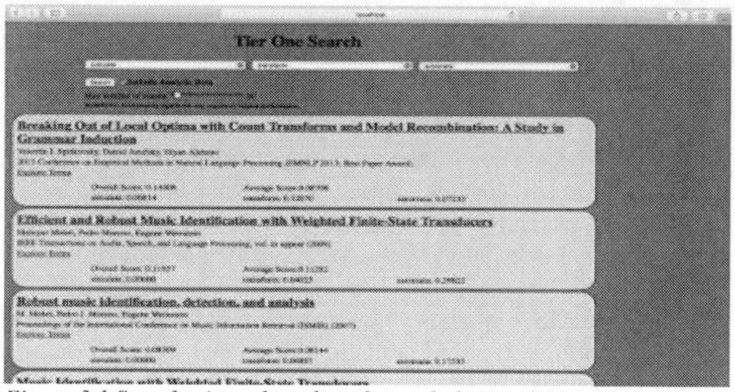

Figure 3.1 Sample view of text based search designed for usability tests

Figure 3.2 shows two searches. The search on the left is the same as the search in figure 3.1. It becomes readily apparent where the two best papers are and how they related to the terms. It also becomes apparent that the world simulate is fairly useless. Using the Tier 2 visualization, we refined the search to use, “grammar,” rather than, “simulate,” giving us the image on the right. This search refinement gives documents of much higher quality, according to the color scale and provides a better distribution in the visualization’s center. Further, the refinement is easier to make in the visual system than a text based one, which would require reading the whole document to find useful terms.

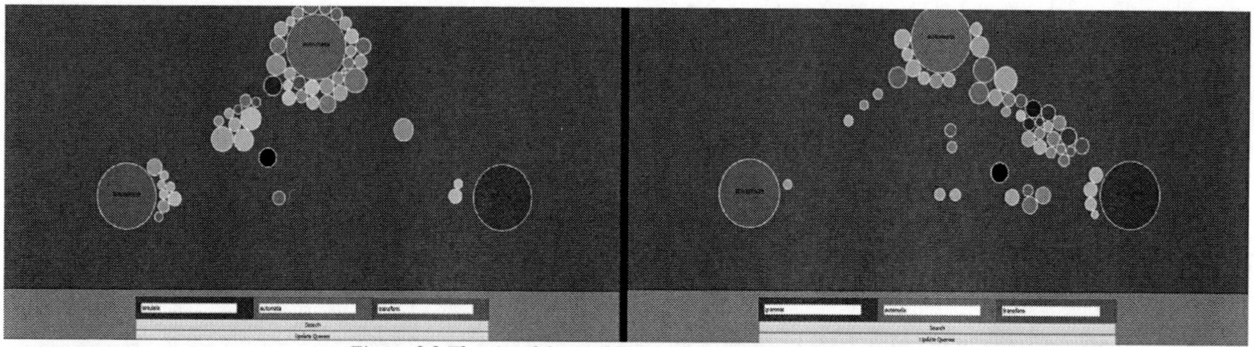

Figure 3.2 The visual form of Figure 3.1 and a refined version

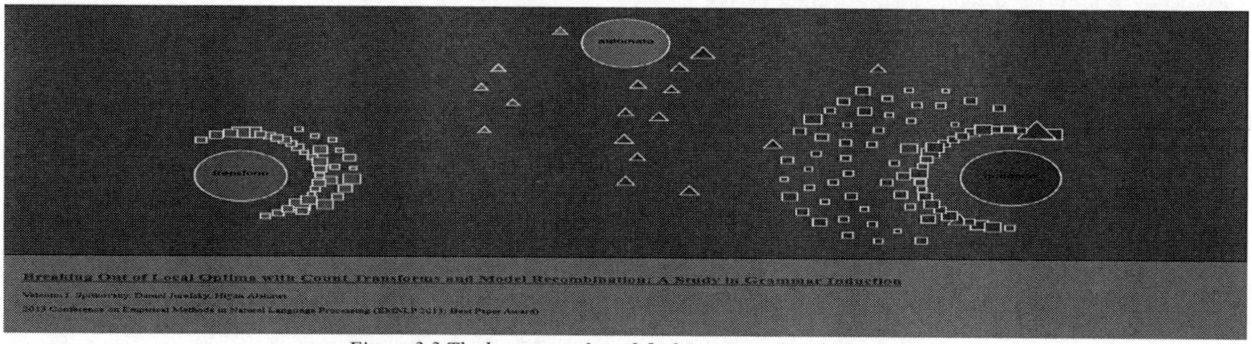

Figure 3.3 The best paper from 3.2 shows some Tier 2 overlap

The Tier 2 visualization succeeds in the goal of providing potential search refinement. It shows all the potentially useful related terms each of the search results have. The figure above directly shows the benefit of search refinement, as previously discussed.

The choice of red, green, and blue for the search term nodes was retained for Tier 2 in order to allow RGB color combinations to show off terms related to multiple documents. This was abandoned in practice, in part because meaningful terms related to two distinct, other terms were rare. This means the colorization here could be changed to represent different information if a better way to show term relation is found. Further, some collision can occur in tier 2 term nodes, which needs addressed in future updates. This can be seen in Figure 3.3, especially around the term “thread”.

FUTURE WORK

The proposed system makes good strides at reaching the goals set out in the introduction. Despite this, there are future work avenues to prove the system works, improve the system, and potentially apply the system in other ways. Some discussion of those angles follows below.

The paper uses searches on a paper database of our own creation. It is built of papers freely accessible on Google's own research papers. There are approximately 1600 of them. In the future, we will apply our visualization to a paid-for paper collection, such as the Text Retrieval Conference Proceedings (TREC). This will give our system a more robust collection to be tested against.

Usability tests are needed to prove that the visualization above is better than a text based system. While we feel the visualization system stands on its own merit, usability tests will add credence to that claim. Our next task will use a custom made, text based search system and compare it to our visualization. We will use a metric based approach to judge effectiveness, as well as judge user preferences. This way, the visualization's greater effectiveness compared to traditional text based interfaces can be proven.

The visualization is not without room for improvement. It would be ideal to take into account more than just the presence of search terms in Tier 1. Ideally, the document ranking algorithm can be altered to take into account all attributes of a document. This means the document's titles, reviews, word count, presence of search terms, and other data will all contribute to a document's relevance score.

Currently, the search is related to three terms. This is left over from earlier work when we were considering using RGB color combinations for paper quality, rather than the current black and white scale. We retained the color usage for Tier 2, but did not find such situations that would benefit from color combination. We are considering allowing an arbitrary N-gon, which will free up RGB colors to be used for different visual elements. Such an N-gon's size will be determined by the user, which a minimum size of two to allow the visualization to remain fully featured.

The potential exists for a third tier: specific term expansion. This tier would allow the user to select a term and see more information about it, including all related terms to that term in the repository, synonyms both in the repository and outside of it, and definitional information. This has yet to be implemented as the usefulness is questionable. It may be sufficient to augment the Tier 2 visualization with word definitions and leave it at that.

Another room for improvement is the clustering algorithm, especially when it comes to the overlapping related terms and the large clusters of low use papers. Some form of blobbing algorithm which combines closely related papers into one node which can then be expanded into the full node set should be considered to make the visualization simpler and more user friendly in such instances.

Finally, future work could include applying our system to other domains. So long as an index can be constructed for the desired data, any form of text-based data could be searched and visualized using the above system. For example, social network posts could be used as documents to search. This would allow the system to search blogs discussions forums, and other forms of social media for the sake of determining user consensus or gathering data for marketing purposes.

CONCLUSION

This paper proposed a visual search on Digital Library systems, specifically targeting journal papers and other research publications. The proposed system targets two goals. The system's first goal is a visualization on an entire document base, to help the user more easily see the best papers available for a given search. The second goal is to aid in search refinement, changing the original search to better suit the user's needs. This unexplored element was addressed by providing a visualization for various forms of related terms. A preliminary indexing step allowed us to apply these visual elements to a collection of unstructured text data; while not our primary research focus, this was still an interesting element and is in contrast to prior visualizations of structured document content which did not require an indexing step.

We developed a two tier system to meet our goals. Tier 1 provides a visualization over the document base for a specific set of three search terms. The papers are positioned and colored based on their relevance to terms and the overall search respectively. Tier 2 provides a visualization of a document's content. It shows how the search terms relate to the underlying content and show other related terms for the sake of search refinement.

By providing these two tiers, we help users with multiple tasks. Tier 1 makes it easy to see if a given search is useful or if a given search is skewed too far to one term. Tier 1 also makes it easy to find the best papers for a given search. Tier 2 allows us to confirm the best paper shown includes the search terms with a high frequency. Tier 2 also lets us refine our searches, allowing users to turn bad searches into good searches by changing a search term or two.

By assisting users with these tasks, our system makes sufficient strides towards our goals. Our last step is fixing the problems mentioned in the discussion section and investigating the improvements mentioned in the future work section. Once this is accomplished, our system will become practical and serve users in their searching of unstructured content in digital libraries.

References

Apache Software Foundation (2015). *Class TFIDFSimilarity*, Available:
https://lucene.apache.org/core/5_2_1/core/org/apache/lucene/search/similarities/TFIDFSimilarity.html

Apache Software Foundation (2015). *Lucene 5.2.1 core API*, Available:
https://lucene.apache.org/core/5_2_1/core/overview-summary.html#overview_description

Bostock, M., Ogievetsky, V., Heer, J. (2011). *D3: Data-Driven Documents* in *IEEE Trans. Visualization & Comp. Graphics.*

Card, S. K., Mackinlay, J. D., and Shneiderman, B. (1999). *Information visualization* in *Readings in Information Visualization: Using Vision to Think,* pp. 1-34.

Dwyer, T. (2009). *Scalable, Versatile and Simple Constrained Graph Layout* in *IEEE-VGTC Symposium on Visualization.*

Fellbaum, C. (2005). *What is WordNet.* Princeton University.

Foley, J., van Dam, A., Feiner, S., Hughes, J. (1996). Computer Graphics: Principles and Practice, Addison-Wesley Publishing Company.

Lin, X. (1996). *Graphical table of contents* in *Proc. of the first ACM Int. Conf. on Digital Libraries,* pp. 45-53.

Marks, L., McMahon T., and Luce, R. (2005). *ActiveGraph: a digital library visualization tool* in *International Journal on Digital Libraries*, vol. 5, no. 1, pp. 57-69.

Rushall, D., and Ilgen, M. (1996). *A context vector-based self organizing map for information visualization* in *TIPSTER: Proc. of a Workshop on held at Vienna, Virginia,* pp. 159-166.

Sacks-Davis, R., Dao, T., Thom, J. A., Zobel J. (1997). *Indexing documents for queries on structure, content and attributes* in *Proc. of International Symposium on Digital Media Information Base (DMIB).*

Shneiderman, B., Feldman, D., and Rose, A. (2000). *Visualizing Digital Library Search Results with Categorical and Hierarchical Axes* in *Proc. 5th ACM International Conference on Digital Libraries*, pp. 57-66.

Short, G., and Kim, B. (2014). *Multi-tiered Visual Interfaces for Book Search with Digital Library Systems* in *Proceedings of the 6th International Conference on Multimedia, Computer Graphics and Broadcasting*, pp.21-24.

Turney, P. D. (2001). *Mining the Web for Synonyms: PMI-IR versus LSA on TOEFL* in *Proc. of the 12th European Conference on Machine Learning (EMCL '01)*, pp. 491-502.

Veerasamy, A., and Heikes, R. (1997). *Effectiveness of a graphical display of retrieval results* in *Proc. of the 20th Annu. Int. ACM SIGIR Conf. on Research and Development of Information Retrieval,* pp. 236-245.

Extended Pixel Representation for Image Segmentation

Deeptha Girish, Vineeta Singh, Anca Ralescu
EECS Department
University of of Cincinnati
Cincinnati, OH 45221-0030, USA
girishde@mail.uc.edu, singhvi@mail.uc.edu, anca.ralescu@uc.edu

Abstract

We explore the use of extended pixel representation for color based image segmentation using the K-means clustering algorithm. Various extended pixel representations have been implemented in this paper and their results have been compared. By extending the representation of pixels an image is mapped to a higher dimensional space. Unlike other approaches, where data is mapped into an implicit features space of higher dimension (kernel methods), in the approach considered here, the higher dimensions are defined explicitly. Preliminary experimental results which illustrate the proposed approach are promising.

Introduction

Image segmentation is a key processes in image analysis. This step is done irrespective of the goal of the analysis. It is one of the most critical tasks in this process. The aim of segmentation is to divide the image into non overlapping areas such that all pixels in one segment have similar features. This representation makes the image more meaningful and makes its analysis and understanding easier. For example, in medical images each color represents a particular stain that is essentially a protein binder that binds to a certain type of molecule. Therefore the different clusters obtained after segmenting such an image according to color can help us identify different biological components in that image. This can help us to do further analysis like finding meta data about each of the structures, finding one structures relative position to the other etc.

One way to achieve this is to cluster similar pixels into one cluster. Therefore, what defines similarity and how it is calculated becomes very important. A lot of research has been done on finding similarity measures for images and videos (Wang et al.(2005)Wang, Zhang, and Feng), (Huttenlocher et al.(1993)Huttenlocher, Klanderman, and Rucklidge), (Gualtieri et al.(1992)Gualtieri, Le Moigne, and Packer). It is important that the measure we use captures the slightest difference in pixels. This plays an essential role in segmentation. K-means (MacQueen et al.(1967)) is a popular algorithm that works well for image segmentation. The aim of the K-means algorithm as stated by Hartigan ET. al. (Hartigan and Wong(1979)) is to divide M points in N dimensions into K clusters so that the within-cluster sum of squares distances is minimized. Thus, distance is an important factor. One of the major difficulties of image segmentation is to differentiate two similar regions which actually belong to different segments. This is because the existing features and the standard distances used to measure the dissimilarity do not capture the small differences very well. Increasing the sensitivity to small differences is the motivation for using the extended pixel representation. Image data is displayed on a computer as a bitmap which is a rectangular arrangement of pixels. The number of bits used to represent individual pixel has increased over the recent years, as computers have become more powerful. Todays computer systems often use a 24 bit color system. The most common color system in use is the RGB space (Red, Green and Blue).

Selecting the right color space for segmentation can be very important. Different parts of the image get highlighted better in different color spaces. It is also dependent on the purpose of the segmentation. To simplify this choice of color space, it is better to know in advance the features that represent maximum variation. This can be done by finding the coefficient of variation for each of the features of different color spaces. For a given data set, the coefficient of variation, defined as the ratio of standard deviation to the mean, represents the variability within the data set with respect to the mean. When selecting features/dimensions, it then makes sense to to take into consideration the coefficient of variation, more precisely, to select the features that have the highest variability. In selecting a color space, it is usual to adopt one (e.g., RGB, HSV) space. This study departs from this policy by selecting more than one color spaces, which further helps in better differentiate between pixels.

Related Work

The idea of extended pixel representation has been used previously to detect and repair halo in images (Ohshima et al.(2006)Ohshima, Ralescu, Hirota, and Ralescu), to calculate the degree of difference between pixels in color images in order to identify the halo region. The extended pixel representation used in (Ohshima et al.(2006)Ohshima, Ralescu, Hirota, and Ralescu) is

Table 1: The original and extended color spaces

Original Color Space	Extended Color Space
$(R\,G\,B)$	$(R\,G\,B\,\rho^{RG}\,\theta^{RG}\,\rho^{GB}\,\theta^{GB}\,\rho^{BR}\,\theta^{BR})$
$(H\,S\,V)$	$(H\,S\,V\,\rho^{HS}\,\theta^{HS}\,\rho^{SV}\,\theta^{SV}\,\rho^{VS}\,\theta^{VS})$
$(Y\,Cb\,Cr)$	$(Y\,Cb\,Cr\,\rho^{YCb}\,\theta^{YCb}\,\rho^{CbCr}\,\theta^{CbCr}\,\rho^{CrY}\,\theta^{CrY})$
$(R\,G\,B)$ $(H\,S\,V)$ $(Y\,Cb\,Cr)$	$(R\,G\,B\,H\,S\,V\,Y\,Cb\,Cr)$

described next. Given a pixel p in the image I, its extended pixel representation of p, is the real-valued vector $(R, G, B, \rho^{RG}, \theta^{RG}, \rho^{GB}, \theta^{GB}, \rho^{BR}, \theta^{BR})$ where RGB are pixel values in the RGB color space, and ρ^{XY} and θ^{XY} are the polar coordinates in the two dimensional color space, (X, Y), with $X, Y \in R, G, B, X \neq Y$. This representation better support image segmentation because it captures the difference between pixels more accurately. In particular, it gives much better results for images with low contrast.

The same extended pixel representation can be implemented in other color spaces as well, as our experimental results for HSV, which uses H for Hue, synonymous to color, S for Saturation, the colorfulness of a color relative to its own brightness, and V for Value which refers to the lightness or darkness of a color. It is known that for most images, HSV color space is more suitable for segmentation and we show that the extended pixel representation for HSV improves the results even for this color space. The $YCbCr$ space uses Y for Luminance, the brightness of light, C for Chrominance, the color information of the signal, which is stored as two color-difference components (Cb and Cr). Table 1 shows the features for each color space used in the experiments.

Current Approach

To illustrate the effect of the extended pixel representation, we consider two experiments as follows.

Sensitivity of distance to the extended space

Two pixels which are almost of the same color and having very similar R, G and B values are selected and their corresponding values in each of the extended pixel representations considered are calculated, using both the Euclidean distance and Manhattan distance. It is seen that the extended pixel representations are more sensitive to the dissimilarity between the pixels irrespective of the distance measure used. This is the idea behind using extended pixel representation. Especially for tasks like segmentation, this is a very efficient way to separate two samples which have similar feature values into different clusters.

Table 2 shows the results for computing the distance between the two fixed pixels, in three standard color spaces, their extensions, and in an extended representation based on three color spaces.

Table 2: Euclidean distance (ED) and Manhattan distance (MD) for two fixed pixels in the original and extended color spaces, and the percentage of change due to the extended representation.

Pixel Representation	ED	MD
$(R\,G\,B)$	54.08	75.00
$(R\,G\,B\,\rho^{RG}\,\theta^{RG}\,\rho^{GB}\,\theta^{GB}\,\rho^{BR}\,\theta^{BR})$	80.47	175.40
% of change	48.78	133.86
$(H\,S\,V)$	5.00	5.13
$(H\,S\,V\,\rho^{HS}\,\theta^{HS}\,\rho^{SV}\,\theta^{SV}\,\rho^{VS}\,\theta^{VS})$	8.59	15.17
% of change	71.69	195.62
$(Y\,Cb\,Cr)$	29.15	32.81
$(Y\,Cb\,Cr\,\rho^{YCb}\,\theta^{YCb}\,\rho^{CbCr}\,\theta^{CbCr}\,\rho^{CrY}\,\theta^{CrY})$	48.24	92.10
% of change	65.52	180.72
$(R\,G\,B\,H\,S\,V\,Y\,Cb\,Cr)$	61.64	112.94
% of change with respect to average distances for the original color spaces	109.58	200.00

Obviously, all distances in the extended space should be larger than those in the original space, because adding more features to the pixel representation in effects adds positive quantities to each of the distances considered and therefore this experiment merely confirms that theoretical fact.

Sensitivity of the distance in the original and extended space when the pixel changes

A second small experiment was run as follows. Starting with two pixels p, and p', ED and MD were computed just as in the previous section. Then p_2 was altered slightly, to obtain p'', and the same distances were computed for p and p'', and compared with those computed for p and p'. Tables 3 and 4 show the results.

Table 3: Changes in the Euclidean Distance (ED) when the pixel p' changes to p''. RGB pixel values are $p = (10, 100, 150)$, $p' = (25, 120, 135)$, $p'' = (30, 125, 130)$.

Pixel Representation	(p_1, p')	(p_1, p'')	diff %
$(R\,G\,B)$	29.15	37.75	29.48
$(R\,G\,B\,\rho^{RG}\,\theta^{RG}\,\rho^{GB}\,\theta^{GB}\,\rho^{BR}\,\theta^{BR})$	54.77	71.24	30.06
$(H\,S\,V)$	15.00	20	33.29
$(H\,S\,V\,\rho^{HS}\,\theta^{HS}\,\rho^{SV}\,\theta^{SV}\,\rho^{VS}\,\theta^{VS})$	25.89	34.52	33.32
$(Y\,Cb\,Cr)$	19.22	24.74	28.68
$(Y\,Cb\,Cr\,\rho^{YCb}\,\theta^{YCb}\,\rho^{CbCr}\,\theta^{CbCr}\,\rho^{CrY}\,\theta^{CrY})$	38.40	49.43	28.70
$(R\,G\,B\,H\,S\,V\,Y\,Cb\,Cr)$	38.01	49.36	29.88

Experiments and Results

Segmentation using the k-means algorithm was implemented for three different images. Each image is in a different color space. Segmentation using K-means was done on these images using the standard pixel representation and the extended pixel representation. The Euclidean distance

Table 4: Changes in the Manhattan Distance (ED) when the pixel p' changes to p''. RGB pixel values are $p = (10, 100, 150), p' = (25, 120, 135), p'' = (30, 125, 130)$.

Pixel Representation	(p_1, p')	(p_1, p'')	diff %
(RGB)	50	65	30
$(RGB\,\rho^{RG}\,\theta^{RG}\,\rho^{GB}\,\theta^{GB}\,\rho^{BR}\,\theta^{BR})$	120.3	155.4	29.17
(HSV)	15.15	20.22	33.39
$(HSV\,\rho^{HS}\,\theta^{HS}\,\rho^{SV}\,\theta^{SV}\,\rho^{VS}\,\theta^{VS})$	45.11	60.16	33.36
$(Y\,Cb\,Cr)$	27.40	35.82	30.73
$(Y\,Cb\,Cr\,\rho^{YCb}\,\theta^{YCb}\,\rho^{CbCr}\,\theta^{CbCr}\,\rho^{CrY}\,\theta^{CrY})$	82.13	106.1	29.22
$(RGB\,HSV\,Y\,Cb\,Cr)$	92.55	121.0	30.77

between pixels (in original color space and extended space) was used. For every image, the number of clusters was decided visually. The same number of clusters was used for all the extended pixel representations. The mean square error, equation (1) and the signal to noise ratio, equation (2) are calculated.

$$MSE(r,t) = \frac{1}{M \times N} \sum_{n=1}^{M} \sum_{m=1}^{N} [t(n,m) - r(n,m)]^2 \quad (1)$$

$$Snr(t,r) = 10 \log_{10} \left(\frac{\sum_{m=1}^{M} \sum_{n=1}^{N} [r(n,m)]^2}{\sum_{m=1}^{M} \sum_{n=1}^{N} [r(n,m) - t(n,m)]^2} \right) \quad (2)$$

where $r(n, m)$ represents the original image and $t(n, m)$ represents the segmented image, both of size $[N, M]$.

Table 5 shows the results of the segmentation and MSE and Snr for each of these segmentations. Inspecting Table 5 it is observed that for all images, even though the distance measure and the number of clusters were same, the mean square error was lower and correspondingly signal to noise ratio was higher when the extended pixel representation was used. It can be seen that the results look very similar to the original image because the clusters are colored with the mean color of all the pixels in that cluster. It can also be observed that the difference in results when the extended pixel representation is used is higher for images of low contrast. The extended pixel representation also performs better for pictures with high texture content.

The smaller changes in color values of the pixels are separated and recognized better in extended pixel representations. Irrespective of the color space used, the extended pixel representation gives lower mean squared error and higher signal to noise ratio than the standard pixel representation for all images. All pixels that are similar in color get clustered into one segment which might represent a particular structure in the image. Thus, this representation adds more meaning to the image.

Conclusion

The segmentation problem considered in this paper can be addressed by using the extended pixel representations. The idea of representing each pixel with more information proved to be successful for image segmentation. It was observed that extended pixel representation can more effectively distinguish similar pixels. Although in the second experiment, it was seen that the percentage change of the euclidean distance between the extended pixel representation and the standard pixel representation when p was changed to p is very small, the effect turns out to be significant in the clustering step.With the same number of clusters and the same distance measure used, the mean square of the segmentation done using the extended pixel representation is lower for all images.

The promising experimental results of this idea encourages exploration of other extended pixel representations in the future. It will be interesting to include texture information like edges or frequency domain information as part of the pixel representation. Tailoring the extended pixel representations for the task in hand and automatic learning of the most important features and optimal number of features to represent a pixel for a particular task is an important idea to be considered for future work.

References

JA Gualtieri, J Le Moigne, and CV Packer. Distance between images. In *Frontiers of Massively Parallel Computation, 1992., Fourth Symposium on the*, pages 216–223. IEEE, 1992.

John A Hartigan and Manchek A Wong. Algorithm AS 136: A k-means clustering algorithm. *Journal of the Royal Statistical Society. Series C (Applied Statistics)*, 28(1):100–108, 1979.

Daniel P Huttenlocher, Gregory A Klanderman, and William J Rucklidge. Comparing images using the Hausdorff distance. *Pattern Analysis and Machine Intelligence, IEEE Transactions on*, 15(9):850–863, 1993.

James MacQueen et al. Some methods for classification and analysis of multivariate observations. In *Proceedings of the fifth Berkeley symposium on mathematical statistics and probability*, volume 1, pages 281–297. Oakland, CA, USA., 1967.

Chihiro Ohshima, Anca Ralescu, Kaoru Hirota, and Dan Ralescu. Processing of halo region around a light source in color images of night scenes. In *Proc. of the Conference IPMU*, volume 6, pages 2–7, 2006.

Liwei Wang, Yan Zhang, and Jufu Feng. On the Euclidean distance of images. *Pattern Analysis and Machine Intelligence, IEEE Transactions on*, 27(8):1334–1339, 2005.

Table 5: Results on segmentation of six images, using each of the three color spaces separately (2nd row), extended pixel representation (3rd row), and all three color spaces (4th row). Bold font indicates the smallest MSE.

a) Original Image

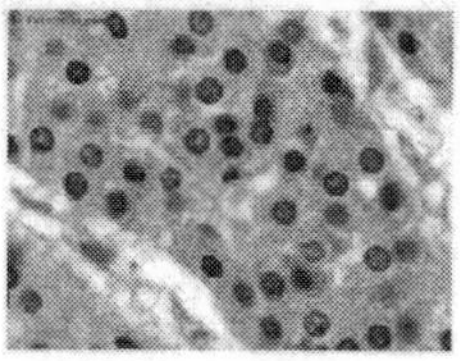

b) Original Image

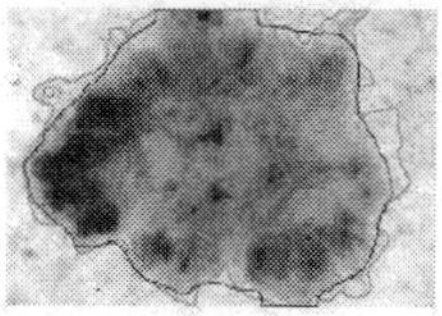

c) Original Image

a) RGB
Snr=35.3260db
MSE=0.0050

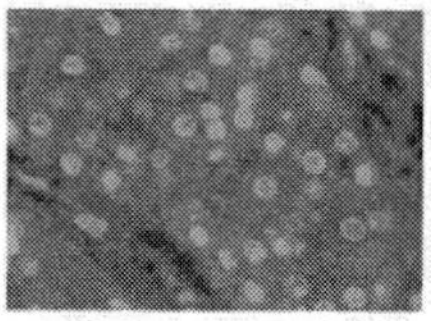

b) HSV
Snr=54.8959db
MSE = 0.0035

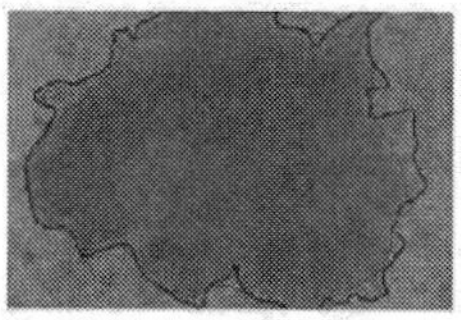

c) YCbCr
Snr=55.8133db
MSE=0.0031

a) RGBρ^{RG} θ^{RG} ρ^{GB} θ^{GB} ρ^{BR} θ^{BR}
Snr=39.3334db
MSE=0.0033

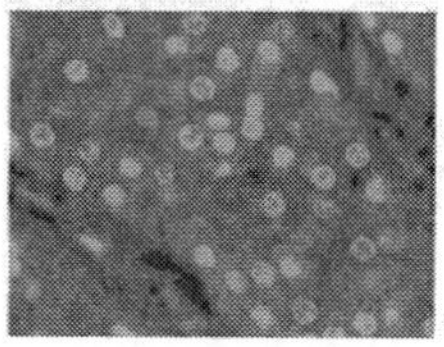

b) HSVρ^{HS} θ^{HS} ρ^{SV} θ^{SV} ρ^{VH} θ^{VH}
Snr=56.1241db
MSE=0.0026

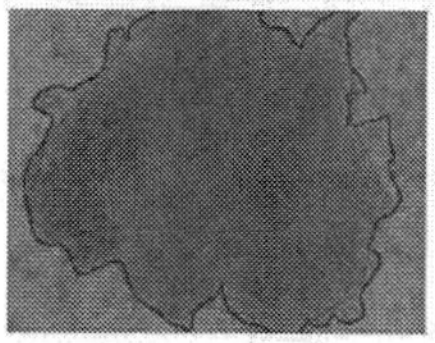

c) YCbCrρ^{YCb} θ^{YCb} ρ^{CbCr} θ^{CbCr} ρ^{CrY} θ^{CrY}
Snr=58.8801db
MSE=0.0015

a) RGB HSV YCbCr
Snr=37.4722db
MSE=0.0173

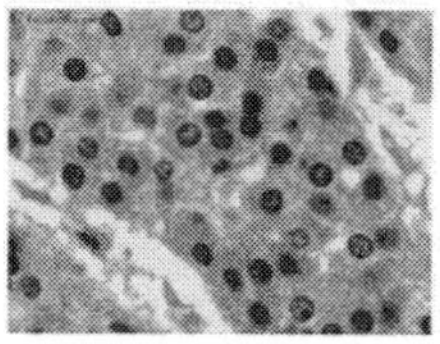

b) RGB HSV YCbCr
Snr=57.064db
MSE=0.0021

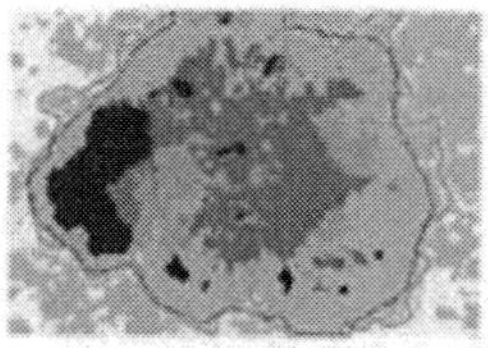

c) RGB HSV YCbCr
Snr=35.4811db
MSE=0.0173

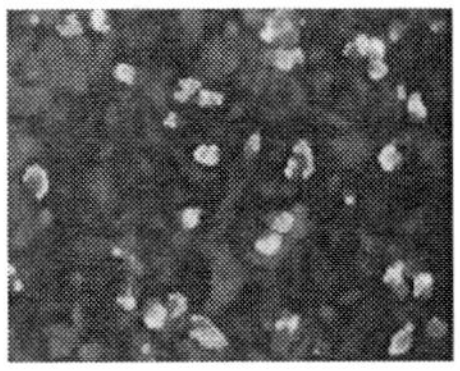

d) Original Image

e) Original Image

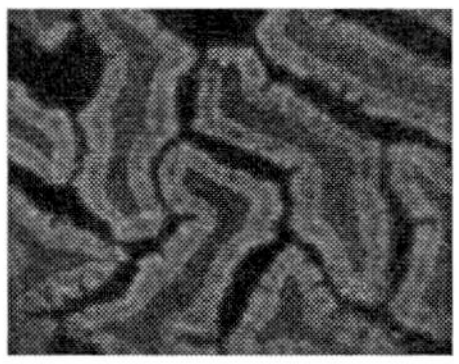

f) Original Image

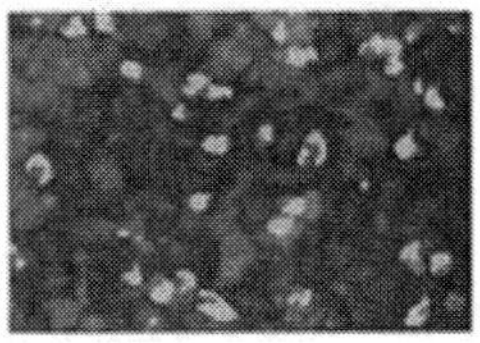

d) RGB
Snr=47.4465db
MSE=0.0014

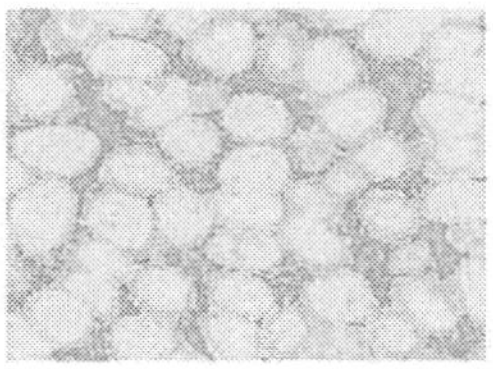

e) HSV
Snr=44.0748db
MSE=0.0062

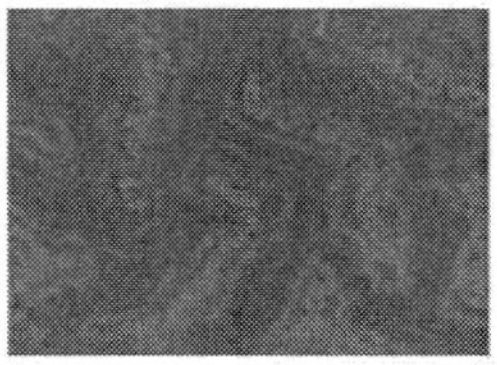

f) YCbCr
Snr=54.3042db
MSE=0.00075

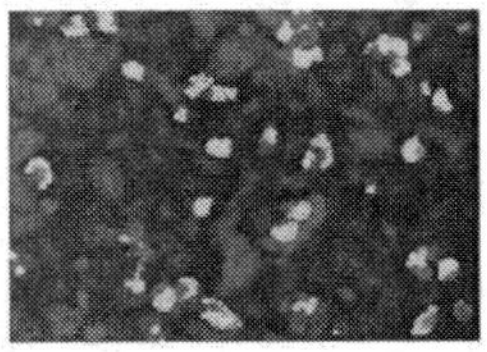

d) RGBρ^{RG} θ^{RG} ρ^{GB} θ^{GB} ρ^{BR} θ^{BR}
Snr=49.2535db
MSE=0.0012

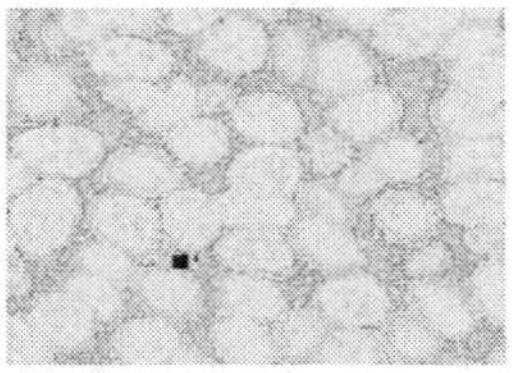

e) HSVρ^{HS} θ^{HS} ρ^{SV} θ^{SV} ρ^{VH} θ^{VH}
Snr=47.3483db
MSE=0.0044

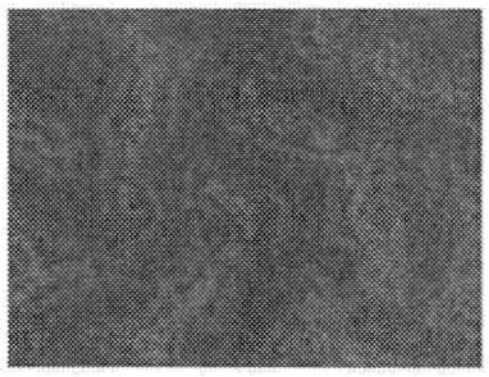

f) YCbCrρ^{YCb} θ^{YCb} ρ^{CbCr} θ^{CbCr} ρ^{CrY} θ^{CrY}
Snr=54.9753db
MSE=0.0007

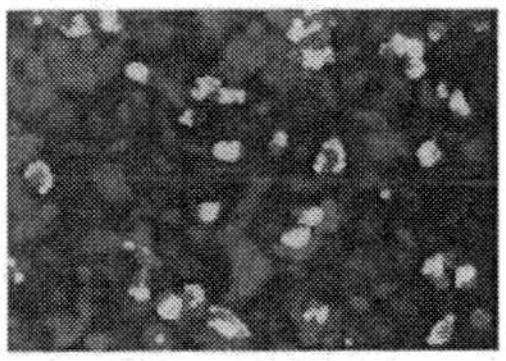

d) RGB HSV YCbCr
Snr=48.1598db
MSE=0.0013

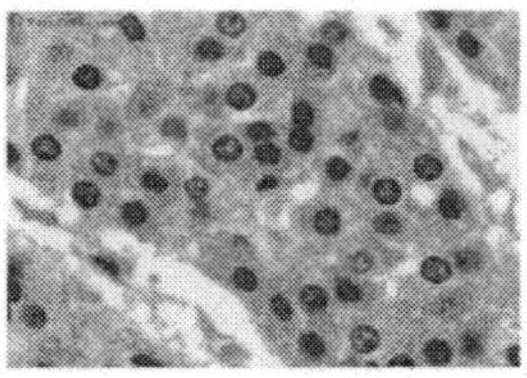

e) RGB HSV YCbCr
Snr=26.9429db
MSE=0.0038

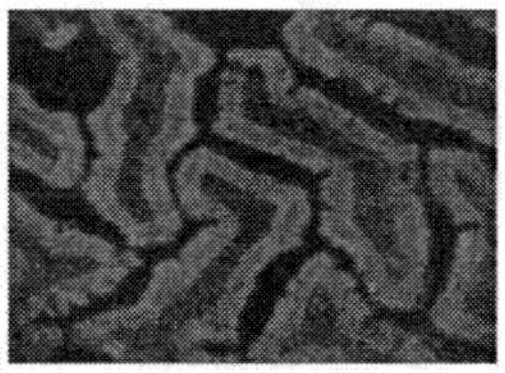

e) RGB HSV YCbCr
Snr=32.4912db
MSE=0.0037

Student Understanding and Engagement in a Class Employing COMPS Computer Mediated Problem Solving: A First Look

Jung Hee Kim
North Carolina A&T State U.
jungkim@ncat.edu

Michael Glass
Valparaiso U.
michael.glass@valpo.edu

Taehee Kim
North Carolina A&T
tkim@ncat.edu

Kelvin Bryant
North Carolina A&T
ksbryant@ncat.edu

Angelica Willis
North Carolina A&T
awillis@aggies.ncat.edu

Ebonie McNeil
North Carolina A&T
eimcneil@aggies.ncat.edu

Zachery Thomas
North Carolina A&T
zithomas@aggies.ncat.edu

Abstract

COMPS computer-mediated group discussion exercises are being added to a second-semester computer programming class. The class is a gateway for computer science and computer engineering students, where many students have difficulty succeeding well enough to proceed in their major. This paper reports on first results of surveys on student experience with the exercises. It also reports on the affective states observed in the discussions that are candidates for analysis of group functioning. As a step toward computer monitoring of the discussions, an experiment in using dialogue features to identify the gender of the participants is described.

Introduction

The second Java programming class, GEEN 165, at North Carolina A&T State University is a bottleneck for many Computer Science and Computer Engineering students. As an experiment in improving student learning and interest, COMPS computer-mediated discussion exercises (Glass et al., 2014a) have been introduced. This paper reports on first measurements of a) student self-efficacy and interest, b) expressions of affect within the discussions. As a test of our ability to have the computer monitor the conversation, the expressions of affect were applied toward the task of using dialogue features to identify the gender of the participant.

GEEN 165 corresponds to the CS2 (second semester) class in the ACM/IEEE curriculum (ACM/IEEE, 2013). The historical success rate for students attempting GEEN 165 is low. From 2003 to 2012, comprising about 1000 student-semesters, approximately 66% of students succeeded well enough (grade C or better) on the first attempt to continue to the next class. The fact that so many students have difficulty makes it potentially a fertile class for experimenting with educational innovation.

Lab-based computer programming classes traditionally permit unstructured group interaction. Students can talk to each other even as they require the students to write their own software. Therefore problem-solving discussions, where students respond to each other in normal dialogue fashion, are a natural addition to the lab component of a computer programming class.

NC A&T has migrated to an objects-later curriculum, meaning that CS2 contains more object concepts than the first semester CS1 class. The student exercises in this intervention are thus oriented toward object concepts.

Expressions of affect have three potential uses for this project. One is they are indications of emotional states that may effect student enthusiasm, self-efficacy and satisfaction. Another is they will be used in studies of group interaction. Finally, they may detectable by machine, contributing to an instructor's dashboard or other assessment of how well the group discussions are working.

Background

COMPS Dialogue Platform and Exercises

COMPS is a web-delivered computer-mediated chat environment (Kim et al., 2013). It permits the instructor (or a TA) to monitor each conversation. The dialogue data from this study comes from log files. Attesting to the interactivity of the COMPS experience, about half of all typing occurs while several students are typing. Even three students at a time can be typing and responding to each other, all contributing to the same discussion, since they can see each other's keystrokes in real time. In spoken conversation productive dialogue does not happen when three people are talking at once, but we have shown that in the chat domain it indeed occurs (Glass et al., 2015).

The exercises in this project involve students solving multiple-choice questions. When implementing these as group collaborations, we pay attention to three principles that promote successful collaborative learning: a structure or activity script for the students to follow, creative interdependence, and individual accountability (Eberly Center, 2016). The activity is structured as follows. The students are instructed to come to consensus on the answer, then have one student approach the instructor or a TA to verify the answer. That student is responsible for bringing the correct answer (or a hint) back to the group, and they must reach consensus again. Creative interdependence means that students should need each other to complete the exercise, it should not reasonable for one or several students to race ahead and finish it and leave the others behind or let them not participate. During the discussion the obligations of discourse require that students explain themselves in the course of reaching consensus. Having conceptual knowledge as the learning goal promotes explanatory dialogue. We have examples where seemingly the weakest student serves as a metacognitive regulator, challenging or directing every reasoning step and becoming a participant in all dialogue exchanges as the other students seem to teach that weakest one (Glass et al., 2013). Individual accountability typically occurs after the group exercise, where the students have a quiz or an exercise utilizing what they have learned. Individual accountability also occurs within the discussion, as the students find themselves responsible for explaining their positions in order to reach consensus.

Addressing Student Learning

Our collaborative inquiry learning exercises are in line with current practices in Computer Supported Collaborative Learning. A key concept is group cognition, where different participants in a conversation contribute different parts of the epistemic knowledge construction task. The Virtual Math Teams project, where students solve math problems through computer-mediated chat, has documented this phenomenon (Stahl, 2009). Learning through group cognition is justified both in terms of learning outcomes and student motivation. There is also research specifically showing that collaborative activity is a desirable pedagogical approach for "relational understanding" or understanding of concepts (Tchounikine et al., 2010). Dialogue that engages in domain reasoning, such as explaining, negotiating, or inferring is observed in these kinds of exercises (Zhou, 2009; Stahl, 2004).

The implication for COMPS technology is that monitoring the health of student conversations could be informed by a) whether students are talking to each other, b) whether they are engaging in reasoning activities.

Addressing Student Interest and Self-Efficacy

Group exercises address many of the components of student interest. Interest refers to an individual's psychological inclination to participate in particular content over time (Hidi & Renninger, 2006). There is a relationship between interest, achievement goals, performance and retention (Harackiewicz et al., 2008). Interest plays a critical role in students' further decisions on engaging and reengaging in the major (Brown, 2012). The four-phase model of interest posits four sequential interest phases: triggered situational interest ("catching"), maintained situational interest ("holding"), emerging individual interest, and well-developed individual interest. Mitchell (1993), as an example, reported that using group work activities, computer-based activities, engaging puzzles, and meaningful activities, were correlated with triggering and holding interest in a mathematics classroom.

Recently Kim and Schallert (2014) have investigated the mediating effect interpersonal interactions have on student interest. It is possible to track student interest in four developmental phases throughout a semester, not just within the time frame of individual activities. It is affected not only by the enthusiasm expressed by the teacher and fellow students, but also by factors such as affiliative motivations: the desire to belong to the group. The social factors enhancing interest were found within college classes in a number of diverse disciplines (e.g. history, chemistry, religion) in both upper and lower level college classes.

Viewed in this light, group exercises should address student motivation issues through social interaction at the same time as they address learning of concepts through group cognition. The exercises are constructed so that students engage with other students, providing the small-group interpersonal contact that best transmits enthusiasm. The students know the teacher is watching the conversations and is taking an active interest in the students' progress, sometimes by intervening and sometimes by providing answers and hints.

The implication for COMPS technology is that monitoring the health of student conversations could be informed by expressions of student affect. Affect, the observable manifestation of emotion, mediates social interaction and is related to student interest.

Self-efficacy, an individual's belief to be capable of performing a particular task (Bandura, 1977), has been widely studied because of its relationship to performance including academic achievement (Choi, 2005; Pajares and Miller, 1995; Wood and Locke, 1987) and even choice of major in college (Hackett, 1985). In accordance with the suggestions of Finney and Schraw (2003), we measured self-efficacy using task-specific survey items rather than generalized questions. This project measures students' self-efficacy both at the level of the skills in individual assignments at the time of the COMPS exercises and overall in the topics of the class at the beginning and end of the semester.

Data and Methods

We have collected data from one semester of the GEEN 165 class. There were 55 students at the start of the semester and 47 at the end. We administered COMPS exercises four times during the semester, with 53 group discussions in total. Most groups had 3 or 4 participants. The bulk of students were assigned to sessions quasi-randomly as students arrived in lab. Cliques of friends, who tended to arrive together, were split into different random groups. We deviated from this protocol by creating a few all female groups, for comparison with the all-male groups. Altogether there were about 8000 dialogue turns. Students were surveyed near the beginning and end of the semester regarding their enthusiasm for the class, their self-efficacy in programming, and their desire to continue. Every COMPS exercise was also accompanied by a survey of the student experiences.

Transcript Processing and Annotation

Table 1 contains an extract from a COMPS discussion. From COMPS log files we extract dialogue turns in spreadsheet format for processing. The text from one dialogue turn is in one line of the spreadsheet. In addition to the metadata such as problem number, turn number, and time stamp, each dialogue turn is tagged with features. Some are derived by software and some are annotated by hand. These features are available for machine learning experiments and for human analysis and study of dialogues. The machine-derived classifiers are available for feeding software that will monitor the health of the conversation.

Some of the existing machine-derived features (Glass et al., 2014b) that have been relevant to transcript studies and machine monitoring of the health of the conversation are:

- The presence of discourse marker words, e.g. "now" or "therefore" near the beginning of a dialogue turn. These are linguistically associated with reasoning, and are therefore possibly indicative of productive discussion.
- The presence of pronouns that include another participant in the dialogue: "you," "we," "us." These are possibly indicative of transactive discussion.
- The presence of question marks.
- The presence of emoticons. It is possible that emoticons are associated with students attending to each others affect.
- The length of a turn in words.
- Whether typing this turn overlapped with other people typing.

Affective States Evinced in Dialogue

Of particular interest are six affective states that we have chosen as initial targets. These are annotated by hand. They were chosen because they may be salient for monitoring both the learning aspects (whether the students are reasoning together) and the social health of the conversation. We show here some of the definitions that the coders have applied for consistency in recognizing and coding.

- Excited.
- Apologetic. Refers to a user expressing regret for previous action. This type of message is usually aimed towards another user or towards the group as a whole.
- Humor.
- Frustrated.
- Confused. User explicitly expressing confusion, or exhibiting confusion e.g. through questions.
- Sad. A negative emotion determined by keywords and sad emoticons that are usually directed at self.

Some of these affective states have been tagged and illustrated in the Table 1 dialogue. Table 2 indicates some of the textual indications for the various states. These are being used by the coders at present, but will become machine-derived features for the purpose of machine-annotating the affective states.

Surveys

The survey administered to all students at the beginning and end of the semester has an interest part and a self-efficacy part. The end-of-semester survey also inquires about student plans for continuing in the major and registering for the next programming class. All items use a 6-point scale. The interest survey items are derived from a survey from Harackiewicz et al. (2008). One of the authors of this paper has utilized these items to assess how much a student's interest in a class is affected by the enthusiasm of fellow students (Kim and Schallert, 2014). Some representative items are "What we are learning in GEEN165 this year can be applied to real life" and "To be honest, I don't find what we do in the GEEN165 class interesting." The self-efficacy items inquire about student confidence in completing 13 tasks corresponding to class topics. This list was obtained from the instructor. A typical item is "Design inner classes that implement event handling interfaces."

The after-COMPS-lab survey had items covering student perceptions in three areas: student interest, whether the student learned from the lab, and how well the group exercise functioned. An example item is "I contributed to the understanding of other students in my group."

Results

Survey Results

Table 3 shows the students' perceptions of interest and efficacy at the beginning and end of the semester. All interest items were combined into one mean and the same for all efficacy items. In total 28 students participated in both pre- and post-surveys.

- Regarding students' interest toward the course, their interest did not change. The averages of students' interest toward the course in the beginning of the semester and end of the semester were 4.33 and 4.32 respectively.

- Self-efficacy with respect to the course content indicated significant improvement between the beginning and the end of the semester, rising from 2.83 to 3.81.

The increase in self efficacy was significant, $p < 0.01$.

Table 4 shows students' perception of the COMPS labs, surveyed immediately after each lab. There seemed to be a clear improvement between the first part of the semester (Labs 1 and 2) and the later part (Labs 3 and 4). Students perceived:

- more effective group work in the second part (means rose from about 3.1 to about 3.4)
- better understanding of concepts in the second half (means rose from about 3.4 to about 3.9).

Multiple one-way ANOVA supports the hypothesis that mean scores are indeed different, $p = 0.03$ for both effectiveness and understanding. Post hoc analyses using the Tukey test for significance indicated that the mean scores of Lab 3 were significantly higher than Lab 2 for both effectiveness and understanding.

However, students' interest in each exercise in the lab sessions seemed to fluctuate throughout the semester. Lab 3 had the highest interest, which corresponded with the highest effectiveness and understanding. But interest in Lab 4 was the approximately the same as Labs 1 and 2.

Affective States by Gender

We annotated the 14 group discussions of one COMPS exercise, comprising 2147 dialogue turns, for the six affective features. In total 199 turns showed evidence of one or more feature, or 9.3%.

As a first test of the utility of these features along with the machine-generated ones, we tried to use them to predict the gender of the participant. Among 49 students we had 16 women and 33 men. First we aggregated all the turns from each student, and looked at statistical differences between the two populations. Two-tailed t-tests revealed that none of the features were significantly different between the genders at the $p < 0.05$ level. However expressions of apology were different at the $p = 0.06$ level. The most common affective feature was confusion, with 62 instances of utterances expressing confusion. Women expressed confusion in 4.6% of turns, and men in 2.2%. It suggests the two genders behave differently, but the $p < 0.22$ level does not show significance. The two genders also showed differences in the amount of participation. Men each uttered an average of 46 turns per dialogue and women 36 turns.

We then trained a J48 decision tree classifier and a multiple-regression linear classifier using the Weka data mining tool (Witten and Frank, 2005). The task is to classify each dialogue turn with the gender of the speaker, to mimic the task of monitoring a conversation in real time turn-by-turn. These classifiers have not been successful. The same features that are statistically correlated with gender are discovered by the decision trees, but accuracy has been quite low.

Discussion and Future work

Survey Results

The students experienced improvement in their experience of the COMPS exercises during the semester. They reported that the groups worked better in the last two exercises and that they learned more. It is not clear why student interest was lower in the last lab. Anecdotally there are two reasons that have been suggested by the instructor and lab TAs who supervised this session. One is that the last lab was optional, presented during Thanksgiving week. That fewer students attended could indicate that the general level of engagement was lower than usual. The other is that perhaps the novelty was wearing off. Some students expressed as much during the session. We will need to find some way to survey the reasons for student interest.

The pre- and post-semester survey is hard to interpret because of low participation rate and dropouts. In the next semester we are enforcing better participation. The increase in self-efficacy was striking, but we do not have yet any comparison with other classes. Future work includes comparing interest and self-efficacy with learning gains on the pre- and post-tests. Future work also includes comparing pre- and post-semester survey results with individual lab surveys, to see whether there are correlations between overall student interest and the situational interest in individual COMPS exercises.

Another analysis in the future will be between the participants of the same group: do they agree about learning and group functioning, do they have similar learning gains.

Affective States in Dialogue

Hand-annotating the remaining 6000 turns of dialogue may result in more reliable statistical correlations. We are also at work toward machine-annotation of these features.

Annotation of the affective states so far has relied entirely on the text of the dialogues. Future work will include extra-linguistic features. In COMPS group exercises in other classes evidence of student engagement sometimes presents through Comic Sans typeface, big or bold fonts, and wild colors. We are also exploring using timing features from the overlapped typing. Students can all type simultaneously while seeing each other's developing chat text (Glass et al., 2015). We think that typing speed, degree of simultaneous typing, and pauses as they look at each other's turns, may provide indications of affective states such as being excited or indications of when they are attending to each other's utterances.

Acknowledgements

Partial support for this work was provided by the National Science Foundation's Improving Undergraduate STEM Education (IUSE) program under Award No. 1504917. Any opinions, findings, and conclusions or recommendations expressed in this material are those of the author(s) and do not necessarily reflect the views of the National Science Foundation.

References

ACM/IEEE. Computer Science Curricula 2013: Curriculum Guidelines for Undergraduate Degree Programs in Computer Science. New York: ACM, 2013.

Bandura, A. (1997). Self-efficacy: the exercise of control. New York: Freeman.

Brown, J. (2012). Developing a freshman orientation survey to improve student retention within a college. *College Student Journal*, 46, pp. 83–851.

Choi, N. (2005). Self-efficacy and self-concept as predictors of college students' academic performance. *Psychology in the Schools*, 42, pp. 197–204.

Eberly Center (2016). Carnegie Mellon, Eberly Center for Teaching Excellence and Innovation. What are best practices for designing group projects? http://www.cmu.edu/teaching/designteach/design/instructionalstrategies/group-projects/design.html. Retrieved March, 2016.

Finney, S. and G. Schraw (2003). Self-efficacy beliefs in college statistics courses. *Contemporary Educational Psychology*, 28, pp. 161–186.

Glass, Michael, Melissa Desjarlais, Jung Hee Kim, and Kelvin Bryant. (2013). COMPS Computer-Mediated Problem Solving Dialogues (poster abstract). International Conference on Computer Supported Collaborative Learning, Madison, WI.

Glass, Michael, Jung Hee Kim, Kelvin Bryant, Melissa Desjarlais, Micayla Goodrum, and Thomas Martin. (2014a). Toward Measurement of Conversational Interactivity in COMPS Computer Mediated Problem Solving. Proceedings of the 25th Modern Artificial Intelligence and Cognitive Science Conference (MAICS-14), Spokane, WA.

Glass, Michael, Jung Hee Kim, Kelvin Bryant, and Melissa Desjarlais. (2014b). Indicators of Conversational Interactivity in COMPS Problem-Solving Dialogues, Third Workshop on Intelligent Support for Learning in Groups (ISLG) at Twelfth International Conference on Intelligent Tutoring Systems, Honolulu, Hawaii, June.

Glass, Michael, Jung Hee Kim, Kelvin Bryant, and Melissa Desjarlais (2015). Come Let Us Chat Together: Simultaneous Typed-Chat in Computer-Supported Collaborative Dialogue. *Journal of Computing Sciences in Colleges*, 31 no. 2, Dec.

Hackett, G. (1985). Role of mathematics self-efficacy in the choice of math-related majors of college women and men: a path analysis. *Journal of Counseling Psychology*, 32, pp. 47–56.

Harackiewicz, J. M., A.M. Durik, K.E. Barron, L. Linnenbrink-Garcia, and J.M. Tauer. (2008). The role of achievement goals in the development of interest: Reciprocal relations between achievement goals, interest, and performance. *Journal of Educational Psychology*, 100, pp. 105–122.

Hidi, S., and K. Renninger. (2006). The four-phase model of interest development. *Educational Psychologist*, 41, pp. 111–127.

Kim, Jung Hee, Melissa Desjarlais, Kelvin Bryant, and Michael Glass. (2013). Observations of Collaborative Behivor in COMPS Computer-Mediated Problem Solving, Proceedings of the 24th Midwest AI and Cognitive Science Symposium, New Albany, IN.

Kim, Taehee, and Diane L. Schallert. (2014). Mediating effects of teacher enthusiasm and peer enthusiasm on students' interest in the college classroom. *Contemporary Educational Psychology,* 39, no. 2 pp. 134–144.

Mitchell, M. (1993). Situational interest: Its multifaceted structure in the secondary school mathematics classroom. *Journal of Educational Psychology*, 85, pp. 424–436.

Pajares, F., and M. D. Miller. (1995). Mathematics self-efficacy and mathematics outcomes: The need for specificity of assessment. *Journal of Counseling Psychology*, 42, pp. 190–198.

Stahl, Gerry (2004). Building collaborative knowing: Elements of a social theory of CSCL. In J. W. Strijbos, P. Kirschner and R. Martens, eds., What we know about CSCL and implementing it in higher education, Boston, MA: Kluwer Academic Publishers, pp. 53–86.

Stahl, Gerry, ed. (2009). Studying Virtual Math Teams, Springer, pp. 57–73.

Tchounikine Pierre, Nikol Rummel, and Bruce M. McLaren. (2010). Computer Supported Collaborative Learning and Intelligent Tutoring Systems. In R. Nkambo, J.Bourdeau, & R. Mizoguchi (Eds.) Advances in Intelligent Tutoring Systems. Chapter 22, pp. 447–463, Springer.

Witten, Ian H. and Eibe Frank. (2005). Data Mining: Practical Machine Learning Tools and Techniques, 2nd Edition, Morgan Kaufmann.

Wood, R.E. and E.A. Locke. (1987). The relation of self-efficacy and grade goals to academic performance. *Educational and Psychological Measurement*, 47, pp. 1013–1024.

Zhou, Nan (2009). Question Co-Construction in VMT Chats. In Stahl, 2009, pp. 141–159.

Table 1: Example of Dialogue Transcript with Affective Features

Turn	Student	Time	Dialogue turn	Affective State
1	A	06:44.2	f and foo are the refernece variables	
2	A	07:05.2	so those together make 16? for the refrence types	
3	B	07:11.9	yup yup	
4	A	07:27.9	16 bytes	
5	C	07:30.2	2a = 20	
6	C	07:36.0	**:D**	**Excited**
7	B	07:39.7	**there ya go lol**	**Humor**
8	D	07:54.9	**Wait where did you get 16?**	**Confused**
9	D	08:05.8	wouldnt it be 48 at least for the main method	
10	D	08:18.3	because the array creates 5 object	
11	A	08:26.1	**oh yeah i looked over that** was just counting m f and foo	**Apologetic**
12	C	08:28.7	those are on the heap not the stack	
13	D	08:48.0	So the objects created by an array are on the heap	
14	A	09:13.8	yeah run time stack = 48	

Table 2: Example of Feature words

Excited	Apologetic	Confused	Frustrated	Sad
:D	sorry	i'm confused	D:<	:(
yay	my bad	how	):<	):
yes!	nvm	why	This is hard	I feel stupid
!!!	whoops	what is		
cool!	i messed up	I don't under-stand		

Table 3: Beginning and end of semester surveys

Time	Interest	Efficacy
beginning of sem.	4.33 / 5	2.83 / 5
ending of sem.	4.32 / 5	3.81 / 5

Table 4: After lab surveys

	Effectiveness of group work Mean / SD		Understanding of concept Mean / SD		Interest in lab Mean /SD	
Lab1	3.17	0.68	3.45	0.96	3.19	0.94
Lab2	3.08	0.93	3.42	1.05	3.08	0.93
Lab3	3.47	0.71	4.03	1.06	3.65	0.76
Lab4	3.40	0.61	3.78	0.85	3.17	0.89

Comparison of Biometric Authentication Software Techniques: GEFE vs. Angle Based Metrics

Robert Stokes, Angelica Willis, Kelvin Bryant, Zanetta Tyler, and Anthony Dobson
Department of Computer Science
North Carolina A&T State University
1601 E Market St. Greensboro, NC 27411
kingstokes@gmail.com, awillis@aggies.ncat.edu, ksbryant@ncat.edu, zrtyler@aggies.ncat.edu, amdobson@aggies.ncat.edu

Abstract

In this paper, we explore three alternatives for developing a biometric authentication software system. The first approach we will consider is a computer vision technique optimized by Genetic and Evolutionary Feature Extraction (GEFE); the second is Angle Based Metrics (ABM); and the third is Angle Based Metrics combined with Genetic and Evolutionary Computation (ABM + GEC). Each of these techniques are research areas which show promise in regards to being able to authenticate users based on their natural mouse movements. When applied to the same data set, the results of our experimentation indicate that both the ABM and ABM + GEC techniques are more accurate than GEFE in correctly verifying genuine users, as well as correctly rejecting impostors.

Keywords – Biometrics, genetic and evolutionary feature extraction (GEFE), angle based metrics

Introduction

Biometric systems are able to authenticate or identify people based on physiological or behavioral characteristics which are unique for each person [5]. As biometric systems become increasingly accurate, they will be selected more often as the option of choice for authentication, intrusion detection, or access control within software systems. One of the most useful applications for biometrics is user authentication. Authentication is a way to prove that a user is who they claim to be. In most systems, authentication involves asking a person to prove who they are by what they know – such as a username and password combination [9]. Biometric authentication attempts to carry out the verification process based on analysis of characteristics that are unique to a given individual. Physiological biometrics include analysis of characteristics such as fingerprint, iris, or facial features. Behavioral biometrics focus on the way in which users interact with their computer device. Some examples are mouse movements [8], keystroke rhythm, and touch screen interaction. The main benefits of biometrics is that they are difficult to mimic and they have an advantage over password authentication in that they are not susceptible to being cracked (via dictionary attacks or brute force attacks), lost, or stolen [11].

An emerging application of biometrics is active authentication (AA). Active authentication is a way of continuously authenticating or verifying a user's identity during a session. Typically, a user is only authenticated at the beginning of a session. If the user steps away from the computer or if the session is hijacked then the secured assets are vulnerable to exploitation. Active authentication attempts to continually verify that a user's biometric patterns (human to computer interactions) are consistent with those demonstrated during their previous sessions [3]. The goal is to determine whether or not the current user is an imposter or the original authenticated user.

In this paper, we compare three different approaches to implementing biometric authentication using mouse movement. The first approach uses Genetic and Evolutionary Feature Extraction (GEFE) [1] to optimize computer vision and evolutionary computation techniques. The second approach, called Angle Based Metrics (ABM) [15], uses angle analysis in order to extract features and distinguish between valid users and impostors. And the third approach, called ABM+GEC is an enhanced version of ABM which utilizes a genetic and evolutionary computation (GEC) technique in order to reduce the size of the extracted feature set. Though both GEFE and ABM+GEC use evolutionary computation as a method of improving the efficiency and success of their root techniques, they are completely independent approaches.

In addition to exploring how these three approaches compare, we also present evidence that GEC is a valuable method of reducing the complexity of systems like ABM, by eliminating irrelevant data from consideration, thus increasing the efficiency and feasibility of Active Authentication. The true acceptance rate (TAR) and false acceptance rate (FAR) results for all three techniques were computed using the same data set. The rest of the paper is as follows. The next section describes GEFE. Following the GEFE section, ABM is introduced. Next, a discussion of how the GEC was combined with ABM is presented, followed by a section that presents the advantages and disadvantages of AMB and GEFE. The last three sections describe how the experiment was conducted, present a comparison of the results and, finally, present conclusions and future work.

GEFE

The GEFE technique involves the use of algorithms which have been adopted from the fields of Evolutionary Computation and Computer Vision in order to be able to classify images [4]. The path of each mouse movement is recorded using the (x, y) screen coordinates and then saved as an image file. The image is then analyzed in a similar biometric manner as a facial image. Images are compared by using image processing techniques to extract features. It is important that the features extracted are useful in distinguishing one image from another. GEFE uses Local Binary Pattern (LBP) [10] for extracting features from the images and storing them into feature vectors/templates. These feature vectors allow images to be mathematically compared to one another to determine how similar they are. Traditionally, the comparison is accomplished by utilizing a distance metric (e.g. Euclidean Distance or Manhattan Distance) to determine how close the images are to each other [7].

LBP works by dividing an image canvas into rectangular regions called patches. Within each patch, the LBP algorithm will iteratively select each interior pixel as a center pixel. Next, the intensity value of the center pixel is compared with its neighboring pixels in order to generate a texture pattern (bit string) for a given pixel. For each neighboring pixel, if the grayscale value is greater than the center pixel's grayscale value then a 0 bit is generated; otherwise, a 1 bit is generated. For each center pixel, an 8 bit binary string is generated that denotes the relationship between the center pixel's grayscale value and that of the 8 neighbors (top, top right, right, bottom right, bottom, bottom left, left, top left). Each patch is then treated as a histogram where the different bins consist of all the texture patterns or bit strings that are possible. The strings for each patch are concatenated in order to form feature sets or feature vectors.

It is possible to designate the number of features that are included in the extracted feature set of a given mouse movement session. For example, GEFE-56 uses feature sets of size 56 (per patch) while GEFE-256 uses feature sets of size 256 for each patch.

GEFE uses a genetic algorithm in order to select the best feature extractor no matter how many features are designated per patch [12]. This means that the genetic algorithm will be able to optimize the feature set to ensure that only the significant features are included in the feature vector. The size of the patches, the center of each patch, and which patches should be included in the feature vector are all decided by the genetic algorithm which evolves the feature extractor as the algorithm is run repeatedly. In contrast, the generic LBP method uses non-overlapping, uniform sized patches for matching.

The process of "evolving" a feature extractor is accomplished via the Estimation of Distribution Algorithm (EDA). An EDA will select a specified number of elites (candidate solutions with the best fitness) to be automatically included in the next population iteration. The remaining offspring in the population will be generated by choosing a subset of the current population to be used to create a probability distribution function (PDF). The PDF is then sampled to generate the remaining offspring for the next population.

The feature vectors for each mouse movement session of a given user will be stored in a profile, and new movements can be compared to the profile of a user to determine if the distance is within a certain threshold. This technique allows users to be authenticated (based on their mouse movements) with a fairly high accuracy rate.

ABM

Angle Based Metrics [15] is an approach to designing a biometric system that focuses on the angles that are generated by the mouse movements of a user. The angles are used to derive useful features or metrics which may be used to distinguish one user from another. The main advantage of this approach is that it works well even if the user's hardware or computing environment changes from one session to the next.

As with most biometric systems, the Angle Based Metrics approach is comprised of four different components: Recorder, Preprocessor (feature extractor), Classifier, and Decision Maker. The Recorder is the simplest of these components and is positioned on the client side of an application to capture user mouse movement events and send that data to the Pre-processor. The Preprocessor executes on the server side and is responsible for translating the data it receives from the Recorder into valuable metrics. There are 3 metrics which our Pre-processor calculates from the mouse coordinates and mouse clicks: the direction angle, curvature angle, and the curvature distance ratio. These metrics are calculated by examining groupings of 3 points -- in the order in which those points were visited by the user's mouse movement. Thus point A is visited before point B, and point B is visited before point C (See figure 1).

- The direction angle (1) is the angle measured from a horizontal line to the line AB. Line AB is formed by traveling from the first point in the group of 3 to the second point.
- The curvature angle (2) is the angle ABC where A, B, and C are consecutive points read into the Preprocessor from the Recorder.
- The curvature distance (r) is as follows: for a line AC, let point Z be the point located from B to AC that is perpendicular to AC. Then the curvature distance is the ratio BZ/AC.

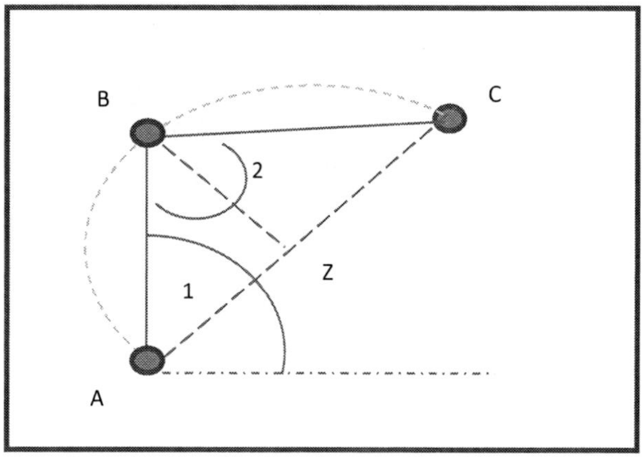

Figure 1: Illustration of Angle Based Metrics

The metrics calculated in the Preprocessor are organized as a cumulative distribution function (CDF), with intervals of direction angle (x), curvature angle (y), and the curvature distance/ratio (r). The CDF is a mathematical model that illustrates which percentage of a user's metrics fall within a given range of values. The percentage values within each CDF bin (interval) are what help to distinguish one user from another and are referred to as "features". The collection of all the features for a given session of user action is referred to as a feature set or template. The feature sets are used as input to the Classifier component of the ABM system.

The main task of the Classifier is to be able to tell whether or not a feature set or group of feature sets belong to a given user or not. There is more than one way to implement the Classifier. One way is to utilize a support vector machine (SVM). A support vector machine is a machine learning component often used for classification [14]. A SVM will take in a group of feature sets derived from a user and utilize them to create a training model of the user's mouse movement characteristics. Then, whenever new mouse data arrives, the SVM can compare the features of that data in order to determine whether the movements belong in the same grouping/classification with the other movements in the user's training model/profile.

Another classification technique utilizes the Normalized Manhattan Distance (NMD). NMD is calculated by taking the sum of the differences between two feature-sets (where each feature set is simply a list of percentages or floating point numbers) divided by the total number of features. For the purposes of our own analysis, NMD was the chosen method for comparison and classification. The NMD value represents how close mathematically a template is to those in a user's profile/training set. That value is sent to the Decision Maker component.

The Decision Maker is the component that is tasked with deciding whether the actions being generated by a user's session are similar enough to those movements saved under the user's profile to be considered a match. One way to do this is to establish a threshold value in order to be able to accept or reject a feature set based on the NMD value. Another approach is to utilize a SVM to determine whether or not a feature set may be classified with the other feature sets known to belong to a given user. The SVM will output a decision value to accept or reject, and that information may be utilized by the security mechanisms within a larger system in order to determine if a user needs to be prompted to re-authenticate or not.

ABM + GEC

All of the main components of the ABM + GEC approach are consistent with that of ABM. In fact, ABM + GEC can be considered an optimized version of ABM. Upon the initial implementation of the ABM system, it was observed that the greatest experimental results were achieved when the CDF bin sizes for the x, y, and r metrics were set to very small values. However, this presented a practicality problem because decreasing the bin sizes results in an increase in the number of features. This is due to an idea known as the curse of dimensionality, where it can be said that, as the number of dimensions in a vector problem increases, so does the complexity of the problem, and therefore, the time devoted to solve the problem increases as well. The natural relationship between the interval sizes and the magnitude of the feature set is an inversely proportional relationship, and so, as the size of the intervals decreased, the size of the feature set grew profoundly. For example, when using x and y intervals of .05, the feature set contained 2683 features. Because features represent the vector dimensionality of the authentication problem, this meant the system incorporated 2683 dimensions, and created an authentication environment that was very slow and difficult to manage. To solve this problem, a genetic algorithm toolset called X-TOOLSS [13] was used. The objective for using X-TOOLSS was to optimize the system by evolving new, smaller feature sets with larger intervals that could produce similar results -- in terms of authentication accuracy -- as the .05 intervals. In addition, X-TOOLSS eliminated redundant features which were non-essential to authentication. This process is called feature masking.

X-TOOLSS uses genetic algorithms (GAs) that, based on the "survival of the fitness" concept, develop optimal solutions for many types of parametric software systems. In this case, the feature masks and interval (bin size) combinations were designated as candidates. The GA evolves a population of candidate solutions by first generating random candidates and assigning fitness values to feature extractors implementing different versions of those candidates. Depending on the type of genetic algorithm being used, different methods are employed to create offspring from high-fitness "parent" candidates, and introduce those offspring into the next generation of the candidate population as a whole. Fitness values were calculated using the authentication accuracy of the candidate system (explained further as the Cumulative Match Curve (CMC) in the Comparisons and Results section). For the ABM + GEC system, a Steady-State GA was used, which stipulates that adding the offspring candidates to the population can only occur when those children have a higher fitness value than their parents. Therefore, the population size remains constant, or steady, throughout the evolution process.

The x, y and r intervals were evolved using double-precision 64-bit floating point values, between a range .5 and (large enough intervals to produce a more manageable volume of features), a population size of 20 individuals, a Crossover Usage Rate of 1.0, a Mutation Usage Rate of 1.0, a Mutation Range of .2, with 1000 total evaluations. These settings evolved new x, y, and r intervals of 6.024, 1.0, and 20.0 respectively. As for the feature mask evolution, the range was limited to the integers 0 and 1, and was applied to each feature in the template, representing either "on" (1) or "off" (0) for that corresponding feature. All other parameters for the Steady-State GA were the same as the interval optimization, save the number of total evaluations, which was 1000. The average results are based off of 10 runs of the GEC.

The evolution of the ABM system produced a remarkable complexity reduction from a 2683-dimensional system to a 283-dimensional system, using interval evolution, and then even further to a 150-dimensional one using the evolved feature mask. This resulted in an overall decrease in complexity of about 94.4%. The evolved system is far faster and more practical for real-world implementation; not only did the efficiency of the authentication system show improvement, the overall accuracy of the authentication improved as well (See Comparisons and Results section).

Pros and Cons of ABM and GEFE

One of the major benefits of both the ABM (including ABM+GEC) and GEFE approach to software biometrics and active authentication is that these techniques are able to effectively verify a user's mouse movements across different platforms without losing a significant amount of accuracy due to differences in hardware devices [15]. This is a major benefit over other metric approaches, such as speed and acceleration that are affected by the user's operating system as well as the mouse or the screen resolution [6]. Speed and acceleration are also poor metric choices due to the endless possibilities of situational diversity. For example, a user may quickly make a decision to advance toward and click a submit button, yet the same user may slowly advance and then pause before clicking a hyperlink on a text-rich web page such as a wiki article.

Another benefit of the ABM authentication approach over other authentication techniques lies in its generated data's minimal impact on user privacy. In the hands of a malicious culprit, mouse movement data would be of little use, as such data would not lend itself to reproduction. The mouse dynamics of a user can be compared to a signature; however, unlike the forging of a signature, where authentication is carried out once, an impostor would be required to continuously mimic the genuine user's biometric behavior throughout the duration of the session [2].

One possible hindrance that could be encountered by ABM authentication involves genuine users who undergo sudden biometric behavioral changes that render them unable to match up to their former biometric profiles. For example, a user could sustain a wrist fracture, causing a sudden change in mouse movement dynamics. Such occurrences, though rare, would possibly require intervention by system administrators to ensure the user is not falsely rejected from the system.

Experiment

The experiment that we developed was closely related to the experiment performed by J. Shelton et al. [12]. The mouse pointer was automatically centered on the screen and users were instructed to move the mouse in order to bring up the login box. The subjects were unaware of the purpose of the experiment.

We obtained and utilized the same data set used by Shelton. The data consisted of mouse movements collected for 16 unique subjects. Each subject had a "profile" comprised of 10 different sessions or sequences of mouse movements. Our experiment was to take a sequence (template) from any user and compare it with the profiles of all other users including the "self" profile to see if we could authenticate or verify a user based solely on their movement pattern. The comparison was based on calculating the NMD between a single sequence and all of the other sequences in each profile. And based on a certain threshold value that we set for the NMD we were able to accept or reject each sequence as belonging to the owner of a certain profile or not. We were able to analyze the TAR and the FAR for ABM, ABM+GEC, and GEFE.

Comparison and Results

Our experimental results consist of the following categories: FAR, FRR, TAR, and the threshold. Note that the threshold is the independent variable but the results are also influenced by the interval that we utilized for the x, y, and r bins (representing the direction angle, curvature angle, and curvature distances respectively) in the CDF that generates the feature vectors. We selected a single template which we designated as a probe and we used all the remaining templates as our gallery set. The probe was then compared to every template in the gallery and if the NMD for probe and gallery member was less than or equal to the threshold value then this would count as an acceptance. True acceptances were those cases where both templates being compared belonged to the same subject and the NMD was below the threshold. A false acceptance occurred if the NMD for probe and gallery template was below the threshold but the templates did not belong to the same subject. And a false reject occurred if the NMD value was above the threshold but the templates were both from the same subject. We iterated through and allowed each of the 160 templates in our data set to have their chance to act as the probe and then designated the remaining 159 templates as our gallery set for each iteration. As we increased the threshold, the TAR value continued to increase towards 100%. Our best results were the ones that minimized FAR and FRR while maximizing TAR. When we set the threshold at .081, it yielded a TAR of approximately 70%, a FAR of approximately 42% and FRR of 30%. Likewise, while using a threshold of .0161 we calculated TAR of 90%, a FAR of 74% and a FRR of 10% (See Figure 2). These results are significantly better than what was achieved with GEFE. When the TAR for GEFE (specifically GEFE-256) approaches 80%, it yields a FAR 76%, and when the TAR reaches 90% it yields a FAR which is close to 90% as well.

We also computed a Cumulative Match Characteristic (CMC) in order to analyze the ABM technique. The CMC uses a single template as a probe and the remainder of the templates from all subjects (including self) in the population as the gallery. The CMC applies a rank for each probe to determine the percentage of templates which are able to find a match which belongs to the same subject on the first probe (rank 1), second probe (rank 2), third probe (rank 3), etc. The percentages on the CMC chart were calculated by letting every template in the population serve as the probe exactly one time. For a given rank, the percentage includes all the matches which were produced using x number of probes where x is less than or equal to the rank number. So rank 3, for example, includes the percentage of probes that found a match within 1, 2, or 3 attempts. A match occurs when a probe is compared with the population gallery and the template discovered to be closest in distance from the probe belongs to the same subject as the probe. If any attempt to find a match results in discovering a template that is closest in distance to the probe but belonging to a different subject, this is a "miss". After any miss, we removed all the templates from the population which belong to the subject which caused the miss.

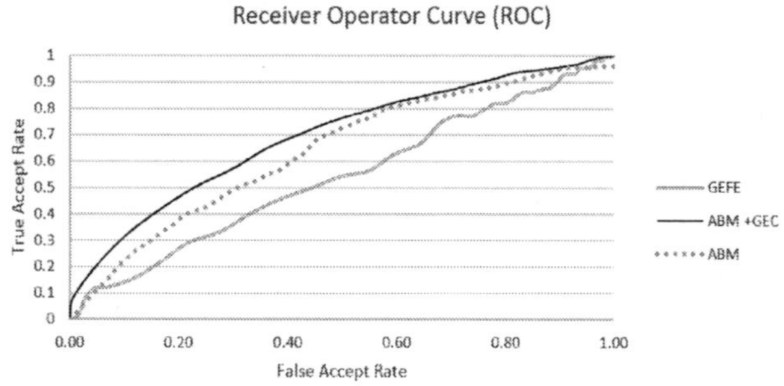

Figure 2: ROC results for ABM, GEFE, and ABM +GEC

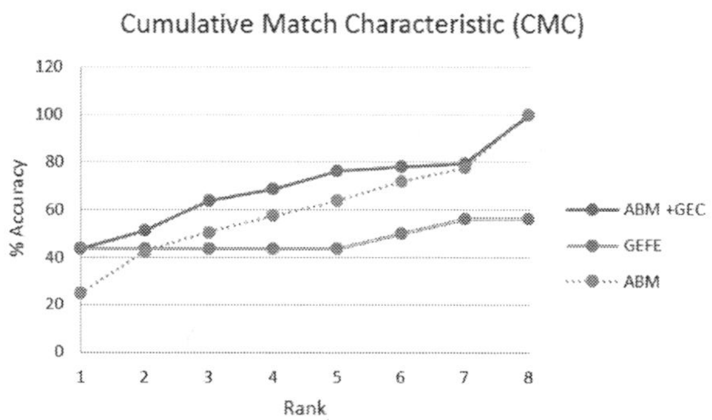

Figure 3: CMC results for ABM, GEFE, and ABM +GEC

The CMC results show that though GEFE has a considerably higher rank 1 accuracy of 43.75%, compared to ABM's 25.0% rank 1 accuracy, ABM begins to substantially outrank GEFE from rank 3, and beyond, including double digit differences in accuracy beginning with rank 4. (See Figure 3 CMC Chart). ABM + GEC further widens the accuracy gap, by matching GEFE's 43.75% rank 1 accuracy and greatly outperforming every other rank for GEFE, including double digit percentage leading from rank 3 and on.

Conclusions and Future Work

Based on the results we have tabulated and displayed in the ROC and CMC curves, it appears that the ABM + GEC technique is more accurate and more effective as a software biometric approach when compared to the GEFE. In addition, ABM+GEC is able to accomplish higher accuracies than standard ABM although using a significantly lower number of features.

Future work needs to be done in order to improve both the GEFE and ABM + GEC techniques if either strategy is going to become applicable to the mainstream authentication. Each approach will have to decrease the FAR while maintaining a high TAR. Also, the entire system needs to be modified and tested in a real time environment in order to better evaluate the feasibility of the technique for deployment in a production setting. The evolutionary computation that GEFE and ABM+GEC undergo can both take hours to run depending on the algorithm parameters. However, each system can be viewed as a feature "update" algorithm which would run as a background component to an AA system, as new data becomes available, to maintain optimal accuracy. Therefore, there should be little impact on user experience due to the speed of completion.

Furthermore, we would like to test the system on a larger pool of users in order to see how that affects the accuracy measurements. Some things to consider in a real time active authentication (AA) system also include: how many templates should be stored in a user's profile during training phase; and how long should each template remain in profile before being "aged out" by new templates.

Acknowledgements

We would like to thank Dr. Gerry Dozier and Joseph Shelton for their consultation on the technical methodology behind prior GEFE research at North Carolina A&T State University.

References

1. J. Adams, D. L. Woodard, G. Dozier, P. Miller, G. Glenn, K. Bryant. "GEFE: Genetic & Evolutionary Feature Extraction for Periocular Based Biometric Recognition," Proceedings 2010 ACM Southeast Conference, April 15-17, 2010, Oxford, MS.
2. A. A. E. Ahmed and I. Traore. A new biometric technology based on mouse dynamics. IEEE Transactions on Dependable and Secure Computing, 4(3):165–179, 2007.
3. Ingo Deutschmann and Johan Lindholm. "Behavioral biometrics for DARPA's active authentication program". BIOSIG 2013: 225-232.
4. Dozier, G., Homaifar, A., Tunstel, E., and Battle, D. (2001). "An Introduction to Evolutionary Computation" (Chapter 17), Intelligent Control Systems Using Soft Computing Methodologies, A. Zilouchian & M. Jamshidi (Eds.), pp. 365-380, CRC press.
5. K. Jain, L. Hong, and S. Pankanti, "Biometric Identification" Commun. ACM 43, 90-98, 2, 2000.
6. Z. Jorgensen and T. Yu. On mouse dynamics as a behavioral biometric for authentication. In Proceedings of the 6th ACM Symposium on Information, Computer and Communications Security, ASIACCS '11, pages 476–482, 2011.
7. Malkauthekar, M. D. "Analysis of euclidean distance and Manhattan Distance measure in face recognition", International Journal of Computer Science and Engineering (IJCSE) ISSN(P): 2278-9960; ISSN(E): 2278-9979 Vol. 3, Issue 4, July 2014, 89- 98.
8. Nazirah Abd Hamid; Suhailan Safei; Siti Dhalila and Mohd Satar. "Mouse Movement Behavioral Biometric Systems"; Kuala Terengganu, Malaysia.
9. L. O'Gorman, "Comparing Passwords, Tokens, and Biometrics for User Authentication," Proc. IEEE, Vol. 91, No. 12, 2019-2040, 2003.
10. Timo Ojala; Matti Pietikainen; Topi Maenpaa. "Multiresolution Gray-Scale and Rotation Invariant Texture Classification with Local Binary Patterns".
11. Douglas A. Schulz, MOUSE CURVE BIOMETRICS, Pacific Northwest National Laboratory, U.S. Department of Energy
12. Joseph Shelton; Joshua Adams; Derrick Leflore and Gerry Dozier. "Mouse Tracking, Behavioral Biometrics, and GEFE"; In Proceedings of IEEE Southeastcon; 2013, p1-6, 6p.
13. Tinker, M. L., Dozier, G. & Garrett, A. (2010). The exploratory toolset for the optimization of launch and space systems (X-TOOLSS). *Available online: http://nxt.ncat.edu/*.
14. S. Tong. Support vector machine active learning for image retrieval. In Proceedings of the ninth ACM international conference on Multimedia, 2001.
15. Nan Zheng; Aaron Paloski; Haining Wang. "An Efficient User Verification System via Mouse Movements"; Williamsburg, VA, USA.

Situations and Evidence for Identity Using Dempster-Shafer Theory

William Nick, Yenny Dominguez and **Albert Esterline**
Department of Computer Science, North Carolina A&T State University, Greensboro, NC 27411
wmnick@aggies.ncat.edu, ydomingu@aggies.ncat.edu, esterlin@ncat.edu

Abstract

We present a computational framework for identity based on Barwise and Devlin's situation theory. We present an example with constellations of situations identifying an individual to create what we call id-situations, where id-actions are performed, along with supporting situations. We use Semantic Web standards to represent and reason about the situations in our example. We show how to represent the strength of the evidence, within the situations, as a measure of the support for judgments reached in the id-situation. To measure evidence of an identity from the supporting situations, we use the Dempster-Shafer theory of evidence. We enhance Dempster-Shafer theory in two ways to leverage the information available in a constellation of situations. One way exploits the structure within the situations, and the other way interprets the information-relationships in terms of argument schemes.

Introduction

We here present our computational framework for identity. State of the art in identity is represented by the Superidentity project (Creese et al. 2013)(Hodges, Creese, and Goldsmith 2012), which developed a model in identity that connects elements from both the cyber and physical universes. In their terminology, an element of identity has a type, and a characteristic is a multiset of elements of identity of the same type. A superidentity is a set of characteristics. Examples of elements of identity include real names and email addresses. An initial superidentity has a seed identity element and is enriched by deriving new elements of identity via functions that transform one or more elements of given types to an element of another type. For example, an email address may be transformed to usernames on social network sites. The enriching continues, creating a directed graph that outlines the provenance of the elements of identity.

It became apparent, however, that the elements of identity and transforms of the Superidentity project do not support the internal structure we require. For an alternative, we turned to situation theory based on Devlins account (Devlin 1995). When we attribute identity, we want something like a legal case. Evidence includes provenance of information, records of how procedures were followed, how information was communicated, and critical narrative detail. Central to our account, a version of Dempster-Shafer theory is used for a quantitative account of the impact of evidence.

The remainder of this paper is organized as follows. The next section introduces situation theory, and the following one outlines the Semantic Web standards we use for representing and reasoning about situations and the information they contain. There follows a section where we describe how we represent and reason about situations and their information, drawing on our running example. We then introduce the Demptser-Shafer theory of evidence and apply it to our running example. The next section outlines how we might exploit the structure of a constellation of situations involved in an identification in combining evidence in Dempster-Shafer theory. The penultimate section outlines another way Dempster-Shafer theory may be applied in situation theory, where a pattern of situations provides the structure for an argument scheme. The last section concludes.

Situation Theory

We follow Devlin's account of situations and information (Devlin 1995). Information is represented using *infons*. An infon is the basic item of information, with the general form $<< R, a_1, ..., a_n, l, t, i >>$, where R is an n-place relation, $a_1, ..., a_n$ are objects appropriate for the corresponding argument places of R, l is a location, t is a temporal location, and i is the polarity, 0 or 1. A polarity of 1 indicates that the objects are thus related in l at t; 0 indicates otherwise. Where s is a situation and σ an infon, $s \models \sigma$ is a proposition and may be true or false; if true, s is said to support σ (σ indeed is information available in s).

A *real situation* is a single entity that is part of reality and supports an indefinite number of infons, while an *abstract situation* is a set of infons. An event is essentially a kind of situation, and an action is a kind of event (involving an agent). We take situations as they relate to identity (*id-situations*) to be those that include identity-relevant actions (*id-actions*). We use situation theory to be able to represent id-situations and the situations that support them.

Situation theory arose as part of the development of situation semantics by Barwise and his colleagues (Barwise and Perry 1981). In situation semantics, one identifies an *utterance situation*, in which a speech act is performed, and a *described situation*, which the speech act is about. Besides supporting information, a situation may *carry information* about another situation. This is made possible by constraints. Some such constraints are natural (as in smoke means fire), and some are conventional, such as those constraints by virtue of which a speech act is about a described situation.

Running Examples

We present a series of situations involved in identifying an individual by mugshot and by fingerprint. Our running example is shown in Figures 1 and 2 and involves six situations (within clouds), s_1-s_6. The situations on the right of each figure (s_1 and s_2) are id-situations that are coordinated in that they result in identifying the same individual (via their "name," actually any identifier unique in the context). Id-situation s_1 has an analyst who matches fingerprints on file with those on a doorknob. Id-situation s_2 has the same analyst matching the face in a group shot to a face in the mugshot. The fingerprints on file were produced in s_3, and the fingerprints on the doorknob were produced in s_4. Situation s_4 is a (spatiotemporal) part of the situation portrayed in the ellipse in the portrayal of s_5, where a group of people is socializing. This situation is in turn part of s_5, where someone takes a picture of the group. In situation s_6, a mugshot of the person of interest is produced. It is used in s_2 to pick out the person in question in the group photo. We thus have two id-cases: the fingerprint case, s_1-s_3-s_4, and the mugshot case, s_2-s_4-s_5.

The dashed lines between situations shown on the left and id-situations connect things produced (left) and used (right). In all cases except where the objects produced are themselves used in the id-situation, there are additional copying or rendering situations not shown in in the figures. In a sense, we have one id-situation made of two coordinated id-situations.

We use the empty prefix : for the namespace in which we define the basic classes and properties. An instance s of class :Situation generally appears as subject in triples identifying the time and location of the situation in terms of subclasses of classes defined in the WGS84 Geo Positioning vocabulary. We thus do not represent time and spatial location in an infon but rather just assume that all infons in a given situation share a common time and place. We move on to using the Semantic Web standards to implement our running examples as per situation theory.

Semantic Web

The Semantic Web is based on two World Wide Web Consortium (W3C) standards: 1) the resource description framework (RDF) and 2) RDF schema (RDFS). These standards are enhanced by the much more expressive OWL (Web ontology language) standard. RDF is a W3C recommendation that provides a data model for annotations in the Semantic Web. An RDF statement (triple) is of the form *subject predicate object*. RDF allows users to annotate web resources in terms of named properties. The values of these named properties can be URIrefs of web resources or literals. Resources that are annotated by RDF are named by uniform resource identifiers (URIs). A URL is a string that identifies a resource on the web. A URI has the same structure as a URL but need not identify a resource on the web. (URLs are URIs but not vice-versa.)A URI reference (URIref) is itself a URI with an optional fragment identifier at the end. URIrefs are written typically as qnames, which are in the form of `prefix:lp`, where the namespace prefix is a URI. A blank node (bnode) is a resource that is not identified by a URIref.

Figure 1: Fingerprint Situation

To represent RDF statements in a machine readable way, the W3C has defined several serializations. One of these serializations is the Notation 3 (N3) serialization. Triples in the N3 serialization are expressed as each of the three components separated by whitespace. When a subject is shared amongst triple, we can abbreviate this by having the subject listed once and separated predicate-object pairs by semicolons:

```
subject predicate1 object1;
    predicate2 object2.
```

RDFS allows for classes and properties to be defined using RDF triples. We state that individual x is an instance of class C with the triple `x rdf:type C`. These individuals could be denoted by a URIref or a bnode. N3 allows "a" to be used as an abbreviation for "`rdf:type`". A class may be a subclasse of other classes, and a property may be a subproperty of other properties. If `p` is a subproperty of `q`, then `x p y` implies `x q y`. If we have `x p y`, then `x` is an instance of the class that is the domain of `p`, and `y` is an instance of its range.

SPARQL is a SQL-like query language for triple stores where a variable is a sequence of alphanumeric characters proceeded by '?', a `WHERE` clause is a sequence of triples each of which might have a variable for its subject, object, or both. SPARQL reports only the variables that appear in the `SELECT` clause.

SWRL is a rule language for the Semantic Web. SWRL rules are in the form *head* → *body* where *head* is the antecedent and *body* is the consequence.

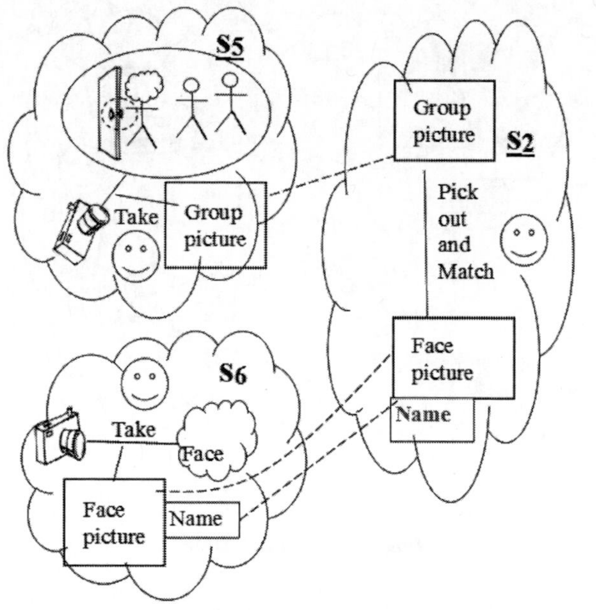

Figure 2: Mugshot Situation

RDF/OWL/SWRL Representation of Examples

That a given situation s has an infon i (an instance of class `:Infon`) is expressed as `s :hasInfon i`. Infon `i` itself has a polarity (property `:hasPolarity`). The various relations are captured by various subclasses of `:Infon`. If R is a relation with roles $r_1, r_2, ..., r_n$, then we define a subclass `:RInfon` of `:Infon` and properties `r1, r2, ..., rn` with domain `:RInfon`. This avoids RDF's restriction of relations to binary relations ("properties") since any instance of `:RInfon` may be a subject of any number of triples with one of `r1, r2, ..., rn` as the property.

The fingerprint id-case involves three situations: `s1` (id-situation), `s3` (taking the fingerprint on file), `s4` (taking the forensic fingerprint). We discuss only `s1` in detail. It has three important infons: `i1`, `i1a`, and `i14`. Like all our infons, they have positive polarity; henceforth we assume this. We discuss only `i1` in detail. It is an instance of `:AnalystMatchingFpInfon`, information that an analyst is matching the forensic fingerprint and the fingerprint on file (no suggestion of objective similarity). Three properties are recorded for it: `:fpObserved`, whose value is the URIref of the forensic fingerprint, `:fpRecorded`, whose value is the URIref of the fingerprint on file, and `:fpAnalyst` is for the officer making the match. In N3, this is (`i1`, like all our infons, is represented by a bnode.)

```
_:i1 a :AnalystMatchingFpInfon;
    :fpAnalyst officer:117;
    :fpObserved forensicfp:822;
    :fpRecorded fpfile:496;
    :hasPolairty :PositivePolarity.
```

Infon `i1a` is an instance of `:SimilarFpInfon`, that the forensic fingerprint and the one on file have a similarity measure of 0.94 according to a certain procedure. Infon `i14` is an instance of `:OnInfon`, that the forensic fingerprint is on the doorknob. Situation `s3` has one important infon, `i3`, an instance of `:TakeFpInfon`, that a given officer takes the fingerprint of our suspect.

The photo id-case also involves three situations: `s2` (id-situation), `s5` (taking the forensic photo), and s6 (taking the mug shot). `s2` is analogous to `s1` but lacks the analogue of the fingerprint on the doorknob. `s6` is analogous to `s3` (taking the fingerprint on file). `s5` is only roughly analogous to `s4`. One of `s5`'s infons, `i5`, is an instance of `:ForensicPicInfon` and is the subject of triples identifying the photographer, the camera, the photo produced, and the situation, `s5a`, caught on camera. One infon that `s5a` has is that our suspect is touching the doorknob; it also has

```
sit:s5a :inSituation group:5342;
```

This says that this group is in the situation but does not identify any information associated with the group, yet infon `i5` includes the information that `s5a` is the situation pictured. We also have (where `insys:201` is our suspect)

```
group:5342 a foaf:Group;
    foaf:member insys:201, insys:563.
```

There is thereby in `i5` the information that `insys:201` is pictured in the photo produced; we do not necessarily have the information that `insys:201` is a member of `group:5342`. And we have (where `foaf:depicts` is an information relation)

```
fshot:812 a biom:GroupImage;
  # The group photo (s2, s5)
    foaf:depicts  sit:s5a .
```

There is also a part-whole (mereological) relation between `s4` and `s5`: `s4`, where the suspect touches the doorknob, is a proper part of `s5a`, the situation caught on film in situation s_5.

Assuming all our information is available (possibly distributed) on the Web, we can issue SPARQL queries that navigate across situations connected by, say, shared individuals.

We have identified a few important infons for each real situation s_1-s_6, but each supports an unbounded number of infons. We need abstract situations as types to classify real situations and constellations in a way conducive to identification. For classifying, we use SWRL rules. Where `C` is a class and `x` is an individual, `C(x)` is true iff the triple `x rdf:type C` holds. Where `p` is a property, `x` is a URIref or bnode, and `y` is a URIref, a bnode, or a literal, `p(x, y)` is true iff the triple `x p y` holds. If certain conditions hold of a situation '`?s`' (note that SWRL variable names begin with '`?`'), we classify it as some subclass of class `:Situation`. Our classifying SWRL rules, then, have the form

```
Situation(?s), ... -> SituationSubClass(?s)
```

The conditions that fill in the ellipsis relate to the infons that `?s` has, one or more sequences like

```
hasInfon(?s, ?i), ...,
  hasPolarity(?i, ?po),
   polarityValue(?pol, ?val), equal(?val, 1)
```

The ellipsis here is filled in with specifics on the roles of the relation represented by the infon. The sequence of atoms after the ellipsis forces positive infon polarity. All our infons have positive polarity, so we ignore this.

The case-type with the photos involves three situation types, identified with the classes `:Mug` (a mug shot is taken), `:Pic` (a forensic picture is taken), and `:PicId` (id-situation type). A situation is of type `:Mug` if it has an infon of type `:TakeMugshotInfon` involving a recorded mugshot, a subject, and an administrative officer responsible for the mugshot. A situation `?s` is of type `:Pic` if it has a `:ForensicPicInfon` involving an officer taking the photo, a group image that is the photo, and a situation captured by the photo and that includes the group depicted in the photo. This describes a situation that references another. A `:Pic` situation, then, is like an utterance situation, best compared to a situation where the "uttering" is writing, although speech and writing abstract away information.

The case-type with fingerprints also involves three situation types, identified with the classes `:FpFile` (a fingerprint is recorded), `:Touch` (a forensic fingerprint is left), and `:FpId` (id-situation type).

Recall that an id-situation together with its supporting situations is an id-case. We form id-case types, abstract versions of id-cases. Generally, an id-case type glues together several situation types, which requires (for connections) exposing more information in the situations than is exposed for the situation types. We define SWRL rules to classify cases as subclasses of a generic `:Case` class.

In the envisioned scenario, the two id-cases are coordinated since the filed fingerprint and mugshot of a single suspect are used to establish his presence in a gathering. We introduce symmetric property `:coordinatedIdCase` whose domain and range are `:IdCase`. We have a SWRL rule for determining that an instance of `MugIdCase` and an instance of `FingerpIdCase` are coordinated by checking not only that the label on the mugshot is the same as that on the fingerprint on file but also that we have one and the same id-situation. The criterion for identity of situations is beyond the scope of this paper.

Dempster-Shafer Theory of Evidence

We want a measure of how the evidence supports the judgment in an id-situation. It should reflect the structure of an id-case and fuse belief constraints from different sources. In our example, s_1 and s_2 are essentially a single utterance situation (the identity judgment), and the situation in the photo in s_5 is the described situation. Imagine that, in s_1, the analyst has access to fingerprints for several likely suspects, each associated with a supporting situation in which a fingerprint was recorded. The RDF for s_1 includes a measure of how similar the fingerprint on file is to the fingerprint from the scene; in the expanded view, it includes such measures for all available fingerprints.

We adapt the Dempster-Shafer theory of evidence (Halpern 2003). The frame of discernment (the set of possible values), W, includes here people who might have left the fingerprint or have their mugshot considered. In s_1, we have a measure of how well the fingerprint on file matches the fingerprint on the scene. We also have similarity measures for other people who might have left the fingerprint on the door in Figure 1, say, Fred, Bill, Sue, and Mary.

Available evidence (e.g., similarity measures) provides some degree of support ("mass"), from 0.0 to 1.0, for subsets of W; those subsets with non-zero mass are called *focal elements*. The sum of the mass for all subsets of W is 1.0. Where $U \subseteq W$, the belief that U holds, $Bel(U)$, is the sum of the support (mass) on subsets of U, a number in [0,1]. Where $m(.)$ is the mass function, $m(U)$ is the probability of observing U, so the definition of the belief function in terms of the mass function is $Bel_m(U) = \sum_{U^* \subseteq U} m(U^*)$.

For our example, suppose that the similarity measures for the singletons {Fred}, {Bill}, {Sue}, and {Mary} to the fingerprint on the doorknob are, respectively, 0.4, 0.075, 0.075, and 0.0. In addition, there is some evidence, mass 0.05, of the fingerprint belonging to {Sue, Bill} (i.e., to Sue or Bill without distinction). And perhaps someone other than the people mentioned left the fingerprint on the doorknob. The evidence for this chance has about half the strength as the evidence for {Fred}; as a singleton set, it receives mass 0.2. We suppose that there is some interest in whether the person is either male or female. Since there is no reason to imply the unknown fingerprint belongs to a male rather than a female or vice versa, we split this mass between a fictional female, Nulla, and a fictional male, Nullus. The sum of the masses so far is 0.8. The remaining 0.2 covers all ways the fingerprint could have got on the doorknob, not only by those mentioned, but perhaps left before or after the situation considered.

Corresponding to the belief function is the plausibility function. The plausibility that U holds, $Plaus(U)$, is the sum of the probabilities of the evidence compatible with the world being in U: $Plaus_m(U) = \sum_{U^* s.t. U^* \cap U \neq \emptyset} m(U^*)$. For $U \subseteq W$, $Bel(U) \leq Plaus(U)$. Note that, where $\bar{U}$ is the complement of U, $Plaus(U) = 1 - Bel(\bar{U})$ and $Bel(U) = 1 - Plaus(\bar{U})$.

Table 1 shows the values of the Dempster-Shafer functions for each focal element for s_1. *All* represents the entire frame of discernment; its mass was not assigned elsewhere. We show the values of the belief and plausibility functions only for focal elements; there are other subsets of W that have non-zero belief and plausibility.

Focal element	Mass	Belief	Plausibility
{Fred}	0.400	0.400	0.600
All	0.200	1.000	1.000
{Sue}	0.075	0.075	0.325
{Mary}	0.000	0.000	0.200
{Bill}	0.075	0.075	0.325
{Nullus}	0.100	0.100	0.300
{Bill,Sue}	0.050	0.200	0.400
{Nulla}	0.100	0.100	0.300

Table 1: Fingerprint Mass, Belief, and Plausibility

For s_2, focal elements are subsets of W with non-zero probability of containing the person whose mugshot matches the picture of the culprit in the forensic picture. Suppose that the mass for the focal elements are Fred: 0.35; All: 0.2; {Sue}: 0.0; {Mary}: 0.05; {Bill}: 0.05; {Mary,Nulla}: 0.15; {Nullus}: 0.100; and {Nulla}: 0.100. Given mass functions m_1 (e.g., for the fingerprints) and m_2 (e.g., for the mugshots) defined on some frame W, we use Dempster's Rule of Combination to construct a new mass function $m_1 \oplus m_2$ that fuses the belief constraints of m_1 and m_2 (e.g., combining the evidence from both the fingerprints and mugshots):

$$(m_1 \oplus m_2)(h) = \Sigma_{U_1,U_2 s.t. U_1 \cap U_2 = U}\, m_1(U)m_2(U)/c$$

where normalizing constant c is the sum of the products $m_1(U_1) \oplus m_2(U_2)$ of all overlapping pairs U_1, U_2:

$$c = \Sigma_{U_1,U_2 s.t. U_1 \cap U_2 \neq \varnothing}\, m_1(U_1)m_2(U_2)$$

Table 2 shows the shows the values of the Dempster-Shafer functions for each focal element of $m_1 \oplus m_2$.

Focal element	Mass	Belief	Plausibility
{Fred}	0.536	0.536	0.610
All	0.074	1.000	1.000
{Sue}	0.028	0.028	0.120
{Mary}	0.018	0.018	0.148
{Bill}	0.058	0.058	0.150
{Mary,Nulla}	0.055	0.194	0.268
{Nullus}	0.092	0.092	0.166
{Bill,Sue}	0.018	0.104	0.178
{Nulla}	0.120	0.120	0.249

Table 2: Combined for fingerprint and mugshot

Dempster-Shafer Theory & Situation Theory

To reflect the structure of an id-case in our account of evidence, we consider the work by Lalmas et al. (Lalmas and Van Rijsbergen 1994), who combine situation theory and Dempster-Shafer theory for an account of information retrieval. They consider constraints as conditionals, $\psi \rightarrow \phi$, where ψ and ϕ are types, with a measure of certainty, $cert(\psi \rightarrow \phi)$. If $cert(\psi \rightarrow \phi) < 1$, then $\psi \rightarrow \phi$ leads from one situation s (say, where there is smoke) to another, $s\prime$ (where there is fire), which may be just an extension of s in that it supports all the infons supported by s. They require that, for type ψ, where C is the set of constraints, $\Sigma_{\psi \rightarrow \phi \in C}\, cert(\psi \rightarrow \phi) = 1$

One of our constraints is that there must be an appropriate supporting situation in which the fingerprint file was produced. We read this, as it were, backwards or teleologically: if there is a situation in which a fingerprint file is produced, then there is a situation in which it is used. Our frame of discernment W is a finite number of fingerprint files. The masses in the singletons are now on the constraints (or sets of constraints). Where $\psi \rightarrow \phi$ leads from situation s to s', Lalmas et al. define the mass of $s\prime$ in terms of the mass of s and the certainty of $\psi \rightarrow \phi$: $m_{i+1}(s') = cert(\psi \rightarrow \phi)m_i(s)$. s' itself may actually be a set of alternative situations the sum of whose masses equals $cert(\psi \rightarrow \phi)m_i(s)$. So we invoke the notion of a frame of discernment W' being the refinement of a frame W; essentially W' is a finer partition of the universe of possibilities than W.

When we impose a constraint that leads from a fingerprint-producing situation, the frame is refined by adding information relevant to the acceptability of the fingerprint file. This might reduce the belief due to matching the fingerprint. Instead of something like Mary as a frame element, we have things like (Mary, off23, 11/25/2007) for a fingerprint purportedly of Mary; the frame is effectively a product space, $Suspects \times AdministeringOfficers \times Dates$. We effectively expand the id-situation to include the supporting situations.

Issues arise with respect to the structure of this product space and how the mass is aggregated to contribute to evidence in the id-situation (where a judgment is made). A focal element is a subset of this product space that is assigned a non-zero mass. We can consider something like marginal distributions: for a given (suspect, administering-officer) pair, we add up the mass across all the dates for that pair. Going further, for a given suspect, we add up all the mass for the triples that involve that suspect.

The certainty on the constraint from the fingerprint-producing situation to the existence of the fingerprint file in the id-situation is a measure of the general acceptability of introducing a fingerprint file into an investigation. What the mass of the supporting situation is taken to be depends on how the evidence is being used. If the investigation engenders suspicion of a given administering officer, then, within the supporting situation, the mass for identifying the suspect would be reduced. These considerations revolve around the relation between the id-situation and a supporting situation as well as the nature of the supporting situation. These are essentially ontological considerations.

Dempster-Shafer Argument Schemes

How evidence regarding supporting situations is incorporated into an overall evaluation can perhaps be answered in a nonontological manner following the work by Tang et al. in combining argumentation with an explicit representation of evidence (Tang et al. 2013) (see also (Tang et al. 2012)). They introduce a logical language L with the usual truth-functional connectives. Atomic propositions are constructed from a finite set of predicate symbols and a finite set of individual constants, with no function symbols, so there are only finitely many possible ground terms. Individual variables occur only in rules (for generality, with uniform substitution across premises and conclusion). The frame of discernment, Ω, is the set of possible truth assignments to all the (ground) atomic propositions: if there are n such propositions, there are 2^n elements of Ω (i.e., rows in the truth table). The interpretation of proposition θ (atomic or not), $I(\theta)$, is a subset of Ω. Propositions θ, $\psi \in L$ are logically equivalent iff $I(\theta) = I(\psi)$. Where $true$ and $false$ are the obvious constants, $I(true) = \Omega$ and $I(false) = \varnothing$. An inference rule δ for L is of the form:

$$\delta = \frac{p_1, \ldots, p_m}{c}$$

where $p_1, ..., p_m; c \in L$. The p_i are the set of *premises* of the rule, and c is its *conclusion*.

It is straightforward to go from a frame of discernment where elements are structures on individuals to a frame of discernment where elements are logical propositions over a finite set of predicate symbols. To take our example $(Mary, off23, 11/25/2007) \in Suspects \times AdministeringOfficers \times Dates$, assume we have one-place predicates $suspect(x)$, $adminOfficer(x)$, and $date(x)$, meaning, respectively, that x is the suspect (whose fingerprint is taken), that x is the administrating officer, and that x is the date (when the fingerprint was taken). Assume also that we have individual constants *Mary*, *off23*, and *11/25/2007* with the obvious denotations. Then our example triple translates to the conjunction $suspect(Mary) \wedge adminOfficer(off23) \wedge date(11/25/2007)$. Set-theoretical operators correspond in obvious ways to truth-functional operators, which again relate to set-theoretical operators on the interpretations of propositions.

We have a set Σ of formulae $\langle h, E \rangle$ where $\langle h, E \rangle$ is an evidence argument that has $h \in L$ associated with supporting evidence E for which there is a mass function, $E = \{e_1 : m_1, ..., e_n : m_n\}$ such that $\sum_{i=0}^{n} m_i = 1.0$. (Note that here a mass function is being associated with a single proposition.) To write a mass function value in isolation, we write $m(E, e_i)$. Given evidence argument $\langle h, e \rangle$, the belief $b(h)$, disbelief $d(h)$, and uncertainty $u(h)$ of h are defined as

- $b(h) = \sum_{I(e_i) \subseteq I(h)} m(E, e_i)$ = the sum of the mass of all the focal elements in E that are part of the evidence for h.
- $d(h) = \sum_{I(e_i) \cap I(h) = \varnothing} m(E, e_i)$ = the sum of all the mass for all the focal elements that are evidence for $\neg h$.
- $u(h) = 1 - b(h) - d(h)$ = the sum of the mass of the formulae that imply neither h nor $\neg h$.

We can define the plausibility of h as $1 - d(h)$. We also have a set Δ of rules $\{\delta, E\}$ where rule δ is associated with evidence E.

For an example of the use of a rule, suppose that the proposition in question is that the fingerprint is Bill's, $fprint(Bill)$, and suppose that the associated evidence is as follows (which duplicates the mass function used in the example in the above example) $E_1 = \{fprint(Fred) : 0.4, fprint(Sue) : 0.075, fprint(Bill) : 0.075, fprint(Nullus) : 0.1, fprint(Nulla) : 0.1, fprint(Bill) \vee fprint(Sue) : 0.05, fprint(All) : 0.2\}$

Suppose also that we have the following rule δ with evidence

$E_5 = \{fprint(X) \wedge thief(X) : 0.8, fprint(X) \wedge \neg thief(X) : 0.2\}$

Note that the proposition constituting the premise is carried down to be conjoined with the stated conclusion; this is to specialize the conclusion to the individual to which variable X is bound.

It is more informative to combine the evidence E_1 as a whole and the evidence E_5, where we take products, instantiating X to the individual constant in the corresponding element of $E1$ (treating $fprint(Bill) fprint(Sue)$ as $fprint(Bill \sqcup Sue)$, where $Bill \sqcup Sue$ is a composite object). The result is shown in Table 3, where a number in a cell is the mass value of $fprint(X) \wedge thief(X)$ or $fprint(X) \wedge \neg thief(X)$, depending on the row, where the value of X is indicated in the column. Note that the sum of all values is 1.0. We have, for example $Bel(fprint(Bill) \wedge thief(Bill)) = 0.06$ and

	Person	Fred	Bill	Sue	Nulla
Thief?	**Yes**	0.32	0.06	0.06	0.08
	No	0.08	0.015	0.015	0.04

	Person	Nullus	Bill or Sue	All
Thief?	**Yes**	0.08	0.04	0.16
	No	0.02	0.01	0.04

Table 3: Result of Applying our Rule δ with evidence E_5

$Plaus(fprint(Bill) \wedge thief(Bill)) = 0.26$. This example is particularly simple, and we intentionally avoided combining evidence to indicate how the rules are applied.

Tang et al. (Tang et al. 2013) consider the several ways of combining evidence that have been suggested in the context of Dempster-Shafer theory, considering them all to fit into the general pattern of:

- A rule pattern in Δ: $\delta = \frac{p_1, ..., p_m}{c}$
- A Dempster-Shafer argument scheme specifying
  - the pattern of the evidence of the premises: $\langle h_1, E_1 \rangle ... \langle h_n, E_n \rangle$
  - optional evidence for rule applicability E_δ
  - an an associated conclusion evidence derivation process: we compute the evidence for the conclusion from the evidence for the premises possibly including the rule evidence

When we go to apply an argument scheme, we ask certain critical questions. Only if the answers to all these questions are affirmative are we entitle to apply the scheme. Each scheme is associated with a particular rule for combining evidence. We have seen the oldest and most common rule: Dempster's rule. Another common rule is Yager's rule (see (Curley 2007) for an intuitive comparison with Dempster's rule), which treats conflicting evidence as uncertainty. See (Sentz and Ferson 2002) for a systematic presentation of various rules for combining evidence.

What we are interested in, however, is how to go from information produced in supporting situations to its use as evidence in an id-situation. (In contrast, the rule above, without combination, used the results of id-actions as evidence for various actors being thieves.) This is usually a combination problem. A closer look, however, reveals that the language used in supporting situation s_3 is different from the language used in the id-situation, s_1. One way they differ is that s_1 is an utterance situation while s_3 is a described situation. In terms of vocabulary, s_3 talks about an administering officer, the time and place the fingerprint is taken, and the method used. And s_1 talks about the fingerprint from the scene, matching the two fingerprints, and the time and place the matching is done. Both situations talk about the fingerprint produced in s_3 and used in s_1 and the person thereby identified. Considering the questions Tang et al. pose, the appropriate rule here is Zhang's center combination rule, which is based on two frames of discernment S and T from two disjoint sublanguage L_S and L_T of L. It assumes that we are concerned with the truth of sentences in L_T but we only have evidence expressed in L_S and in $L_S \in L_T$. For $A_T \cup L_T$, we are given two pieces of evidence, E_1 in L_S and E_2 in $L_S \cup L_T$. This scheme can be used where question 1 for Demster's rule is answered "no" since the evidence does not directly support the conclusion of interest because of the change in language. Zhang's rule is especially useful in transforming the evidence from a source domain L_S into a targeting domain L_T with the connection evidence in their super domain $L_S \cup L_T$.

There is, however, more than combining evidence going on as information supported by s_3 is taken as evidence in s_1. How this fitting into a forensic picture contributes to the resulting mass function must be captured by the rule $\delta \in \Delta$ that is applied. This plays a role similar to that of a constraint, $\psi \rightarrow \phi$, along with its level of certainty, in the application of Dempster-Shafer theory to situations.

Conclusion

We have presented a computational framework for identity based on situation theory, where we identify id-cases, each consisting of an id-situation (where an identity judgment is made) and supporting situations. We have shown how to encode in RDF information supported by a situation in terms of infons (items of information). We have shown how to use OWL and SWRL to define rules that classify situations thus encoded under types (i.e., abstract situations). We have also defined SWRL rules for identifying types of id-cases and coordinated id-cases. We also address quantifying the evidence that supports the judgment in an id-situation. For this, we use the Dempster-Shafer theory of evidence, applying it to our running example. To capture how supporting situations contribute to the evidence for a judgment, we considered two approaches. One approach associates a certainty with a constraint by virtue of which one situation carries information about another, and it introduces a refinement of the frame of discernment related to the target situation. The second approach sees the support that situations provide for the id-situation in the framework of argument schemes framed in terms of Dempster-Shafer theory.

Following the argument-schemes approach, we wish to approximate the outcomes of informal reasoning and largely capture the post hoc rationalizations by which actors justify their decisions. The classic here is Toulmin's *The Uses of Argument* (Toulmin 1958), which presents a diagram for directing one's analysis of arguments. The subject is sometimes known as informal logic. There is a coherent literature under the rubric "argumentation theory" (cf., e.g., (Walton 2013)(Van Eemeren et al. 1996)). Argumentation is central to the law, and legal scholars have addressed evidence in this context (Twining 2006) (Anderson, Schum, and Twining 2005). Note that a legal perspective may be central to ones view of individuals and numerical identity: Locke famously called "person" a forensic term (and held personal identity, or self, to be founded on continuity of consciousness not of some [unknowable] substance) (Locke 1689).

On the other hand, capturing the constraints and refining the frame of discernment would have the benefit of associating evidence with the inherent structure of the case. Future work, then, besides including enhancements to the implementation, will attempt to reconcile these two approaches to how supporting situations contribute to the evidence for a judgment.

References

Anderson, T.; Schum, D.; and Twining, W. 2005. *Analysis of evidence.* Cambridge University Press.

Barwise, J., and Perry, J. 1981. *Situations and attitudes.* The MIT Press.

Creese, S.; Gibson-Robinson, T.; Goldsmith, M.; Hodges, D.; Kim, D.; Love, O.; Nurse, J. R.; Pike, B.; and Scholtz, J. 2013. Tools for understanding identity. In *Technologies for Homeland Security (HST), 2013 IEEE International Conference on*, 558–563. IEEE.

Curley, S. P. 2007. The application of dempster-shafer theory demonstrated with justification provided by legal evidence. *Judgment and Decision Making* 2(5):257.

Devlin, K. 1995. *Logic and information.* Cambridge University Press.

Halpern, J. 2003. *Reasoning about uncertainty*, volume 21. MIT press Cambridge.

Hodges, D.; Creese, S.; and Goldsmith, M. 2012. A model for identity in the cyber and natural universes. In *Intelligence and Security Informatics Conference (EISIC), 2012 European*, 115–122. IEEE.

Lalmas, M., and Van Rijsbergen, C. 1994. Situation theory and dempster-shafers theory of evidence for information retrieval. In *Incompleteness and Uncertainty in Information Systems.* Springer. 102–116.

Locke, J. 1689. *An essay concerning human understanding.* Penguin.

Sentz, K., and Ferson, S. 2002. *Combination of evidence in Dempster-Shafer theory*, volume 4015. Citeseer.

Tang, Y.; Hang, C.-W.; Parsons, S.; and Singh, M. 2012. Towards argumentation with symbolic dempster-shafer evidence. *Computational Models of Argument: Proceedings of COMMA 2012* 245:462.

Tang, Y.; Oren, N.; Parsons, S.; and Sycara, K. 2013. Dempster-shafer argument schemes. *Proc. of ArgMAS.*

Toulmin, S. E. 1958. *The uses of argument.* Cambridge University Press.

Twining, W. 2006. *Rethinking evidence: Exploratory essays.* Cambridge University Press, 2nd edition.

Van Eemeren, F. H.; Grootendorst, R.; Henkemans, F.; Blair, J.; Johnson, R.; and Krabbe, E. 1996. al. 1996. fundamentals of argumentation theory. a handbook of historical backgrounds and contemporary developments. In *A Handbook of Historical Backgrounds and Contemporary Developments.* New Jersey: Lawrence Erlbaum.

Walton, D. 2013. *Methods of argumentation.* Cambridge University Press.

The WebID Protocol Enhanced With Group Access, Biometrics, and Access Policies

[*]Cory Sabol, [€]William Nick, [€]Maya Earl, [€]Joseph Shelton, and [€]Albert Esterline
[*]Dept. of Computer Science & [€]Dept. of Computer Science
[*]University of North Carolina at Greensboro & [€]North Carolina A&T State University
Greensboro, North Carolina
cssabol@uncg.edu, {wmnick, mnearl, jashelt1}@aggies.ncat.edu, esterlin@ncat.edu

Abstract

The WebID protocol solves the challenge of remembering usernames and passwords. We enhance this protocol in three ways. First, we give it the ability to manage groups of agents and control their access to resources on the Web. Second, we add support for biometric access control to enhance security. Finally, we add support for OWL-based policies that may be federated and result in flexible access control.

Introduction

The primary way of authenticating users on the Web is via username and password. This is a rather secure and time-tested method, but it is cumbersome and error prone. A user may forget their username or password, requiring them to choose the ever so prevalent "forgot password" option. If the way a password reset is handled is insecure, then this opens up an entirely new attack surface for malicious actors to gain information about a user. This is where alternatives such as OpenID (Wang Chen & Wang, 2012), EMCSSL (Emercoin, 2015), and WebID (W3C, 2015) come into play. These systems are distributed platforms that provide a user with, ideally, a simple way of asserting their identity on the Web. In this paper, we focus on the WebID protocol, identification for groups and some ways in which the security of WebID can be improved for applications in which it is deemed necessary.

The remainder of this paper is organized as follows. The next section presents Semantic Web standards (such as RDF and OWL), which are used for representation in our protocols. Next is a section that introduces the WebID protocol and its use. Next, we introduce the problem of group access with WebIDs, and the following section presents our solution. The next section discusses our use of access policies, reasoning about policies, and enforcing policies. Next, we present biometrics (the use of a person's physiological and behavioral characteristics for authentication) and our biometric enhancement of the WeID protocol. The penultimate section briefly discusses implementation technologies, and the last section concludes with a summary of this paper.

Semantic Web Standards

RDF/RDFS/OWL

Our enhancements make heavy use of the Resource Description Framework (RDF). RDF is a specification for managing metadata of resources on the Web. In RDF, all information is represented as triples of the form *subject, predicate, object* (Broekstra, Kampman & Harmelen, 2002). The subject is the resource in question, and the predicate might describe a characteristic that the subject has, in which case the object is the value of that characteristic. Or the predicate describes a relationship between the subject and the object, as in *Tim knows Sarah*, where *Tim* is the subject, *knows* is the predicate, and *Sarah* is the object.

RDF lets us create a model of a resource and the relationships it has with other resources. RDF is also machine-readable so that we can build applications that leverage it and the power of linked data (see below) to make the use and discovery of data much easier and consistent across platforms. RDF is also expressible in various serializations, such as RDF/XML, for better machine consumption. The Turtle serialization is a subset of the N3 serialization and is meant for ease of human reading and writing. All RDF examples throughout this document are written in N3 syntax for ease of reading.

The Resource Description Framework Schema (RDFS) provides a way to construct RDF vocabularies by allowing one to define RDF classes, properties, and relations tailored to one's needs. One such RDFS vocabulary used in the research reported here is FOAF, which stands for Friend Of A Friend. Another such vocabulary is ACL, or the Access Control Language. Both vocabularies are discussed below.

Linked Data

Linked-data is a set of best practices regarding the publication and connection of structured data on the Web (Broekstra, Kampman & Harmelen, 2002). Linked-data aims to provide a consistent and uniform way for agents on the web to consume and publish data, machine and human alike. The key to this is that data is published in a consistent format and that all data links to other appropriate data so that the discovery and consumption of further data is easy and encouraged. The main format in which linked-data is published in RDF.

FOAF

FOAF is a powerful RDF vocabulary that allows for the concise description of people and their social networks in a semantic and machine-readable manner (OpenSSL, 2007), It allows us to compute over the relationships and programmatically make conclusions about a person and those to which they are connected. The conventional namespace prefix for FOAF is `foaf:`.

FOAF is, of course, applicable to more than just people and their social networks. It is applicable to any agent on the web. An agent could be a person or it could be a software agent that acts on the behalf of a person or organization. FOAF is also useful for representing the subtle status of a group of agents. We leverage the semantics of the `foaf:Group` class in order not only to allow a group to act as a collection of agents but also for the group itself to be treated as, as well as act as, an individual within an application or service. This is the crux of allowing for authentication of a group's agents based on the group asserting its identity as an individual.

ACL

The Access Control Language (ACL) is a simple RDF vocabulary that allows the specification of access control rules to be tied to resources on the web and presented in a machine-readable manner. It allows for a fairly flexible and broad range of rules to be specified regarding a resource. It also allows for the rules to be specified and determined in a decentralized manner. A resource can have its access control rules easily derived from another resource's ACL file on the web. The rules can even be maintained simply via a separate service, thanks to the power of linked data. Table 1 depicts the various modes of access offered by ACL.

Table 1 – ACL access modes

Mode:	Actions Allowed:
Read	Read the contents (including querying, etc.)
Write	Overwrite contents (including deleting or overwriting parts of it)
Append	Add information to the end without overwriting any part
Control	Set the access control rules for the resource

This ACL-RDF vocabulary, which is defined with RDFS, includes properties of authorization (W3C, 2015). It allows the administrator to specify access control modes, which are essentially classes of operations. The WebAccessControl protocol states that the user authenticates to the server through the implementation of WebID+TLS.

However, ACL can in some cases be rather rigid, which is why we introduced a policy ontology written in OWL (web ontology language) that we developed. The main advantage of this ontology is that it can be used in tandem with a reasoner service such as Apache Jena, which can make inferences based on the rules derived from the ontology.

OWL

OWL (Antoniou & van Harmelen, 2004) extends the power of RDFS and is used to represent ontologies on the Semantic Web. "Ontology" is a term that is borrowed from philosophy referring to a conceptualization of a domain, describing entities in the world and how they relate to each other.

WebID and Its Use

WebID

WebID is a W3C proposed protocol which provides a way for an agent to be identified using standard web technologies (W3C, 2015). At its most basic level, a WebID is simply a unique URI (uniform resource identifier) that represents some resource or agent on the web. When the URI is dereferenced, an RDF or human readable format of the document that describes the resource or agent in question is returned. (Derefencing means to retrieve the resource to which the URI points.) The version of the file that is returned is determined by content negotiation and CoolURIs (Ayers & Völkel, 2008), along with fragment identifiers or 303 redirects, to determine and return the appropriate representation of the document representing the resource that the WebID represents. Typically, HTML is served to human users and RDF to machines. The service that is implementing WebID can of course decide how this is to be handled; it could be that a human agent has reason to view the RDF representation of a resource and a machine needs to consume the HTML representation.

WebID + TLS

WebID + TLS is the protocol that describes the implementation of WebID. It has the following general steps (W3C, 2015):

- Initially, the client must establish a TLS connection, which the server authenticates itself, using the standard TLS protocol.
- Next, the client on a specific resource can perform an HTTP GET, PUT, POST, or DELETE action.
- At this stage, the guard, or server agent, can grant or deny access according to the access control rules.
- Now, if the resource requires authentication for access, the client's identity is linked to a private key and public key pair. This pair should be embedded in the client's certificate to be verified. The client has the option to automate which certificate to send from its browser when the TLS agent makes a certificate
- The TLS agent matches the certificate's public key with the public key in the user's profile document on the server.
- The Verification Agent, defined in (W3C, 2015), verifies that the WebID in the WebID certificate knows the given public key.
- The Verification Agent extracts the public key and the URIs from the *Subject Alternative Name* property field in the certificate.
- With the WebID collected, the guard can check if one of the URIs is authorized by the access control rules. If access is granted, then the guard can pass on the request to the protected resource.

The Group Problem

There are several problems that this work addresses, including group access control using WebID as well as strengthening access control on the web by coupling the policy ontology we have developed with a Jena-based reasoner to help decentralize the security logic of determining access to resources on the web. We also present a solution to one of the main security flaws of WebID by creating a system that couples a user's biometric data with their WebID to create a two-step authentication process.

We start by describing the problem surrounding group access control on the web. As it stands, delegating access to agents on the web is a process that relies heavily on static access control lists and security logic that is heavily integrated into the application logic of the service. Furthermore, we have a natural notion of trust in a group's head member, often allowing them to assert their identity and subsequently allowing for the knowledge to validate the identity of the group's other members. Capturing this in a computational environment is a challenge, but we have several solutions. We implemented a system that can allow for group owners to authenticate themselves as well as establish the trust needed to more easily authenticate the group's members. This is primarily accomplished by making use of the FOAF term `foaf:Group` and the subtlety that allows a `foaf:Group` also to be an individual agent. Also, one can specify a class associated with a group so that elements of that class are automatically of that group and vice versa.

We now address decentralizing web access control further than was done in our initial implementation. Developing secure code is often difficult, especially when the security logic of the application is tightly knit into the implementation. In our access to resources based on semantic rule lists, decoupling some of the security functionality from the main application logic allows for the application logic to be developed and maintained much more easily. We remove the rigidity of our original solution to authenticating groups and expand it into a more generalized and extensible system with the use of OWL and a Jena reasoning service that can also easily apply to individual agents. The OWL policy ontology that has been developed in our lab is also more robust and flexible than ACL as a means of expressing access control rules.

Our Solution to the Group Problem

To solve the problems of group access control, we began experimenting with the notion of authenticating a group of agents by dereferencing the WebIDs of the group's members, which are presented in the group's profile document. In order for this to work, however, we must make certain that a group is explicitly defined to avoid ambiguities in discerning whether or not the agent that is asserting its identity is indeed a group. This is where we make use of the `foaf:Group` term. Figure 1 is a simple example of a `foaf:Group` defined in RDF using N3 syntax. The profile explicitly asserts that the agent is a `foaf:Group`. The profile document also contains the agent's public key, as all WebID profiles must. And it contains a list of the WebIDs belonging to its member agents. This is critical to the verification process, which allows the group to assert its identity and authenticate the group members too.

```
@prefix foaf: <http://www.xmlns.com/foaf/spec/#> .
@prefix cert: <http://www.w3.org/ns/auth/cert/#> .

_:webidcommunitygroup a foaf:Group;
    foaf:name "webidcommunitygroup";
    foaf:member[/*group member WebID's here*/];
    cert:PublicKey "MIICQ...EstKg==" .
```

Figure 1 – Simple Group Profile Document

We can allow a WebID that represents a group to serve as an entry point to the authentication process. We do this by first dereferencing the WebID to get the profile document. With this we determine whether or not the agent is a group by checking if the profile contains the `foaf:Group` term. From there, we parse the WebIDs contained in the `foaf:member` list and individually verify the WebID of each member and determine the access to the resource in question based on the access rules tied to the resource. We then use server-side caching techniques to cache this access information for a limited time to the service so that, when an agent that is a member of a previously authenticated group requests access to the resource, the service may simply validate their WebID and then perform a simple lookup against the cached access data to determine what type of access should be allowed.

We expanded our initial algorithm to include use of the policy ontology and a reasoner, which was implemented using Apache Jena. This got rid of the rigidity of the algorithm and its close ties to the limited ACL vocabulary in favor of the flexibility that our OWL-based policy ontology offers. Figure 2 shows the updated version of the high-level group access algorithm, which makes use of a response returned from the reasoner.

Defining and Enforcing Policies

OWL-based Policy Ontology

The major advantage of using XML to represent policies is that it is straightforwardly extensible (Bradshaw, Uszok and Montanari, 2014), but the problem with XML, as with many other representations, is that its semantics is mostly implicit. One problem with implicit semantics is that the conventions on which it is based are potentially ambiguous. For that reason, semantic technologies are being used. There are many advantages to using OWL to represent policies. Ontologies allow for policies to be easily extended by simply adding new concepts.

```
define function grantAccess(AgentURI, ResourceURI):
  if (Agent's WebID not valid) then
    Deny access to ResourceURI, prompt resource owner that
    AgentURI
    has requested access to the resource.
    return access denied
  end

  Define AProile := dereference(AgentURI)
  Define ResACL := dereference(ResourceURI)
  Define AGraph := toGraph(AProfile)
  Define ResACLGraph := toGraph(ResACL)

  if (AgentURI is in ResACLGraph OR
      Agraph.class is in ResACLGraph) then
    return access type specified in ResACL
  end
  else
    Deny access to ResourceURI, prompt resource owner
    that AgentURI has requested access to the resource.
    return access denied
  end
end

forEach (Member m in Group g) do
  accessCache.add(m, grantAccess(m, Resource.URI))
end
```

Figure 2 – Group Access Delegation Algorithm

Using ontologies to describe policies enables the system to use concepts that describe the entities and environments that are being controlled. This simplifies their descriptions and improves the system's analyzability. The result is that policy frameworks can take advantage of powerful features such as policy conflict detection and harmonization. As with databases, there is the possibility of accessing the information provided by querying the ontology based on the ontology schema.

The KAoS policy service framework (Uszok, Bradshaw & Jeffers, 2004) is a mature general-purpose policy management system developed by the Florida Institute for Human and Machine Cognition (IHMC). It makes use of OWL and OWL-based tools for specification, analysis and enforcement of policies that are constrained across a variety of distributed computing platforms. KAoS has support for obligations and authorization policies as well as mechanisms for other kinds of policies. This enables analysis, management, specification, and enforcement of policies. Use of OWL-based policies allows term and policy federation. We are importing the KAoS policies and extending it in order to create our own policies.

Jena/Reasoning

Jena is a Java-based Semantic Web framework (McBride, 2002). It can read all RDF serializations and add data to RDF graphs, and it can write RDF graphs to all common serializations. A number of inference engines and reasoners can be used in Jena. With these engines, additional RDF assertions can be derived from an original RDF document. Languages such as RDFS and, for possibly sophisticated ontologies, OWL are supported; additional facts can be inferred from instance data using these languages. SWRL rules (Horrocks et al., 2004) are supported if one installs the Pellet reasoner (Parsia, 2004). Pellet is an open-source Java-based OWL 2 reasoner. One of the main points of this framework is that it is intentionally general so as to be applicable for virtually any problem.

Apache Thrift

Thrift is an interface definition language and binary communication protocol that is used to define and create services for numerous languages. It is used as a remote procedure call (RPC) framework and was developed at Facebook for "scalable cross-language services development" (Apache, 2007). It is incorporated into our code through the use of RDF and triples. The RDF file information goes to the server, which infers triples and then returns more triples. Whatever access the person has will be inferred by the reasoner. The Thrift service uses Pellet for reasoning about our policies.

Extension Using Biometrics

Biometrics

Biometrics is the study of identifying an individual based off of their physical characteristics (Jain and Ross 2008). It is useful in many authentication systems due to its inherent advantages over other types of authentication. Unlike a knowledge-based system (Zhang and Li 2011) that uses a password or some other key phrase to grant access, a biometric system uses an individual's biometric, such as their face, iris or fingerprint. These biometrics cannot be as easily misplaced or stolen as a password can. A token-based systems (Hao & Yu, 2010) use some physical token such as a key or smart card to grant access. However, tokens can also be misplaced or stolen.

A biometric system is composed of some sensor, such as a camera or scanner, a module that extracts features from what was taken from the sensor, a module that stores the extracted features in a database, and a module to compare extracted features to enrolled features (Jain and Ross 2008).

WebID + Biometric protocol

This section describes the WebID+Biometrics protocol, which is built off the WebID protocol but uses the disposable feature extractors created by the GEFE technique developed by Shelton et al. (2012) for biometric verification. WebID+Biometrics also uses OWL-based policies, as described above. One possible scenario where this protocol might be used is where a person tries to login to a social network service. For example, William is a user of Joseph's social networking site. Figure 3 shows the sequence diagram for the WebID+Biometrics protocol for this scenario. The scenario assumes authentication for a RESTful web service. A RESTful web service communicates using the HTTP protocol in a way similar to (but more involved than) the way a web browser gets a web page from a server.

William's client sends a TLS request to Joseph's social networking service. Then Joseph's social networking service requests a certificate from William's client. William's client sends a certificate to Joseph's social networking service and dereferences William's profile from William's server from the URI that was provided in William's certificate. Joseph's social networking service then queries the RDF that is William's profile and checks whether or not the modulus and exponent from the profile on William's server match the modulus and exponent from William's certificate. If they match, then Joseph's service will send the RDF for the particular feature extractor that has been generated at random. William's client will ask William to submit, for example, a picture from which it will extract the feature vector and serialize it to an RDF serialization. That RDF will be sent to Joseph's service, which will dereference a document on William's server that contains William's biometric information. Joseph's service will then verify that William's biometrics matches the enrolled feature vectors. Finally, if the biometrics submitted to Joseph's social networking service matches the biometrics from the RDF document on William's server, then Joseph's service will notify William's client that he may access it.

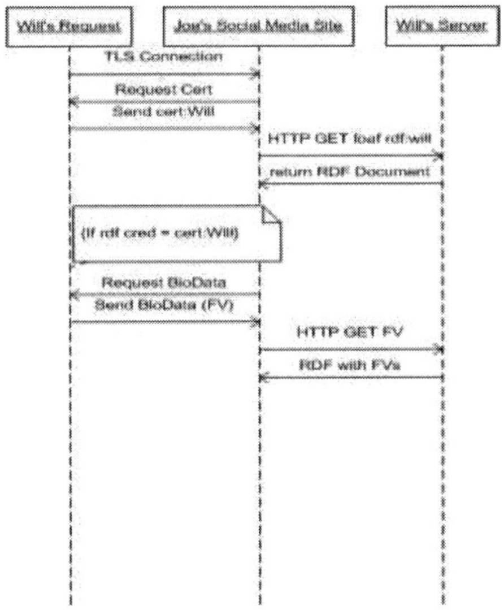

Figure 3- The sequence diagram for the WebID+Biometrics Protocol

Unlike the WebID protocol, we use policies, which are expressed in OWL. This allows us to infer roles and to infer how access is delegated. To illustrate this, consider another example, where a user, Renee, is trying to access a resource controlled by William. Renee is part of the same organization as William, and William has also delegated access to a resource to Renee. Renee's client requests to login and access a resource controlled by William. The service requests Renee's certificate and gets the RDF profile document from Renee's server from the URI in the certificate. The service checks whether the modulus and exponent in the certificate match the modulus and exponent in the profile document. The Service requests Renee's client to submit her biometric credentials using a particular disposable FE. If the biometrics for Renee matches the biometrics on Renee's server, then the server will pass Renee's policy document to a reasoning service. The reasoning service will reason about the document based on a policy ontology. The result will determine whether Renee will gain access to the system.

Like the WebID protocol, our protocol allows for profiles to be decentralized. Unlike the WebID protocol, however, our protocol is able to handle biometric verification. This allows users to bring their own biometrics. Unlike the WebID protocol, our protocol reasons about permissions using policy documents expressed in OWL.

Implementation

Node.js was used to build a client application from which agents may try to authenticate for access to resources that have access rules expressed using the OWL based policy ontology. The client also acts as the WebID authentication service. We paired the Node.js client with an Apache Jena based reasoner service, which accepts the access rules and makes inferences based on them, returning the type of access to a resource that is to be granted to the client. The reasoner used is Pellet, and Apache Thrift provides RESTful access to it.

Conclusion

We addressed the way group access control and group based authentication might be handled on the web and created a high-level algorithm for authenticating a group and its members and caching the access decisions to the server for a limited time. This allows for a more natural notion of a group to exist and interact with web services, just as in real life a group owner's identity is validated and then trust is established and propagated to the group's members. We also improved the security of the WebID protocol by coupling it with biometrics. This mitigates the threat of somebody having access to a device in which an agent's WebID certificate is installed. We also add support for OWL-based policies that may be federated and result in flexible access control. What is reported here leads to future work aimed at the notion of a network of trust.

References

Antoniou, G., & van Harmelen, F. (2004). Web ontology language: Owl. In *Handbook on ontologies* (pp. 67-92). Springer Berlin Heidelberg.

Apache Software Foundation. *Apache Thrift.* 2007.http://thrift.apache.org/.

Ayers, D. and Völkel, M. 2008. *Cool URIs for the Semantic Web.* Cool URIs for the Semantic Web.

http://www.w3.org/TR/cooluris/.

Bizer, C., Heath, T., and Berners-Lee, T. 2009. *Linked Data—The Story So Far.* International Journal on Semantic Web and Information Systems. pp. 1–22.

Bradshaw, J.M., A. Uszok, and R. Montanari. 2014. *Policy-Based Governance of Complex Distributed Systems: What Past Trends Can Teach Us about Future Requirements.* Adaptive, Dynamic, and Resilient Systems, CRC Press.

Broekstra, J., Kampman, A. and Harmelen, F. V. 2002. *Sesame: A Generic Architecture for Storing and Querying RDF and RDF Schema.* Proceedings of the First International Semantic Web Conference on the Semantic Web. Springer-Verlag, London, UK, UK, 54-68.

Emercoin. 2015. *EMCSSL. Decentralized identity management, passwordless logins, and client SSL certificates using Emercoin NVS.* Emercoin International Development Group.

Hao, Z., & Yu, N. 2010. *A Security Enhanced Remote Password Authentication Scheme Using Smart Card.* 2010 Second International Symposium on Data, Privacy, and E-Commerce, 56-60.

Horrocks, I., Patel-Schneider, P.F., Boley, H., Tabet, S., Grosof, B., Dean. M. 2004. *SWRL: A Semantic Web Rule Language Combining OWL and RuleML,* W3C Member Submission, W3C. http://www.w3.org/Submission/2004/SUBM-SWRL-20040521/.

Jain, A. K., Ross, A. 2008. *Introduction to Biometrics.* Handbook of Biometrics. Springer. pp. 1–22.

McBride, B. 2002. *Jena: A Semantic Web Toolkit.* IEEE Internet Computing 6(6): 55-59 (2002)

OpenSSL Software Foundation. *OpenSSL Project.* The OpenSSL Project Homepage, 2007.

< https://www.openssl.org/>

Parsia, B., Sirin, E. 2004. *Pellet: an OWL DL reasoned.* Proc. DL-2004, 2004.

Shelton, J., Bryant, K., Abrams, S., Small, L., Adams, J., Leflore, D., & Dozier, G. 2012. *Genetic & Evolutionary Biometric Securi-*

ty: Disposable Feature Extractors for Mitigating Biometric Replay Attacks. Procedia Computer Science, 8, 351-360.

Uszok, A., Bradshaw, J. M., & Jeffers, R. 2004. *KAoS: A policy and domain services framework for grid computing and semantic web services*. Trust management: Second international conference, iTrust 2004, Oxford, UK, March 29–April 1, 2004. Proceedings. Vol. 2995 of Lecture Notes in Computer Science., (pp. 16–26). Springer-Verlag, Berlin, Heidelberg

W3C. ed. 2015. *WebID-TLS*. Authentification over TLS.

Wang, R,. Chen, S., Wang, X. 2012. *Signing me onto your accounts through Facebook and Google: A traffic-guided security study of commercially deployed single-sign-on web services*. IEEE Symposium on Security and Privacy.

Zhang, H., & Li, M. 2011. *Security vulnerabilities of an remote password authentication scheme with smart card*. 2011 International Conference on Consumer Electronics, Communications and Networks (CECNet), 698-701.

Comparison of Recent Machine Learning Techniques for Gender Recognition from Facial Images

Joseph Lemley
Computer Science Department
Central Washington University
Ellensburg, WA, USA

Sami Abdul-Wahid
Computer Science Department
Central Washington University
Ellensburg, WA, USA

Dipayan Banik
Computer Science Department
Central Washington University
Ellensburg, WA, USA

Răzvan Andonie
Computer Science Department
Central Washington University
Ellensburg, WA, USA
and
Electronics and Computers Department
Transilvania University
Braşov, Romania

Abstract

Recently, several machine learning methods for gender classification from frontal facial images have been proposed. Their variety suggests that there is not a unique or generic solution to this problem. In addition to the diversity of methods, there is also a diversity of benchmarks used to assess them. This gave us the motivation for our work: to select and compare in a concise but reliable way the main state-of-the-art methods used in automatic gender recognition. As expected, there is no overall winner. The winner, based on the accuracy of the classification, depends on the type of benchmarks used.

Introduction

A major goal of computer vision and artificial intelligence is to build computers that can understand or classify concepts such as gender in the same way humans do.

Automatic classification of gender from frontal face images taken under contrived conditions has been well studied with impressive results. The variety of methods published in the literature show that there is not a unique or generic solution to the gender classification problem.

Applications of gender classification include, image search, automatic annotation of images, security systems, face recognition, and real time image acquisition on smart phones and mobile devices.

The state-of-the-art gender classification methods generally fall into the following main categories: Convolutional Neural Networks (CNN), Dual Tree Complex Wavelet Transform (DTCWT) + a Support Vector Machine (SVM) classifier, and feature extraction techniques such as Principal Component Analysis (PCA), Histograms of Oriented Gradients (HOG) and others with a classifier (SVM, kNN, etc). The SVM approach is natural, since we have a two class problem. The CNN is related to the well-known deep learning paradigm. The DTCWT provides approximate shift invariance and directionally selective filters (properties lacking in the traditional wavelet transform) while preserving the usual properties of perfect reconstruction and computational efficiency with good well-balanced frequency responses (Kingsbury 2001).

To assess gender classification techniques, two types of benchmarks may be used: standard posed datasets (with well defined backgrounds, lighting and photographic characteristics) and datasets containing "In the wild" images that exhibit the diversity of subjects, settings, and qualities typical of everyday scenes.

The diversity of the methods and benchmarks makes a comparison between gender classification a challenging task, and this gave us the motivation for our work. We compare state-of-the-art methods used in automatic gender recognition on two benchmarks: the most popular standard dataset Facial Recognition Technology (FERET) (Phillips et al. 2000) and a more challenging data set of "in the wild" images (Adience) (Eidinger, Enbar, and Hassner 2014).

We only compare the accuracy of the classification and not other performance measures (precision, recall, F1 score, etc). The main reason is that the misclassification cost in this particular problem is the same, regardless if we misclassify a male or a female. We also do not compare the running time, since the experiments are performed on different computer architectures (the CNN is implemented on a GPU).

Related work: recent gender classification methods

Classifiers such as SVMs and feedforward NNs are often used to classify images after the faces have been cropped out from the rest of the image, and possibly aligned and normalized. Various feature extraction methods such as Principal Component Analysis (PCA), independent component analysis, Fischer linear discriminants (Belhumeur, Hespanha, and Kriegman 1997) (Wu et al. 2015), and edge detection algorithms can be used to encode useful information from the image that is fed into the classifier, leading to high levels of accuracy on many benchmarks. Other approaches use hand-crafted template features to find facial keypoints such as nose, eyes etc, while also using edge detection methods (Sobel) and line intensities to separate facial edges from wrinkles. The resulting feature information, when fed into a feedforward neural network, allows age and gender to be classified with overall 85% accuracy on two test sets with a total of 172 images in the FERET and FGNET databases (Kalansuriya and Dharmaratne 2014).

LDA (Linear Discriminant Analysis) based approaches to the face recognition task promise invariance to differing illuminations (Belhumeur, Hespanha, and Kriegman 1997). This has been further studied in (Bekios-Calfa, Buenaposada, and Baumela 2011). Fisher linear discriminant maximizes the ratio of between- class scatter to that of within-class scatter. Independent component analysis has been used on a small subset (500 images) of the FERET dataset, leading to 96% accuracy with an SVM classifier (Jain, Huang, and Fang 2005). Likewise, PCA has been used in conjunction with a genetic algorithm that eliminated potentially unnecessary features. The remaining features were then fed to a feedforward neural network for training, and an overall 85% accuracy was obtained over 3 data sets (Sun et al. 2002). Various information theory based metrics were also fused together to produce 99.13% gender classification accuracy on the FERET (Perez et al. 2012). To overcome the challenge of inadequate contrast among facial features using histogram analysis, Haar wavelet transformation and Adaboost learning techniques have been employed, resulting in a 97.3% accuracy on the Extended Yale face database which contains 17 subjects under 576 viewing conditions (Laytner, Ling, and Xiao 2014). Another experiment describes how various transformations, such as noise and geometric transformations, were fed in combination into a series of RBFs (Radial Basis Functions). RBF outputs were forwarded into a symbolic decision tree that outputs gender and ethnic class. 94% classification accuracy was obtained using the hybrid architecture on the FERET database (Gutta, Wechsler, and Phillips 1998).

HOG (Histogram of Oriented Gradients) is commonly used as a global feature extraction technique that expresses information about the directions of curvatures of an image. HOG features can capture information about local edge and gradient structures while maintaining degrees of invariance to moderate changes in illumination, shadowing, object location, and 2D rotation. HOG descriptors, combined with SVM classifiers, can be used as a global feature extraction mechanism (Torrione et al. 2014), while HOG descriptors can be used on locations indicated by landmark-finding software in areas such as facial expression classification (Déniz et al. 2011). One useful application of variations in HOG descriptors is the automatic detection of pedestrians, which is made easier in part because of their predominantly upright pose (Dalal and Triggs 2005). In addition, near perfect results were obtained in facial expression classification when HOG descriptors were used to extract features from faces that were isolated through face-finding software (Carcagnì et al. 2015).

A recent technique proposed for face recognition is the DTCWT, due to its ability to improve operation under varying illumination and shift conditions when compared to Gabor Wavelets and DWT (Discrete Wavelet Transform). The Extended Yale B and AR face databases were used, containing a total 16128 images of 38 human subjects under 9 poses and 64 illumination conditions. It achieved 98% classification accuracy in the best illumination condition, while low frequency subband image at scale one (L1) achieved 100% (Sultana et al. 2014).

Recent years have seen great success in image related problems through the use of CNN, thereby seeing the proliferation of a scalable and more or less universal algorithmic approach to solving general image processing problems, if enough training data is available. CNNs have had a great deal of success in dealing with images of subjects and objects in natural non-contrived settings, along with handling the rich diversity that these images entail. One investigation of CNN fundamentals involved training a CNN to classify gender on images collected on the Internet. 88% classification accuracy was achieved after incorporating L2 regularization into training, and filters were shown to respond to the same features that neuroscientists have identified as fundamental cues humans use in gender classification (Verma and Vig 2014). Another experiment (Levi and Hassner 2015) uses a convolutional neural network on the Adience dataset for gender and age recognition. They used data augmentation and face cropping to achieve 86% accuracy for gender classification. This is the only paper we know of that uses CNN on Adience.

A method recently proposed by (Eidinger, Enbar, and Hassner 2014) uses an SVM with dropout, a technique inspired from newer deep learning methods, that has shown promise for age and gender estimation. Dropout involves dropping a certain percent of features randomly during training. They also introduce the Adiance dataset to fulfill the need for a set of realistic labeled images for gender and age recognition in quantities needed to prevent overfitting and allow true generalization (Eidinger, Enbar, and Hassner 2014).

As we can see, most of the state-of-the-art methods for gender classification fall into the categories described in Section .

Data sets

A number of databases exist that can be used to benchmark gender classification algorithms. Most image sets that contain gender labels suffer from insufficient size, and because of this we chose two of the larger publicly available datasets: Color-FERET (Phillips et al. 2000) and Adience (Eidinger, Enbar, and Hassner 2014).

Figure 1: Randomly selected images from the Adience dataset illustrating the wider range of photographic conditions found.

Color FERET Version 2 was collected between December 1993 and August 1996 and made freely available with the intent of promoting the development of face recognition algorithms. Images in the FERET Color database are 512 by 768 pixels and are in PPM format. They are labeled with gender, pose, name, and other useful labels.

Although FERET contains a large number of high quality images in different poses and with varying face obstructions (beards, glasses, etc), they all have certain similarities in quality, background, pose, and lighting which make them very easy for modern machine learning methods to correctly

Figure 2: Randomly selected images from the FERET dataset show similarities in lighting, pose, subject, background, and other photographic conditions.

classify. We used all 11338 images in FERET for which gender labels exist in our experiments.

As machine learning algorithms are increasingly used to process images of varying quality with vast differences in scale, obstructions, focus, and which are often acquired with consumer devices such as web cams or cellphones, benchmarks such as FERET have become less useful. To address this issue, datasets such as LWS (labeled faces in the wild) and most recently Adience have emerged. LWS lacks gender labels but it has accurate names from which gender can often be deduced automatically with reasonable accuracy.

Adience is a recently released benchmark that contains gender and approximate age labels separated into 5 folds to allow duplication of results published by the database authors. It was created by collecting Flickr images and is intended to capture all variations of pose, noise, lighting, and image quality. Each image is labeled with age and gender. It is designed to mimic the challenges of "real world" image classification tasks where faces can be partly obscured or even partly overlapping (for example in a crowd or when an adult is holding a child and both are looking at the camera). Eidlinger, et al published a paper where they used a SVM and filtering to classify age and gender along with the release of Adience (Eidinger, Enbar, and Hassner 2014).

We used all 19370 of the aligned images from Adience that had gender labels, to create our training and testing sets for all experiments that used Adience.

Using the included labels and meta data in the FERET and Adience datasets, we generated two files containing reduced size 51x51 pixel data with values normalized between 0 and 1, followed by a gender label. We choose to resize the images to 51x51 because this produced the best quality images after Anti-Aliasing

Classification methods

We compare the accuracy of CNN and several SVM based classifiers. We limit ourselves to methods involving these two approaches because they are among the most effective and most prevalently used methods reported in the literature for Gender Classification.

Gender classifications with SVM perform on the raw image pixels along with different well known feature extraction methods, namely DTCWT, PCA, and HOG. Training is done separately on two widely differing datasets consisting of gender labeled human faces: Color FERET, a set of images taken under similar conditions with good image quality, and Adience, a set of labeled unfiltered images intended to be especially challenging for modern machine learning algorithms. Adience was designed to present all variations in appearance, noise, pose, and lighting, that can be expected of images taken without careful preparation or posing. (Eidinger, Enbar, and Hassner 2014)

We use the following steps in conducting our experiments:

- Uniformly shuffle the order of images.
- Use 70% as training set. 30% as testing set.
- Train with training set.
- Record correct classification rate on testing set.

Steps 1-4 are repeated 10 times for each experiment using freshly initialized classifiers.

We report the results of 18 experiments, 16 of which use SVMs and two of which use CNN.

SVM classification

Both linear and RBF kernels were used, with each constituting a separate experiment using the SVC implementation included as part of scikit-learn(Pedregosa et al. 2011) with $C = 100$ parameter set.

In one experiment, raw pixels are fed into the SVM. Other experiments used the following feature extraction methods: PCA, HOG, and DTCWT. Feature extraction was applied to images uniformly without using face finding software to isolate and align the face.

Histogram of Oriented Gradients

HOG descriptors, combined with SVM classifiers, can be used as a global feature extraction mechanism (Torrione et al. 2014), while HOG descriptors can be used on locations indicated by landmark-finding software in areas such as facial expression classification (Déniz et al. 2011).

One application of HOG descriptors is the automatic detection of pedestrians, which is made easier in part because of their predominantly upright pose (Dalal and Triggs 2005). We use the standard HOG implementation from the scikit-image library (van der Walt et al. 2014).

For every image in the Adience and FERET databases, HOG descriptors were uniformly calculated. 9 orientation bins were used, and each histogram was calculated based on gradient orientations in the 7x7 pixel non-overlapping cells. Normalization was done within each cell (i.e., 1 x 1). The result was fed into a SVM (SVC class from scikit-learn).

Training and testing on both Adience and FERET was performed separately. 30% of images in each database were used for testing, and the rest for training. For each database, after reading the data into arrays, the arrays were shuffled and then the testing and training set were separated. Training and testing were repeated 10 times with freshly shuffled data.

Principal Component Analysis

PCA is a statistical method for finding correlations between features in data. When used on images of faces the resulting images are often referred to as Eigenfaces. PCA is used for reducing dimensionality of data by eliminating non-essential information from the dataset and is frequently used in both image processing and machine learning.

To create the Eigenfaces we used the RandomizedPCA tool within scikit-learn, which is based on work by (Halko, Martinsson, and Tropp 2011) and (Martinsson, Rokhlin, and Tygert 2011). The resulting Eigenfaces were then used in a linear and RBF SVM.

Convolutional Neural Network

For the learning stage we used a convolutional neural network with 3 hidden convolutional layers and one softmax layer. The training was done using a GTX Titan X GPU using the Theano based library Pylearn2 and CUDNN libraries. Stochastic gradient descent was used as the training algorithm with a momentum of 0.95, found by trial and error. Learning rates under 0.001 did not show any improvement. Increasing the learning rate above around 0.005 results in decreased classification accuracy.

A general outline of the structure of our CNN is:

- Hidden layer 1: A Rectified Linear Convolutional Layer using a kernel shape of 4x4, a pool shape of 2x2, a pool stride of 2x2 and 128 output channels. Initial weights are randomly selected with a range of 0.5.
- Hidden layer 2: A Rectified Linear Convolutional Layer using a kernel shape of 4x4, a pool shape of 2x2, a pool stride of 2x2 and 256 output channels. Initial weights are randomly selected with a range of 0.5.
- Hidden layer 3: A Rectified Linear Convolutional Layer using a kernel shape of 3x3, a pool shape of 2x2, a pool stride of 2x2 and 512 output channels. Initial weights are randomly selected with a range of 0.5.
- Softmax layer: Initial weights randomly set between 0 and 0.5. Output is the class (male or female).

Experimental results

Tables 1 and 2 summarize the classification accuracy of each approach on each data-set after random shuffling and separation into 70% training and 30% testing sets. For each method the grayscale pixels were used as the features, either directly to the classifier, or to the filter mentioned. For example, HOG+SVM[RBF] indicates that we use the pixels as input to a HOG filter, the output of which is used as the input to a SVM with an RBF kernel.

DTCWT was both the second best method (after CNN) and the very worst method we examined; its performance has the greatest degree of variability depending on the dataset. It performs very well when objects are consistent in location and scale. CNN outperformed all methods. Even the worst CNN experiment on the most difficult dataset performed better than the best of any other method on the easiest dataset. This is not a surprising outcome. We wanted to see if HOG alone was sufficient to increase classification accuracy as a filter. We found that HOG filters with SVM, without the usual additional models, provide no benefit on their own over raw pixel values for this experimental setup.

Table 1: Mean Classification accuracy and Standard Deviation for different methods on the Adience dataset over 10 runs. 70% of images used for training and 30% used for testing.

Method	Mean	SD
CNN	96.1%	0.0029
PCA+SVM[RBF]	77.4%	0.0071
SVM[RBF]	77.3%	0.0046
HOG + SVM[RBF]	75.8%	0.006
HOG+SVM[linear]	75%	0.0053
PCA+ SVM[linear]	72 %	0.0032
SVM[linear]	70.2%	0.0052
DTCWT on SVM[RBF]	68.5%	0.0059
DTCWT on SVM[linear]	59%	0.0046

Table 2: Mean Classification accuracy and Standard Deviation for different methods on the FERET dataset over 10 runs. 70% of images used for training and 30% used for testing.

Method	Mean	SD
CNN	97.9%	0.0058
DTCWT on SVM[RBF]	90.7%	0.0047
PCA+SVM[RBF]	90.2%	0.0063
SVM[RBF]	87.1%	0.0053
HOG+SVM[RBF]	85.6%	0.0042
HOG+SVM[linear]	84.6%	0.0024
DTCWT on SVM[linear]	83.3%	0.0047
PCA+SVM[linear]	81%	0.0071
SVM[linear]	76.5%	0.0099

PCA ties with DTCWT on the best performance on FERET but performs better than DTCWT on Adiance. As expected RBF methods performed better than linear SVM classifiers, however unexpectedly this did not hold true for Adiance, where differences in filters were enough to cancel out the effect of RBF in some cases. Every time we used a filter on FERET RBF was better than linear with filters. This did not hold for Adience. None of the filters worked particularly well on Adience, with only PCA slightly outperforming raw pixels for the RBF classifier.

On the FERET dataset DTCWT is better (90% vs 86%). On Adience, it is worse ($\tilde{6}7\%$ vs 77%). This would lend support to the idea that DTCWT seems to work better (in theory) on images that are more similar to FERET (uniform lighting, no complex backgrounds, no extreme warping, pixelation, or blurring).

Using an initial momentum of 0.95 tended to promote fast convergence without getting stuck in local minimum. We use a momentum of 0.95 and a learning rate of 0.001.

Using this setup we have achieved an average valid classification rate of 98% on FERET and 96% on Adience which is better than the previous highest reported results according to (Levi and Hassner 2015) on Adience, but we do not recommend direct comparison of our results with theirs because of different experimental protocols used.

One of our aims is to investigate the use of the dual tree

complex wavelet transform (DTCWT) on the face feature classification task. Several recent papers report success in using DTCWT in gender recognition from frontal face images citing the benefits of partial rotation invariance. It is somewhat unclear how to best use this for "In the wild" images.

Conclusions

Much of the previous work on automatic gender classification use differing datasets and experimental protocols that can make direct comparisons between reported results misleading. We have compared nine different machine learning methods used in gender recognition on two benchmarks, using identical research methodology to allow a direct comparison between the efficacies of the different classifiers and feature extraction methods. In addition to providing updated information on the effectiveness of these algorithms, we provide directly comparable results.

The aim of our study was to explore gender classification using recent learning algorithms. We carried out experiments on several state-of-the-art gender classification methods. We compared the accuracy of these methods on two very different data sets ("In the wild" verses posed images).

To the extent of our knowledge, this is the first use of DTCWT on a large $\geq 15,000$ database of "in the wild" images, specifically addressing gender classification. We have achieved an average accuracy of 98% (FERET) and 96% (Adience), which is better than the previous highest reported results (according to (Levi and Hassner 2015)) on Adience using a CNN.

The DTCWT seems to work better ($\approx 90\%$) on images that are more similar to FERET (uniform lighting, no complex backgrounds, no extreme warping, pixelation, or blurring).

The Adience and FERET data sets are relatively large and this may explain why the CNN method generally outperforms other methods: it is known that deep learning performs well when large training sets are being used. It is interesting to determine in this particular application what "large" actually is.

References

Bekios-Calfa, J.; Buenaposada, J. M.; and Baumela, L. 2011. Revisiting linear discriminant techniques in gender recognition. *Pattern Analysis and Machine Intelligence, IEEE Transactions on* 33(4):858–864.

Belhumeur, P. N.; Hespanha, J. P.; and Kriegman, D. J. 1997. Eigenfaces vs. fisherfaces: Recognition using class specific linear projection. *Pattern Analysis and Machine Intelligence, IEEE Transactions on* 19(7):711–720.

Carcagnì, P.; Del Coco, M.; Leo, M.; and Distante, C. 2015. Facial expression recognition and histograms of oriented gradients: a comprehensive study. *SpringerPlus* 4(1):1–25.

Dalal, N., and Triggs, B. 2005. Histograms of oriented gradients for human detection. In *Computer Vision and Pattern Recognition, 2005. CVPR 2005. IEEE Computer Society Conference on*, volume 1, 886–893. IEEE.

Déniz, O.; Bueno, G.; Salido, J.; and De la Torre, F. 2011. Face recognition using histograms of oriented gradients. *Pattern Recognition Letters* 32(12):1598–1603.

Eidinger, E.; Enbar, R.; and Hassner, T. 2014. Age and gender estimation of unfiltered faces. *Information Forensics and Security, IEEE Transactions on* 9(12):2170–2179.

Gutta, S.; Wechsler, H.; and Phillips, P. J. 1998. Gender and ethnic classification of face images. In *Automatic Face and Gesture Recognition, 1998. Proceedings. Third IEEE International Conference on*, 194–199. IEEE.

Halko, N.; Martinsson, P.-G.; and Tropp, J. A. 2011. Finding structure with randomness: Probabilistic algorithms for constructing approximate matrix decompositions. *SIAM review* 53(2):217–288.

Jain, A.; Huang, J.; and Fang, S. 2005. Gender identification using frontal facial images. In *Multimedia and Expo, 2005. ICME 2005. IEEE International Conference on*, 4–pp. IEEE.

Kalansuriya, T. R., and Dharmaratne, A. T. 2014. Neural network based age and gender classification for facial images. *ICTer* 7(2).

Kingsbury, N. 2001. Complex wavelets for shift invariant analysis and filtering of signals. *Applied and Computational Harmonic Analysis* 10(3):234 – 253.

Laytner, P.; Ling, C.; and Xiao, Q. 2014. Robust face detection from still images. In *Computational Intelligence in Biometrics and Identity Management (CIBIM), 2014 IEEE Symposium on*, 76–80. IEEE.

Levi, G., and Hassner, T. 2015. Age and gender classification using convolutional neural networks. In *Proceedings of the IEEE Conference on Computer Vision and Pattern Recognition Workshops*, 34–42.

Martinsson, P.-G.; Rokhlin, V.; and Tygert, M. 2011. A randomized algorithm for the decomposition of matrices. *Applied and Computational Harmonic Analysis* 30(1):47–68.

Pedregosa, F.; Varoquaux, G.; Gramfort, A.; Michel, V.; Thirion, B.; Grisel, O.; Blondel, M.; Prettenhofer, P.; Weiss, R.; Dubourg, V.; Vanderplas, J.; Passos, A.; Cournapeau, D.; Brucher, M.; Perrot, M.; and Duchesnay, E. 2011. Scikit-learn: Machine learning in Python. *Journal of Machine Learning Research* 12:2825–2830.

Perez, C.; Tapia, J.; Estévez, P.; and Held, C. 2012. Gender classification from face images using mutual information and feature fusion. *International Journal of Optomechatronics* 6(1):92–119.

Phillips, P. J.; Moon, H.; Rizvi, S. A.; and Rauss, P. J. 2000. The feret evaluation methodology for face-recognition algorithms. *Pattern Analysis and Machine Intelligence, IEEE Transactions on* 22(10):1090–1104.

Sultana, M.; Gavrilova, M.; Alhajj, R.; and Yanushkevich, S. 2014. Adaptive multi-stream score fusion for illumination invariant face recognition. In *Computational Intelligence in Biometrics and Identity Management (CIBIM), 2014 IEEE Symposium on*, 94–101. IEEE.

Sun, Z.; Yuan, X.; Bebis, G.; and Loui, S. J. 2002. Neural-network-based gender classification using genetic search for eigen-feature selection. In *Neural Networks, 2002. IJCNN'02. Proceedings of the 2002 International Joint Conference on*, volume 3, 2433–2438. IEEE.

Torrione, P. A.; Morton, K. D.; Sakaguchi, R.; and Collins, L. M. 2014. Histograms of oriented gradients for landmine detection in ground-penetrating radar data. *Geoscience and Remote Sensing, IEEE Transactions on* 52(3):1539–1550.

van der Walt, S.; Schönberger, J. L.; Nunez-Iglesias, J.; Boulogne, F.; Warner, J. D.; Yager, N.; Gouillart, E.; Yu, T.; and the scikit-image contributors. 2014. scikit-image: image processing in Python. *PeerJ* 2:e453.

Verma, A., and Vig, L. 2014. Using convolutional neural networks to discover cogntively validated features for gender classification. In *Soft Computing and Machine Intelligence (ISCMI), 2014 International Conference on*, 33–37. IEEE.

Wu, Y.; Zhuang, Y.; Long, X.; Lin, F.; and Xu, W. 2015. Human gender classification: A review. *arXiv preprint arXiv:1507.05122*.

An Autonomic Computing System based on a Rule-based Policy Engine and Artificial Immune Systems

Rahmira Rufus, William Nick, Joseph Shelton and **Albert Esterline**
Department of Computer Science, North Carolina A&T State University, Greensboro, NC 27411
{rsrufus, wmnick, jashelt1}@aggies.ncat.edu, esterlin@ncat.edu

Abstract

Autonomic computing systems arose from the notion that complex computing systems should have properties like those of the autonomic nervous system, which coordinates bodily functions and allows attention to be directed to more pressing needs. An autonomic system allows the system administrator to specify high-level policies, which the system maintains without administrator assistance. Policy enforcement can be done with a rule based system such as Jess (a java expert system shell). An autonomic system must be able to monitor itself, and this is often a limiting factor. We are developing an automatic system that has a policy engine and uses Artificial Immune Systems (AISs) to sense its environment and to monitor its components and performance. AISs emulate the natural immune system to defend the body against external malicious entities. The proposed system monitors itself without human intervention and thus addresses the problem of systems complexity.

Introduction

With more systems and devices networked together, more system administrators are required to monitor and maintain these networks, and maintenance becomes costly and time consuming. Yet it may not be clear how a complex system may manage itself in the absence of a human. We here report on an autonomic system we are developing for a network-connected computer system that self-manages by using mechanisms similar to the autonomic nervous system of the body to achieve the so-called self-CHOP properties: self-configuring, self-healing, self-optimizing, and self-protecting. A rule-based policy enforcement engine is used (like the body's hypothalamus) to regulate the autonomic system, and the system has artificial immune systems (AIS) that mimic the functions of the sensory and motor subsystems.

The remaining sections of this paper are organized as follows. The next section provides background on autonomic computing, AISs, and rule-based systems. We then discuss the motivation for implementing an AIS. There follows a section that presents the architecture of our autonomic system. This is followed by the AIS sensoring agent section, where we describe how the AIS aids the autonomic system with its self-CHOP capabilities via anomaly detection. The context monitor is then described, followed by a section describing how the self-CHOP properties are realized by our system. The final section presents the conclusion and future work.

Background

Autonomic Computing

IBM, in a 2001 manifesto, compared complex computing systems to the human body, which has an autonomic nervous system that removes the tasks of consciously coordinating bodily functions (Huebscher and McCann 2008). Complex computing systems should have autonomic properties that independently take care of tasks of regular maintenance and optimization tasks, thus reducing the workload on the system administrator.

IBM also articulated the four self-CHOP properties. Self-configuration is defined as components and systems being configured as per high-level policies (Kephart and Chess 2003). When a component is introduced into a system, it is incorporated seamlessly, and the rest of the system adapts to the presence of the new component. With self-optimization, components and systems continually seek to improve their performance and efficiency. Self-healing is defined as a system automatically detecting, diagnosing, and repairing problems in software and hardware. Finally, self-protection is defined as a system being able to automatically defend against malicious attacks or cascading failures. Kephart et al. (Kephart and Walsh 2004) came up with three types of policies for autonomic computing: 1) action policies, 2) goal policies, and 3) utility function policies. Action policies specify what actions should be taken based on the current state of the system. A goal policy specifies either a desired state or a set of criteria for a desired state. Utility function policies are objective functions that provide a utility value for each possible state.

Artificial Immune Systems

The natural immune system is a defense mechanism that can learn about foreign entities that enter the body and respond to them by creating defensive antibodies. This concept has been artificially simulated for intrusion detection, resulting in an approach known as an artificial immune system (AIS) (Hofmeyr and Forrest 2000). Similar to the biological immune system, the goal of an AIS is to distinguish between self and non-self entities. The natural immune system that this system imitates depicts self as a cell that is innate or safe for the body while non-self is not. One can associate this mapping with detecting or sensing what is as opposed to what is not; this mapping is also known as a detector.

AISs have also been applied to the problems of fault diagnostics, fraud detection and detecting viruses (DasGupta 1993). There are a few methods for using an AIS. One is the negative selection algorithm (Forrest et al. 1994).This technique randomly generates a set of detectors that are trained to match any non-self entities for any system and not match any self entities. More specifically, the detectors are first applied on a set of self entities and the ones that detect the self entities are discarded. The idea is that, if a detector does not match self, it has a better chance of detecting non-self, which would be any anomaly in the system. The surviving detectors can then be applied on non-self to observe how much of the set can be detected.

Rule-Based Systems

The classical application of rule-based systems is in expert systems, which typically use a human experts knowledge for solving real world problems (Abraham 2005). This expert knowledge is often expressed in the terms of rules. These rules and data constitute a rule-based expert systems. Such systems have played a role in modern artificial intelligence and other applications such as fault monitoring. The Ponder rule-based policy language (Bradshaw, Uszok, and Montanari 2014) is the broadest and most widely used policy language.Its policies are rules that define system behavior choices that reflect on objectives set by system managers. Other rule-based policy enforcement systems use the event-condition-action rule paradigm. An example of this is Bell Labs' policy description language, in which a policy is a function that maps a series of events into a set of actions.

Carey et al. created a composite service execution engine for composing web services (Carey, Lewis, and Wade 2004). The policy engine for this execution engine uses the Jess rule engine (Friedman-Hill 2013). The rules are executed to refine goals into service policies. Before the policy engine can execute, additional information is required such as the name of the service and the finite state machine (FSM) models for each of the constituted services. Goals are refined by Jess rules triggered when the state used in high-level policy matches the state in the FSM of the composite service.

Requirements

We aim for a system capable of adapting to unforeseen occurrences in the operating environment. This includes adjusting to situations in a proactive manner as well as reactively supporting system recovery. Here pro-action amounts to perceiving danger then preempting harm or any compromised system state. Fault tolerance in the operating environment permits system execution to continue without interruption, while preempting failure from a system-wide perspective presupposes the occurrence of a compromised system component or operation.

Anomaly detection can be a key component to properly assessing whether events are uncharacteristic of a system's configuration (De Castro and Von Zuben 2000). Furthermore, accompanying this detection method with a response procedure that reduces the damage of the compromised component is crucial, but also crucial is simultaneously permitting uncompromised system components to continue. One goal of this research is to provide a sensoring component that promotes the self-CHOP requirements for an autonomic system.

One immunity-inspired algorithm of interest focuses on danger theory, which extends the role of the innate immune system for discriminating between 'self' and 'non-self' but employs the acquired immune system to react to danger (Brownlee 2011). Sensing danger lets a system protect, recover or heal, optimize and determine whether a reconfiguration assessment is necessary. Unlike Fail2ban, our system will learn new malicious and unwanted traffic to protect itself from malicious and unwanted traffic in the future.

System Architecture

Figure 1 shows our proposed system, which realizes the self-CHOP properties. The external world feeds information into the system through a series of sensors. AISs are used as detectors that identify anomalies from the outside world. The input from the external world also feeds into a rule-based policy engine. The rule-based policy engine connects to a rule base of policies. This engine accepts as input sensor data from the AISs as well as the context monitor, which is the component collecting information about the state of the system's context by monitoring network connections and system resources. In addition to providing status information to the context monitor, the system resources also provide status information to the AISs to help inform the detectors. The system is maintained in a proper state by the rule-based policy engine.

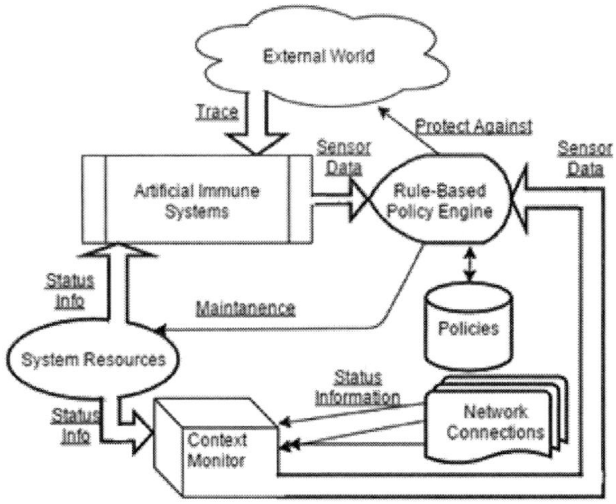

Figure 1: AIS & Autonomic System with Rule Based System

AIS Sensor Agents

We here discuss how the AISs contribute to the self-CHOP properties. Note that sometimes we refer to a single AIS while other times we partition the functionality among several AISs. Although we refer to sensing, note that the AISs detect both external and internal state. The AIS sensoring apparatus will consist of detector populations that monitor system activity as does a network sniffer or intercepting proxy. The AIS component will deploy detectors that compare system activity against normal system behavior. The detection methods behave as intrusion detection systems (IDSs) that detect system irregularities not stated in the innate system configuration. The detection method can also adapt to changes in the system.

The detector set will become a new feature vector for detecting danger in the system. The new vector will allow the system to recognize system behavior that has been previously labeled as dangerous. The new danger vector is then propagated throughout the system to scan for stress levels that are approaching this danger state.

Each round, the AIS will acquire more knowledge about the operating environment via the detector populations. The cloning process allows one generation to be more adept than the previous. The acquired immunity that aids the AIS in determining the health of the system is expressed via the number of danger vectors that have been detected and mitigated properly, with more emphasis on the mitigation process.

Following the detection of a stress level threshold being met, the policy engine will determine whether the system is in danger based upon the signal that the AIS found to indicate danger. If danger is confirmed, then the policy engine will determine what the system needs to repair or heal itself. For each consecutive detection round, the AIS will monitor the healing process by executing a subset of detectors for repair monitoring.

The system will adapt to the configuration expected of systems and components as per high-level policies during self-configuration (Kephart and Chess 2003). Conversely, within the configuration assessment module, the AIS will initially transmit a response to the policy engine that the need for repair or healing is not foreseeable. During the healing or repair process, the repair subset monitors the healing of the system via the change from affinity to a danger vector to the self set. Excessive danger is the signal to the policy engine to determine whether the system should limit the usage of the system component because the component might cause other components to be compromised. To increase the fault tolerant capabilities for the autonomic system, the AIS will monitor the affinity to danger or self for all system components involved or related to this configuration assessment.

Context Monitor

The environment of a computer system can undergo changes for any number of reasons. To deal with this, one exploits context awareness, a computer sensing and reacting to changes in its environment (Abowd et al. 1999). The environment that is monitored by some context-aware device is generally external; however, there is no reason that the environment cannot be the internal workings of a system. There are several consistent workings of any system that are consistent, such as CPU usage, amount of memory available, and network traffic to name a few.

Rule-based Policy Engine

For our rule-based policy engine, we used Jess (Java Expert System Shell) (Friedman-Hill 2013) . The policies use if-then rules as is standard with Jess. The variables in the rules are values provided by the AIS and the context monitor. The rule-based system will control switches and various resources. The sensor data from the AIS and the context monitor will be fused using the Dempster-Shafer theory of evidence (Shafer 1976). Based on the fused data, policies that are appropriate will be executed.

One of the purposes of our proposed system is intrusion detection. With this in mind, there are policies that are focused on this activity. For one thing, if packets from the network come in and the timestamp of these packets are a certain time away from the system's current time, a flag will be raised. If continuous traffic is coming from one specific IP address, it could be indicative of a Denial-of-Service attack. In this case, the system may block packets from that particular IP address. For any input coming into the system, it is assumed that the input is in a standard format. However, if the input appears to be irregular, such as a password having many symbols not numerical or alphabetical, then a warning flag may be raised. There are also policies related to internally monitoring the system. The system should run fairly consistently, where the CPU usage may spike or idle depending on certain actions occurring on the system. If there are times when the CPU spikes or peaks and none of the activities that normally causes this are occurring, then the system may take actions to run a diagnostics check on it. If enough memory is consumed, the system may run a heuristic to delete items that it considers to no longer be necessary. The AISs in the machine are developing detectors to detect anomalies externally and internally. The policies can have additional steps that state that if it catches anything the detectors from the AISs do not, it will prompt the AISs to adjust its detector creation strategy.

enough memory is consumed, the system may run a heuristic to delete items that it considers to no longer be necessary. The AISs in the machine are developing detectors to detect anomalies externally and internally. The policies can have additional steps that state that if it catches anything the detectors from the AISs do not, it will prompt the AISs to adjust its detector creation strategy.

Within any automated system, faults can occur. Faults can be described as unexpected changes from the normal system condition. The area of research dedicated to detecting faults is referred to as the Abnormal Event Management (AEM) in research done by Laurentys et al. (Laurentys et al. 2010). More specifically, the AEM deals with detecting, diagnosing and correcting abnormal conditions in real-time. An AIS can develop detectors that have a great information processing capability, pattern recognition and learning ability. These abilities can be applied towards creating detectors that can detect faults and take appropriate action. In the scope of our problem, the faults would be internal such as if something goes wrong with disk mirroring, or memory swapping from the disk. The self set of a detector would be the "normal" state of the system, and non-self would be anything that is different enough from the baseline of the system.

Realization of the Self-CHOP Properties

A major aspect of protection is sensing attempted intrusion, which is a standard task for AISs, detecting "self" and "non-self." We can generalize this function to perceiving danger (in the environment) in general and perhaps even to recognizing a need to adapt to a change in the environment. The general notion is that of monitoring the environment to protect self. The intent is that an AIS will identify a threat and characterize it sufficiently so that the policy engine may activate resources as per the applicable policies. The expert system may consult with AISs in the course of enforcing a policy.

In a similar vein, we can have the AISs detect when the system is not "itself" and in need of repair; this is the heal CHOP attribute, and what is monitored is self. The role of the AIS here is to identify faulty behavior and to characterize it so that the expert system may activate resources as per the applicable policies. Again, the policy engine may consult with AISs in the course of enforcing a policy.

This vigilance regarding the system's own behavior may extend to self-optimization if we have a baseline reading of system behavior. An AIS would help us distinguish acceptable patterns that deviate from this pattern (as when some resource is accessed) from unacceptable patterns. Something similar could address self-configuration. The most obvious occasions for self-configuration, however, are where a new device is attached. In such cases, a simple signal from a context monitor would suffice to provide the policy engine all the information needed to apply policies.

Conclusion & Future Work

We have sketched the autonomic system we are developing that uses artificial immune systems (AISs) augmented with a context monitor to provide data to a rule-based policy engine. The architecture is conceptualized as the AISs and context monitor providing sense data to the policy engine, but not that the data is also from the internal state of the system. We discussed how the system supports the self-CHOP properties: self configuring, self-healing, self-optimizing, and self-protecting.

We are implementing our autonomic architecture on a stock workstation that is attached to the Internet (inviting intruders) and to which we can attached multiple accessories (requiring self-configuration). In the future, we plan to investigate autonomic cyberphysical systems. In the future, we shall look into other biological metaphors and implement some into our system.

References

Abowd, G. D.; Dey, A. K.; Brown, P. J.; Davies, N.; Smith, M.; and Steggles, P. 1999. Towards a better understanding of context and context-awareness. In *Handheld and ubiquitous computing*, 304–307. Springer.

Abraham, A. 2005. Rule-based expert systems. *Handbook of measuring system design.*

Bradshaw, J. M.; Uszok, A.; and Montanari, R. 2014. Policy-based governance of complex distributed systems: What past trends can teach us about future requirements. *Agile Computing.*

Brownlee, J. 2011. *Clever algorithms: nature-inspired programming recipes.* Jason Brownlee.

Carey, V. K.; Lewis, D.; and Wade, V. 2004. Automated policy-refinement for managing composite services. *M-Zones White Paper June* 4:114–130.

DasGupta, D. 1993. *An overview of artificial immune systems and their applications.* Springer.

De Castro, L. N., and Von Zuben, F. J. 2000. Artificial immune systems: Part i–basic theory and applications. *Universidade Estadual de Campinas, Dezembro de, Tech. Rep* 210.

Forrest, S.; Perelson, A. S.; Allen, L.; and Cherukuri, R. 1994. Self-nonself discrimination in a computer. In *null*, 202. Ieee.

Friedman-Hill, E. 2013. Jess, the rule engine for the java platform. *Java Expert System Shell, http://jessrules.com, United States.*

Hofmeyr, S. A., and Forrest, S. 2000. Architecture for an artificial immune system. *Evolutionary computation* 8(4):443–473.

Huebscher, M. C., and McCann, J. A. 2008. A survey of autonomic computingdegrees, models, and applications. *ACM Computing Surveys (CSUR)* 40(3):7.

Kephart, J. O., and Chess, D. M. 2003. The vision of autonomic computing. *Computer* 36(1):41–50.

Kephart, J. O., and Walsh, W. E. 2004. An artificial intelligence perspective on autonomic computing policies. In *Policies for Distributed Systems and Networks, 2004. POLICY 2004. Proceedings. Fifth IEEE International Workshop on*, 3–12. IEEE.

Laurentys, C.; Ronacher, G.; Palhares, R. M.; and Caminhas, W. M. 2010. Design of an artificial immune system for fault detection: a negative selection approach. *Expert Systems with Applications* 37(7):5507–5513.

Shafer, G. 1976. *A mathematical theory of evidence*, volume 1. Princeton university press Princeton.

AUTHOR INDEX